TOP FACES BG

OLD SCHOOL TERRACE LEGENDS

TOSH MCINTOSH   GILLY BLACK
MILEN PANAYOTOV

Britain's Next
BESTSELLER

Contents

Foreword   xi
Introduction   xvii

Part I

Hools vs Ultras   3
The Different Point of View   8
Musical   11
Skinheads' subculture, movement and style   25

Part II   97

Interviews   99
Tosh and Gilly   100
Profile - fighters   103
.   117
Other representatives   123
.   191
Interviews   265
Epilogue   284
Opinions   290
Authors   307

Dedication, acknowledgements
and special thanks

Dear readers,

What you are holding in your hands is not just another book that you are going to quickly read and quickly forget. No, it isn't! You are about to become familiar with an experiment that is unprecedented not only for Bulgaria, but also for the entire region we know so painfully well where we were destined to be born and live by God's will. And we are about to introduce you to a challenge, a challenge that we faced ourselves when we came up with the extravagant idea to collect into a single almanac the stories of people who, at first sight, are not only different but are each other's exact opposite in terms of environment, philosophy, belonging, etc. what you are browsing through, however, is not a collection of saints' lives. On the contrary! The participants in this experiment are everything else but saints!

They aren't good boys, either, but … there are no good boys anyway. They just haven't been caught! Are they sinners? They might be, but in any case, they are no bigger sinners than you! Actually, what they really are is up to you to decide!

But whatever you decide they are, they will never, ever, give a fuck at all. Because they don't give a fuck about anyone and anything! Because if they gave a fuck they wouldn't have accepted the challenge in their lives! Because they are the Bulgarian hardcore lads!

When I first came to know the idea for this project, truth to tell, I was a wee confused, not to use the word 'shocked'. I wasn't a great optimist, either. To gather round representatives of the cores of different Bulgarian mobs, add to them some other 'informal' nutters, representatives of more or less known subcultures initially seemed to me like mission impossible. Then it began to seem to me like making a dangerous cocktail, something like a Molotov cocktail. However, when the interviews with those blokes started coming in, each of them having been made without the interviewee's knowledge of what the other participants were asked and what they answered, or even who the other human guinea pigs actually were, I gradually started not only think more seriously about it, but also to become seriously amazed… With every interview read, my mouth would open wider and wider with surprise. What surprised me was that those interviews were so similar that some were even to the point of being identical, as if they were copy-pasted and then only certain words were replaced, for example "pigs" with "cattle", "parrots" and other derogatory words specifying rival fans. Actually, it turned out that though radically different at first sight, those people have so much in common that they even don't suspect it. It turned out that those people feel the same extent of love, passion, hatred, etc. It was just that the direction of that palette of emotions was different.

It turned out that they think alike, dream alike and share similar attitudes. And no matter how blasphemous it may sound, those people started looking to me like people who have so many things in common that probably the only thing different was the colour of the club they love so madly.

In addition to that incredible, deep and completely blind love they have for their relevant clubs, what those blokes also share is their unlimited and unconditional love for their people and fatherland. What they do share is their willingness to sacrifice for that love! What they do share is the way they perceive life and its hardships. What they do share is the denial of one's own self in the name of the common welfare and the common goal! What they do share is their courage, defiance, and sometimes madness in pursuing and defending their philosophy! What those men do share is the well-developed senses of patriotism, honour, dignity and justice. What they also share are their common enemies, first of all what people call 'police' and the individuals meant by this meaningless, useless and mindless concept and then any other degenerates, politicians, minorities and other leaches and last but not least, traitors…

So gradually I became convinced in the meaning and the point of what we are doing. I became convinced in the difficulties that lay ahead but come to think of it… our path has never been easy, our path and the path of all those men who agreed to take part in this unique for Bulgaria project! If we had taken the easy paths and if we had quitted in the face of difficulties, we wouldn't have left any legacy! Because the easy path is the path of the weak, of the fake, of the spineless, of the cowards. And the people whose words you are about to read on the pages that follow are anything else, but weak, spineless cowards! And they are the last you'd call fake! Because unlike some modern-day heroes from Internet sites and pathetic forums, those people stand up before you with their 100% authentic stories! For that they get our huge thanks! We sincerely thank those lads who were lucky enough to find the way of life they loved and found and still find the courage to live it their own way, the way they love and want! Great thanks to all those tough lads for their choice to live and not just exist!

We'd like to thank all the participants in our project 'TOP FACES BG', namely S. S., M. N., V. V., Y. D., K. G., I. P., S. R., C. N., V. M., T. T., I. I., K. I., E. T., B. B., K. A., A. S., Y. B., D. H., Y. G., I. I., T.P., K. D., V. R., T. P., I. E., K. A., N. Y., M. M., M. M., G. D., V. M., M. P., as well as to all our foreign special guests S. D., S. H., P. F., and all those involved who helped this book be published!

Last but not least, we'd like to express our gratitude to the people who have stood closest to us and have been incredibly patient and resolute in their support for us and those people are our families.

We'd also like to thank all our relatives, friends and like-minded lads!

We'd also like to thank all those tough lads who are no longer with us, but who paved the way and left their marked tracks in the history of Bulgarian fandom!

The fellas who used to be our teachers and whose example we followed and still try to follow nowadays on the terraces! May their memory lives forever! We won't list or name them because now there are too many of them and we'll surely skip someone! You are not forgotten, mates! This book is dedicated to all of you! See you on the other side some day! And then we'll once again party like we did here, on this Earth!

Without all of the aforementioned people, this experiment of ours would have surely been impossible! And only time can tell whether it will be successful or not.

Because the time is not only the best healer, but also the most reliable, accurate and independent assessor and judge. Not people, but time!

Enjoy the book!

Milen Panayotov

The following lines are dedicated to
all our fellow brothers, fellows and
followers, who recently went to play
the hooligan game at some other
place ... somewhere beyond ... And
our next book, 'Dying Breed', will be
entirely dedicated to them all ...
See you on the other side, fellas!

Foreword

THE VOICE OF THE FAN

From father to son

from V. V.

"My father first took me to a football ground and he was the one who made me embrace the idea! However, the older lads from the mob made me the proper fan I am today. In those times, i.e. the 1970s and 1980s, there were no groups and firms like nowadays and everybody stuck together as a whole. Dad used to take me from a very early age to every home game along with my mother and my sister. We would always sit at one and the same place, the north-east stand of 'The Big House'. We'd arrive a few hours before kick-off time. Dad would play cards with his colleagues and I'd watch the crowds coming in. The ground would gradually fill to its capacity and I'd get particularly excited every time an older boy wearing a black-and-white scarf or carrying a flag would pass me by. They all used to go to the upper tier of the north stand, where our mob used to stand. I loved watching the flags fly. The interesting thing is that those are my first memories from the games of my favourite club. I was 10 or 11 years old when I started attending games on my own and naturally the north stand became my favourite place. I remember my first scarf and then my first flag. One of my classmates had an older sister and she took a piece of green 100/70 cm cardboard they'd sell in bookstores and made a template with the name of our beloved team. We met up, cut a white sheet in two and carefully, using the template and a black marker, we wrote the sacred four letters and then we added thin diagonal lines. Our excitement and pride in what we'd done were so great that we could barely wait for our next home game. If I have to tell you exactly when I felt a real part of the mob, saying to myself that it was the family I had always wanted to belong to, it happened at some point in the mid-1980s, 1987 if I'm not mistaken. There was a game... What I remember we were 0-3 down at half time. A sudden summer shower started and we, younger boys, decided to look for shelter on the lower tier. Then some of the older lads, our role models, stood up, came up to us and I'll never, ever, forget what they told us, 'Boys, please stay! We need you, the team needs you, no matter we are down, we still have the second half to play! Let's support the boys!'... I don't know about the others, but to me, the way those older lads addressed us, 'bedwetters' and the respect they showed really meant a lot! They fact that they made us feel important and valuable was what made me think that from that very moment on, whatever happened, those were my mates and that was my club. I don't know whether those older lads were aware that they had won me over forever, but afterwards I realised that those were the usual relations among our supporters back then. There was this incredible mutual respect, no matter if you're old, young or different. It made us totally united at both home and away games.

The feeling of being part of it was simply indescribable! I could hardly wait for the Saturdays to come; the fever would get hold of me as early as mid-week. Little by little, after a few years, I was already quite active, of course not like the oldest lads, but more like those who were about my age. On match days, we'd meet up at different places, most often it would be construction sites or abandoned houses. The memories I have are usually from some semi-dilapidated houses surrounded by iron fencing. They were meant to be pulled down, I believe. Those streets could easily be used as a setting for a World War II film depicting bomb sites. So, we'd find a gap in the fencing and we'd squeeze in and go upstairs. We'd have a beer or two and make some bombs out of red lead and white bronze, a few smoke bombs, etc. Then we'd set off for the ground chanting and blowing up horns. And there all of us would stand together, young and old as one! No matter win or lose, everybody would do their best to support the lads on the pitch. I'll never forget this home game; we were 0-2 down at half time. As our players were coming out for the second half, someone gave us a song and everybody on our stand rose and started singing frantically to support the team in. The referee blew his whistle and the chants and cheers became even more encouraging, so our players went on ferocious attacks, literally elated by the support they were getting. About 10 minutes into the second half, a boy of my age standing next to me burst in tears screaming 'Woooow! Because of 10 minutes like these I'll support this team forever!' ... We lost the game, but you know ... it was not our first or last defeat. It did not matter much at all! What really mattered was that the crowd was ready to support their players till their last breath and the players, in turn, were ready to die on the pitch for their club and supporters. No matter whether they'd lose or win. It did not matter because we, up there on the terraces, knew that they had done their best for us. I can still name all our starting line-ups from 1980s and 1990s.

In their majority, our players were products of our own youth academy. Boys who grew up in the town, boys you'd met or could meet in the street, boys you'd studied in one and the same school with, boys from your own neighbourhood. I'll never forget the excitement of meeting or just seeing them. I still remember the joy I felt when I and a mate of mine got an autograph from one of our best defenders. They were famous and recognisable for the entire population of our town."

from K. G.

"I don't remember very well the first time I set foot in this home as I was quite young, but what I do remember is that it felt good, really good. Kinda strange home it is as you can go inside from August to May and one Saturday it is open and the next one it's closed... Sometimes it is also open on weekdays. There's always been a big green garden in this home. Sometimes it's well-kept and sometimes it's not, but it's always bright green. It is a garden I couldn't set my foot in, but it felt good watching it. When I first entered it, I didn't know anybody in, but I had the feeling that everybody knew me. One could often hear songs in this home.

Songs that are loud, proud and clear... sometimes the zeal is gone, but then quickly regained. There's no place for apathy in this home and whoever steps inside should not do it out of fashion or because it is visited by friends. Whoever lives in this home knows its rules, keeps them and protects them. I have experienced some awesome moments there. I have always entered it enthusiastically, I often leave it overjoyed and sometimes saddened. I knew it better than I knew myself. I always approach it at a brisk pace feeling proud that I'm about to go in. Some say that a game is better watched on TV, at home. I don't get it! Hasn't the home of football always been here!? How could those fellas talk about different stuff? I don't get it! I'd rather jump for joy for a few seconds without having seen a goal scored in front of the opposite end instead of watching several TV replays of it from different angles. I'd rather be in the crowd asking 'Who scored? Who scored?' I'd rather not see anything when it's a matter of fast counterattack. I'd rather watch fragments of the game only as a huge flag is being flown in front of me. Nothing can put me off, this is my home and I'll never leave it. I'll stay here till the end. Go on inventing TV channels, satellites and any kind of decoders you'd like. I was born at a football ground and I will die on a football ground. I'll keep on skipping lunch and dinner in order to watch football in the flesh. I'll keep on staying at home on Fridays and Saturdays in order to save money for away games. I'll keep on getting up early taking the risk to feel sleepy along the way. I'll be coming home late at night or even early on the next morning and I'll keep on wearing my scarf in winters and pouring cold water on my head in summers. And now there are lads banned from entering this home. Lads whose only fault is they love it too much. And because of that great love they are forced to stay away from it. They are its only and proper keepers. They are the same lads who have sacrificed everything they had to protect it without wanting anything in return. Just a grove, a few entrances, an asphalt alley and some steep stairs that you'd always go up running. It's the best home in the world!"

For the team

from Y. D.

"For all those sleepless nights we spent ahead of big games! For all my mates on the terraces! For the euphoria that begins in the weeks ahead of the start of this madness! For the 8–hour coach, car and train trips! For going mental after yet another goal scored in the dying seconds! For ending up in ER after yet another wave of emotions! For all the friendships made! For all the months of preparations for derby games! For all the beers drunk ahead of games! For the 'respect breeds respect' idea! For thinking over and over how to play truant in order to be a part of this madness! For all those adults who spend yet another weekend at football grounds. For a behind closed doors game for which you travel to your hometown from the other corner of the world just to be in the boozer with your mates! For travelling to a faraway town and the coach driver busting you ahead of kickoff time and going back on his own! For each and every good initiative!For coming home at 5:00 am when the game finished at 7:00 pm! For the joy you see in everybody's eyes after a goal is scored! For the team spirit! For all these things I have never thought twice what I'd like to do at the weekend!"

For the cause

from Y. D.

"Seen a lot, suffered a lot… lots of lads are gone, some were not for real and they so quit when times got tough, giving up the cause easily!!! A cause that became a way of life for those who have been called all kinds of names and labeled as yobs, thugs, scum of the Earth… labels that they have given them a bad name throughout their lives!!! But it is them who did not betray the cause even for a second and it is them who really know the score when it comes to true love and deep hate, to fighting and standing up for your cause …Yes, the cause that has become our way of life has its name and has its voice. A voice of will, a voice of victory, a voice that tells you, 'WE SHALL NEVER SURRENDER'.

Loving an Ultras!

from I. P.

"You won't forget him. No matter how many men in suits and expensive fragrances pass you by, it is him that you won't forget. This man has no name. You won't see his face… what you'll only see will be two eyes looking at you, seeing through you like a storm, but you'll turn around to look at him. His hood conceals his entire world, the scarf across his face is all you see, and you won't judge much by his clothes. It seems like he's coming from Hell, but he just passes you by going to or coming back from the football ground. The flare in his hand is his light. His chant is his soul. And you think he's a hooligan. You think he's a criminal… But if you fall he'll help you up. If you're in need of something he'll lend a hand, no matter that he doesn't know you. He'll give food to the beggar. He wouldn't hurt a fly and his entire shocking existence for you will make sense. And then you'll understand that this man is actually the best you could be destined to and you'll be sorry that society made you mistake him for a villain. You'll get interested in him, he'll look at you a few times and it'll be enough for you to want to see his face. And if you're real enough to be with a man like him, he'll take off his hood, he'll put his scarf on your shoulders and he'll take your hand. He'll love you like no one else did before, he'll love you the only way he can. If you make him choose you'll hurt him bad and he'll take his scarf back, he'll put his hood back on and you'll never see him again. He'll hate you the only way he can. He won't run away, that's not the way he's been taught. He'll leave with dignity and you'll start to hate yourself too. Ultras hates to choose and his love is strong equal for those who he loves... once you hurt him he'll destroy you without even touching you. You love an Ultras once and he'll love you forever, giving you all that you need just like the way he does it every weekend at stadia."

Introduction

FOOTBALL HOOLIGANISM

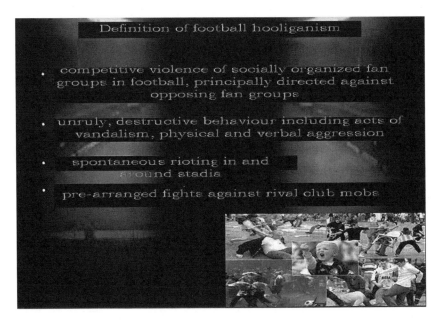

Definition of football hooliganism

Competitive violence of socially organised fan groups in football, principally directed against opposing fan groups. In order for hooligan rivalries to exist and develop there must be at least one similar opposing group. It is manifested mainly through violent, destructive behaviour of hardcore football supporters and includes acts of vandalism, physical and verbal opposition and aggression.

Taken from our first book Beyond the Hatred:

"Football hooliganism is spread all over the world, but in general England is believed to be the homeland not only of the game, but also of hooliganism. Football is the English national sport and occupies a major part of the English way of life. Hooliganism has existed since the beginning of football in general. It is hard to specify the exact date that marked the start of venting the anger that still reigns over stadia. The more popular and important football became in social aspect, the more brutal the very hooligans became. The farther back we look into English history, the more understandable becomes the conclusion that besides their good manners and deep faith in personal rights, the English are distinguished for their natural aptitude for rioting. In the spirit of this clearly outlined trend, the number of hooligan acts quite naturally increased in the 1950s and 1960s and going through the naughty 1970s and 1980s they reached our modern times. Hooliganism has turned into a game following its specific rules and a certain informal code of honour. Football hooligans are also football fans. Football is in their blood. Those who indulge in violence do it because it allows them to experience the extremes of any emotion known to man. Football hooliganism is a kind of extreme sport".

Globally, football hooliganism is known as the 'English disease' for a number of reasons. However, the spread of this 'disease' is not limited to England only. A number of other countries, incl. Bulgaria, also face serious problems related to hooligans. As already said, the term 'hooliganism' was coined in the late 1950s by the media and tabloids in particular. Since then, they have been extremely flexible in attributing the 'hooliganism' label to different types of incidents.There are also numerous 'social types' of riots that have been labeled as 'football hooliganism', but if we have to define the label in question within the football related violence frame, then it would be: Typically low-level offences committed by football fans during, ahead of or after games, spontaneously or deliberately and absolutely intentionally involving violence organised by football related groups (or the so called today 'firms'), which are the leading part (core) of the more extreme football supporters who fight against like-minded supporters of other clubs. However, the views and ideas of some diehard fans of different clubs quite often are similar or the same so here is the question we raised in our first book called 'Beyond the Hatred':

"Do any of those people understand hooligans' messages?! Sociologists, journalists... all of them just love writing about the phenomenon".

The roots of the issue are very different. The word 'hooligan' does not mean some kind of barmy, wacky thug. Hooligans are the outcome of the world we live in. The essence of hooliganism is to be found in what fans have to state. If it is a game related clash, the reason is some kind of difference. If it is rampage, it is a sign of disagreement. A hooligan's mentality comes down to what he can do and show the world. Who he is and what he wants from it. Our society is way too hypocritical to be able to impartially discuss such controversial topics like the issue of hooliganism. Indeed, hooligans are a pain in the society's ass, but not a single problem can ever be solved without first being become aware of, understood and discussed.

Football related violence and hooliganism have always been inseparable parts of football ever since the game appeared, but they were not object of sensation until the press decided to cover the issue and report the riots happening during games. There's no easy answer to the question why violence and hooliganism were so common back in those days and still are. One may claim that the roots are to be found in the first working class generations after World War II and the advent of the longest regime in our history. From dawn till dusk, in severe working conditions, poverty and starvation, lack of any funds whatsoever – a picture depicting a clear notion of what life was for people back then. A class of people literally tyrannised by the evil communist regime and the government of a brutal dictatorship for more than 40 years. Those in power nipped in the bud any opposition by the poor and the workers fighting for a piece of bread and better conditions of life. Moreover, intellectuals who dared to express freely an opinion on what a normal life should be were sent to camps. In case you did not seem aggressive or discontent with the government regarding their bad policies, you remained passive, became reconciled with being tormented and stayed hungry. Aggression is usually the result of one's way of life, social status, fears and education. It is a behaviour that leads to encroachment upon the personality of others. Its aim is domination over others and undermining their self-confidence and free will. Those are the effects of the regime. Even after the fall of communism in 1989, the government promised a better standard of living but actually continued the old Stalin-like method of government and for that purpose they created a subclass of underpaid people. There was a problem with the shortage of jobs and loss of self-respect and generally the life of misery and sufferings continued. As expected, such people would turn to aggression and revolt. They would be censured, punished and sent to prisons and camps. You would be caught in a vicious circle and there would hardly be any way out. Naturally, you only fight violence with violence."

That was how we tried to explain in brief the phenomenon called football hooliganism in our book 'Beyond the Hatred', the very first of its kind to be published in Bulgaria. In the lines that follow we will try to give readers a clear idea of what actually an 'old school' diehard football (and in particular Bulgarian) fan (hooligan) is. How and in what ways the cumulative character that he undoubtedly is was shaped? What cultural, subcultural and countercultural movements, trends and styles have had their effects on him, etc.? We'll do it comprehensively, but with no claims to any scientific and academic verbosity. By doing this we have absolutely no intention to encourage anyone or promote anything whatsoever! We do not want our endeavours to be perceived as educational efforts and we are not describing anyone in particular. We will just make a general profile and draw a general picture (the way we've seen it through all the years) with the purpose of trying to explain things in depth and from the inside, using certain definitions and concepts. Quite naturally, we did ask for the assistance of number of mates (two of them being psychologists) and we also used the numerous online sources of information (Google) and, of course, the good old books being reliable source of both information and inspiration.

The phenomenon

The football hooliganism phenomenon first appeared in Bulgaria in the late 1980s and the early 1990s. Individual hooligan acts and clashes between rival fans were also witnessed before the advance of democracy. Their small number and low profile were not a major threat to the law and order in society. Serious and significant acts of violence and vandalism and escalation of antisocial behaviour by football crowds were witnessed not earlier than the mid-1990s.

One cannot go deep into the football hooliganism topic without taking into consideration the nature of youth communities in Bulgaria. In modern times youth is tolerated, but not all young people manage, or simply are not willing, to fit into the society and its norms and rules. Some of them form their own groups dominated by their specific tastes and interests and so they become a kind of closed communities where their culture is created. Provisionally this culture is treated as subculture insofar as on the one hand it is a subtype of what is generally accepted, and on the other hand the term is slightly negatively charged as a definition of a lower culture. Thus, youths belonging to this category turn out to be at the same time modern-day society insiders and outsiders. What all those youth subcultures share is their longing to challenge conformity and the generally adopted patterns of society.

Bulgarian football fans are in the first-place spectators. However, some of them find the role of a spectator they are assigned inadequate. What they really want is to openly show their affinity and so become a part of the very game. Not all football supporters can be attributed to some kind of subculture. The level of involvement, of belonging to the group; the feeling of solidarity; the developed group identity determines each fan's standing within the subculture. Quite often supporters are called, or they call themselves, ultras or hooligans. In Bulgaria, where the emergence of most subcultures, incl. football ones, is the result mainly of copycatting already existing patterns, both types of hardcore football fans often overlap. The majority of them in our country prefer to call themselves ultras following the Italian football fandom traditional practice. They have their own moral norms that can be defined as loyalty to their own club and hatred for their opponents, but quite often to the officials and management of their own club. Other hardcore supporters call themselves 'hooligans' following the English example in terms of clobber and behaviour. Age also varies widely and in no way football fan communities can be fully attributed to youth subcultures. Naturally, a large part of active football fans are definitely aged between 18 and 30, but in the very core of the subculture we can find people in their thirties and forties. Solidarity among the members of such a core leads to such strong emotional bonds that fans often call the others in their group 'brothers' and treat them as their new family that deserves respect and absolute devotion. In their subculture world built on either real or imaginary identity, they proclaim their affinity with their club, loyalty to their firm, their love for freedom and any other emotions. A football ground is at the same time their home and temple, their beloved club is their cause and their firm is their family.

When ordinary people look at some ultras they can hardly understand him, but he also does not want to be understood by them and so he would not give any explanations regarding what one should be or not be. Each ultra is different as there are those who wear their clubs or firms colours and there are others who have never worn anything more than a single pin. There are those who stick to their group and there are others who go on their own (lone wolves), but when in a group they tend to become leaders. Ultras are different, but they are united by their love for their club. They can stand in the rain or cold for 90 and more minutes but they are united in warming themselves by singing their hearts out, they are united by the feeling of security offered by their mates' backs; they are united by their stroll, heads up high, in yet another strange town on an away day; they are united in their joy upon departing and weariness upon arriving back; they are united by the shared sandwiches and fags; they are united by the looks they exchange following another fist fight against their rivals; they are united by the adrenaline and their very mentality. Ultras is not violence, it is the protection from a life full of violence, from the police brutality, pay TVS, modern generations' extravagances, TV programs and most of all repressions. Ultras will always be misunderstood by ordinary people, who prefer living behind a screen instead of shattering it and entering the real world no matter how cold and rainy it may be. Being ultras is not a fashion; it is a way of life. Ultras are very similar to English hooligans and feel great affiliation with their club colours and are strongly attached to the popular culture of supporting their clubs.

In particular, if we are to discuss the reasons behind football hooliganism escalation in Bulgaria… there are quite a lot of them, starting from the quality of Bulgarian football and ending up with the suspicions of corruption, fixed games and bribes given to referees, etc. The media also add loads of fuel to the fire. All of those make fans prejudiced when going to football grounds. They accumulate a lot of negative energy and hatred inside, be it hatred for their superiors at work or hatred for rival clubs. Another significant source of aggression and negative emotions is refereeing. The public opinion regarding the Bulgarian referees' corruptness is notorious. Other relevant reasons could also be the constant stress and aggression everyone encounters in their lives.

The modern way of life becomes increasingly hectic, strenuous and giving rise to conflicts. Sometimes one cannot take the pressure and all the anger built up inside is let off. That is exactly the reason why so many people attend games, i.e. so that they could let off the emotions that have built up inside them, be it positive or negative. Society needs this so called 'social vent' in order to 'let off steam'. Those numerous negative factors like aggression, hatred, detestation, etc. that meet at the ground result in starting fights with the rivalry fans or the police, ripping off seats, blowing up bombs and other antisocial behaviour. But for the majority of football hooligans or ultras fighting for their club is just a matter of honour. The adrenaline involved is simply unbelievable. However, we don't think anyone can understand such powerful levels of passion. Power for them is like heroin and they become addicted see their role as one of extreme importance for the football game.

In Bulgaria there are several football clubs whose supporters have organised firms that can be openly called hooligan or ultras. Among the supporters of Levski and CSKA, Plovdiv clubs Lokomotiv and Botev, Varna clubs Spartak and Cherno More, Bourgas clubs Neftochimic and Chernomorets, as well as clubs like Beroe, Lokomotiv GO and Etar, there are firms that identify themselves with hooligan concepts.

In recent years, crowds and firms have significantly increased and are dominated by youngsters interested in this subculture and willing to join the firms.

Contemporary psychological research allows us to make up a collective image of hardcore football supporters. They are usually young men possessing increased levels of impulsiveness, arrogance and verbal and physical aggressiveness. Confronted by criticism, fear, and shame of being humiliated, disregarded and misunderstood by the rest, with their own distinct ideas of the world around them and hence their lack of tolerance to different opinion. The research carried out on the hooligan's personal profile reveals low levels of compatibility with the rest and high levels of aggressiveness.

Socio-demographic profile

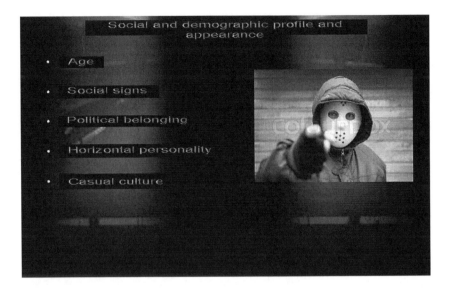

Originally hardcore fans used to be 16-20 years of age (apart from the ringleaders), usually (but not always) working in the shadow economy and belonging to the lower social strata. What they share appears to be their 'perception of low social status'. In general, men of lower social status tended to develop aggressive and violent features and manners displaying them far more often than men of higher standings. This kind of behaviour can originate from premature socialisation, domestic violence, or adolescence spent among peers in street gangs. In most societies, group members of lower social status are less prone to high individuality and more willing to start up intense relations with other like-minded individuals and identifications that include equally intense hostility against outsiders.

However, there has been a current change in the profile of hardcore football fans – they are no longer youngsters only closed within their fanatic subculture. What we witness these days is the so called 'horizontal person' capable of finding and virtually integrating followers and organising antisocial acts against 'the others' using the modern social networks. Also, one can more frequently meet fans with prestigious jobs (lawyers, doctors, dentists and fire fighters), who take an active part in fights against rival sets of fans, street riots and antisocial acts like violence, public disorder, arsons, etc.

Football subculture is not related to any political ideologies. Different fans belonging to one and the same firm may have different political views, i.e. left wing, right wing, liberal and even apolitical. It is not necessarily connected to a certain kind of music, either. Fans have quite varied music tastes, e.g. Mod, revived Mod style, Ska, Dub, Indie Rock, Rave, New Rave, Punk, Post Punk, Heavy Metal, Britpop and their varieties.

Appearance

Initially, fans were easily recognised due to their skinhead style of clothes, and in the distant past even workwear, but modern-day supporters now wear designer labels on a daily basis (the so called 'casual' style), which makes them much more attractive. A football jersey and a scarf are no longer sufficient signs of belonging to a certain set of supporters. Fans themselves are critical to each other when wearing cheap or out-of-fashion clobber. The modern-day fans' attire is rather aimed at attracting instead of repelling others. An absolute favourite with casuals is the expensive Italian Stone Island brand with its large logo on the left-hand sleeve depicting a compass, which has become an absolute must for all football firm members. The other two uniform-like elements are the white trainers and the checks in shirts, scarves and hats manufactured by English designer brands. The competition between warring sets of fans thus included appearance, i.e. which fans would look better. However, these days there is an opposite trend as supporters now go for a simpler, plainer clobber with no excessive signs and traits and their only item related to club belonging is a small (about 1 cm) pin.

Group identification

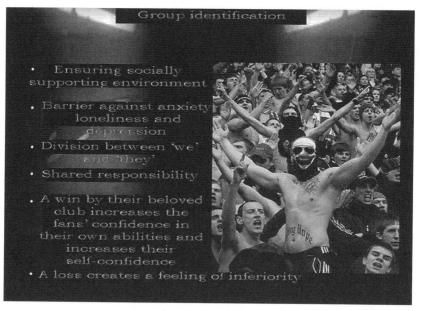

Separate individuals join groups for a number of reasons, the major one being to satisfy their basic need of social belonging. There is the feeling of 'our own lot' and 'the others'. Research performed by Cardiff University shows that sometimes *"a feeling of inferiority can be reduced through group identification where one is perceived as 'strong' and having 'high status' and at the same time the other groups are defamed so that one can feel 'higher'."*

Identification with a certain club provides a socially supporting environment ensuring a barrier to anxiety, loneliness and depression. There is evidence that those who settle in such social groups even have enhanced protection against physical illnesses. Dutch research shows that there is a 'satisfaction with one's love for a club' , which can be sometimes hard to find in one's personal life. When in a group, one is less responsible for any wrong choice as responsibility is shared and there is either conscious or subconscious division of 'we' and 'they'. In every country fans believe they are the 'twelfth' member of a football team. A win by their favourite club increases fans' faith in their own abilities and their self-confidence while a defeat provokes the opposite feelings.

'Life without my club is pointless; life without my club is failure. My club is what I have. My club is my paragon!'

Of course, now when football is largely commercialised, one could hear sentences like 'To hell with modern football' and a number of supporters attend games only for the thrill, the feeling of belonging and the group identification in question.

The violence

Bill Buford, a famous American author (Among the thugs) and journalist sees violence in the fans' behaviour as follows: "They do it for the same reason that another generation drank too much, or smoked dope, or took hallucinogenic drugs, or behaved badly or rebelliously. Violence is their antisocial kick, their mind-altering experience, an adrenaline-induced euphoria that might be all the more powerful because it is generated by the body itself, with, I was convinced, many of the same addictive qualities that characterise synthetically -produced drugs."

It is ridiculous to claim that all hardcore fans are drug addicts and pissheads because they 'produce' their 'kick' internally with the help of adrenaline. Just like the rest of fans and the ultras they look for 'peak' or 'high tide' experiences; they feel not like ordinary football supporters, but like playing a more active and rewarding role of direct participants. They search for high levels of emotional excitement by taking risks in response of boredom. There's also the aspect of getting hooked on hooliganism.

Hooliganism is a kind of measure of masculinity, a fight for territory and a quest for thrills. They see it as a major source of importance, status or reputation and even satisfactory emotional excitement. They talk of respect within the group and they hope that being members of such groups, that excitement will increase their adrenaline and aggression levels just like the sexual excitement they talk about comparing the feeling they get after having sex with the feeling they have after taking part in a football related fight, claiming that the latter feels even much better!

In this context, since the ability and willingness to fight are criteria for group membership and prestige, they learn to associate the adrenaline rush and any actions performed in such situations with pleasure and satisfaction instead of guilt and reproach that the rest of the society usually associate violence with.

A number of firm members use various substances ahead of games, but that does not make them some brainless creatures; on the contrary it just intensifies their 'kick'. For them the opportunity to end up in risky situations, pump up adrenaline and alcohol in their blood cells, experience the feeling of triumph over rival clubs is not only a way of life, but the essence of existence. They see fandom as a kind of a job and realisation they cannot always achieve in their daily routines. The life of a football supporter influences those lads just like drugs would do. They feel they are not capable of leaving it and they always go for it taking more and more risks.

Part I

Hools vs Ultras

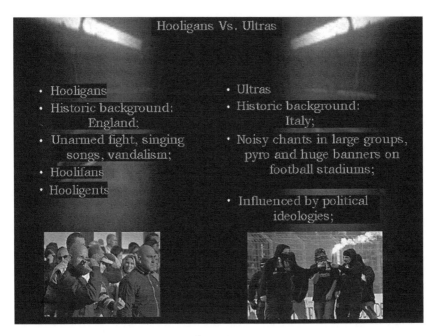

Comparison

History

THE HOOLIGANISM PHENOMENON originated in the UK (named after a 19th century English gang notorious for its aggressiveness), developed historically and the former unruly vandalism is now relatively controlled by means of strict legislation sanctioning such behaviour. Hooliganism, a.k.a. the 'English disease' is widely spread and nowadays there are strong hooligan firms in countries like Serbia, Turkey, Italy, Russia, Poland, Holland, Bulgaria, Croatia, Greece, Argentina. They get involved mainly in singing songs in support of their beloved clubs, unarmed fights and vandalism. There are several kinds of football hooligans, e.g. 'hoolifans' (admirers of hooliganism, but also knowledgeable fans of their favourite club) and "hooligents" (gentleman-type hooligans who don't like violating the public order and would not go rioting in the presence of ordinary supporters, women, kids, etc.)

What matters in their case is being differentiated from the Ultras movement (or a kind of more modern type of extreme hooliganism), which originated in Italy. What we've got here are sports fans known for their fanatic support for their favourite clubs, noisy, attention attracting acts in support of their favourites such as singing and chanting in large groups, using pyro ('Pyro is Not a Crime'), banners and huge flags across stadia. The purpose of those acts is to create the appropriate atmosphere and cheer for their beloved teams, as well as to intimidate rival players and supporters. The behaviour of ultras can sometimes be too extreme, as well as influenced by different political ideologies, racism, etc. to such an extent that at some point their genuine support for their clubs may be taken to the background.

In recent years ultras and hooligans subculture was permeated by a trend against commercialisation in sports and football, in particular. Parts of that movement are slogans like 'Against Modern Football', 'Fuck FIFA/UEFA' etc.

Ultras have no names for the outside world and it is only their close friends who know them. They have no faces as hoods often cover them. They don't wear designer clothes like hooligans following the casual culture and they don't follow fashion, but rather ignore. Older ultras serve as examples for younger ones and the latter respect them to a certain extent, but there is not strict hierarchy and in recent times we witness a change on the terraces, where the change of generations leaves a gap between the older and younger ones and there is a definite lack of succession. Youngsters are no longer grateful that the older lads could stand beside them, teach them and positively criticise them, though actually they are proud of them. Most young ultras nowadays believe they were born erudite, their time would never end (they'd be young and strong forever) and don't need any monotonous lecturing of the 'Do you know how things used to be in the good old days?' type as they consider it outdated and old-fashioned. When ordinary folks see such an ultra aggressive, modern, self-confident (cocky) bloke, they naturally misunderstand him (not that they ever understood old-school hooligans), but in turn, he wouldn't like to be understood either, on the contrary, he'd hardly be willing to give anybody, even his forerunners, any explanations of what he is. Each ultras is different as there are those dressed in the colours of their beloved clubs or firms, and there are others who have never worn such an attire. Ultras are fans who stick to their firms, but ultras are also those who are natural born leaders, though in general leadership among modern ultras is not approved, respected and esteemed much. Moreover, there are often internal conflicts and separation into different factions only because some do not agree with the opinion of others and would not like to follow any leaders. On the whole, ultras have different characters (some are quite quick tempered), share different attitudes and ideas, so what actually unites them is their love for their club and their ability to withstand for 90 minutes any kind of weather extremes jumping, singing and cheering for their teams.

The ultras movement came from Italy and the term 'ultra' is often translated into English as 'hooligan'. But if we check the meanings of those two words we'll see they are different. As mentioned above the word 'hooligan' is derived from the name of the English gangs' active in the late 18th century, notorious for their aggression. The term describes this type of fans as thugs, while the word 'ultra' means much more. It comes directly from politics and it is related to political extremism. In different countries the movement took different paths according to the local culture and social and political situation in the country. In particular, the ultras phenomenon proved to be different from the English model to such a degree that in the late 1980s it became an example for other European countries.

In Italy, the advance of the ultras groups becomes strongly related to politics and reaches its peak between the end of World War II and the 1970s. Political conflicts spread all over the country and took over the entire social life. Sports events became a means of expressing conservative (often considered as pro-fascist) or left-wing, communist views. This opposition is clearly seen in football where clubs are differentiated on grounds of their fans' social status and their geographical location. For example, in the city of Milan, Milan AC represents the working-class club, while FC Inter is the middle-class club and has connections with conservative right-wing movements. The first FC Inter ultras group was established by young Italian Social Movement supporters. Taking into account the strong political context, the emergence of young rebels in the 1960s and the subsequent formation of ultra groups are not only the consequences of social and cultural trends, but also the result of the political situation.

In England, Rock music related street subcultures facilitated the appearance and advance of organised hooliganism the typical features of which are strong attachment to territories, strict entry criteria, and protection from outsiders, aggressive behaviour, etc. Those rules spread across the rest of the continent in different ways. In Italy, some of those youth rules became known at the time of students' protests and street riots caused by factory (blue-collar) workers. On grounds of those protest movements, young people started form small and medium-sized groups taking over streets and squares, facing the constant opposition from the police and organised right-wing groups. As a result, political views started blending and gave rise to new ideas and styles. Another subculture was born to combine the rebelliousness, so typical of youth, with anti-conservative ideas. That's how ultras groups appeared.

All of those groups were fascinated by English hooliganism. The first Italian ultras stood out from the rest wearing particular attire and standing at definite sections of the ground that gradually became inaccessible for the other (the rank-and-file) supporters. They also supported their clubs by constant singing throughout games and had hostile attitude towards rivals.

Although ultra groups are fond of violence (just like English hools), they made friends or enemies with other supporters on grounds of traditional links existing between clubs and cities. Besides, ultras directly copycatted the attire worn by politically affiliated groups, i.e. camouflage jackets with numerous pins, blue jeans, balaclava style hats, etc. In addition, ultras began to use metal drums during games, which they borrowed from rallies and marches and used them to accompany their songs and chants. The fans' chants and slogans were also borrowed from politics. Flags and huge banners, typical of political demonstrations, also started appearing across stadia. Also, ultras groups are much more open to the world than the British hooligans. Unlike the English, they accepted a number of female supporters in their groups.

Ultras are very similar to English hools and feel strongly attached to their club colours and related to the popular club support culture. They buy the cheapest seats and watch the games standing. They use bombs, smoke canisters and flares when their favourite teams come out on the pitch, which eventually became part of almost every choreo. The adoption of some popular cultural influences, along with other characteristics of ultras, made this culture highly appealing to youths and facilitate the achievement of their goal, i.e. to rule wield power. Those features were typical of the ultras movement born in the 1970s. As time went by, the development of this movement went hand in hand with a significant increase in the number of clashes between rival sets of supporters. Then it came the second period in the ultras movement development, i.e. from the late 1970s to the mid-1980s. During that period, the rest of Europe witnessed a significant increase of violence due to the growth of hooligan firms. The skinhead style became predominant across stadia in North Europe as a result of growing xenophobia and racism trends. It led to increased anger and isolation in people, which afterwards resulted in violent clashes between fans and police. Stadia saw an increase in the use of illegal arms such as knives, iron bars, etc. The names of those new groups were still greatly influenced by the political situation as a lot of groups were named 'brigades' after the names of terrorist groups active in that period. Their symbols also appeared on flags and banners. More and more often, ultras groups started to arrange fights outside stadia in order to avoid the police attention. They also gained full control over the terraces. Before being admitted into the elite or the cores of such groups, young and inexperienced members had to stand a number of trials in order to prove their reliability and loyalty not only in terms of fights, but also in terms of organisation and overall behaviour. Outbursts of violence was witnessed only at games between clubs that had been traditional rivals. In that way violence was somewhat controlled. If anyone turned out to be inefficient, ignored older members and in that way threatened group safety, he would simply be expelled. In that period, the numbers of ultras increased, and their organisational structure was improved. The established connections with football clubs and benefitted from ticket allocation and organisation of away day trips. Belonging to a certain social class no longer mattered as more and more guys with good jobs and education, boys from wealthier backgrounds and married men joined the ultras. Also increased was the control over travelling groups of fans. In addition, the first change of generations in the hierarchy of ultras occurred. Certain charismatic leaders who were also politically active left the stage due to increased police repressions. Others lost their influence as a result of drug addiction. As a result, grounds witnessed the arrival of new groups formed by much younger boys (14-16 years old), often disliked by the other groups. In the end, those new groups had success and earned their place on the terraces standing behind their own flags. Those new groups appeared in a society dominated by hedonism and discontent of the political and social situation. All of them appeared in the late 1990s (still appearing up to this day) and they proved to be even more experienced in evading police measures. They easily evade the police by changing their appearance. They were not interested in existing alliances and so violated them, causing trouble due to their uncontrollable violence and frequent use of weapons. Those characteristics of theirs helped a number of those groups follow the 'monopoly on violence' principle, which they still do up to this day.

The Different Point of View

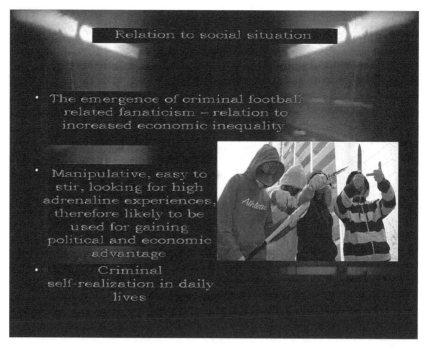

Relation to the social situation

THE EMERGENCE of criminal football related fanaticism is also facilitated by more serious hidden reasons, in particular the increasing economic inequality. Historically, it was shaped up in low culture and poor backgrounds, where different inferiority complexes are caused by social injustice. Martin Luther King Jr said something of the kind, 'There is nothing more dangerous than to build a society with a large segment of people in that society who feel that they have no stake in it; who feel that they have nothing to lose. People, who have stake in their society, protect that society, but when they don't have it, they unconsciously want to destroy it '. The identification of fans with sports clubs is psychologically significant for a lot of people, especially in our extremely unstable times. 'I have a group of mates who are just like me because we support one and the same club and this gives me some networks of valuable relations ', says one of them. Group identification becomes particularly intensive in cases of great ordeals during sports events, when the entire group is loaded on adrenaline.

It can explain why those young people are in constant conflicts with others, who don't share their ideologies, like other clubs' fans, for instance. Their behaviour often involves radicalism, group narcissism, aggression, cynicism, focus on violence and show of force. The increased conformity of acting as part of a mob and the group identity prevailing over self-identity also contribute to the fans' antisocial behaviour.

Crime related self-realisation in the daily routines of some mob members is one of the factors that sometimes results in fan groups becoming part of organised crime. Another important issue is the fans' increasing use of cold weapons and firearms (they call 'arguments'). "

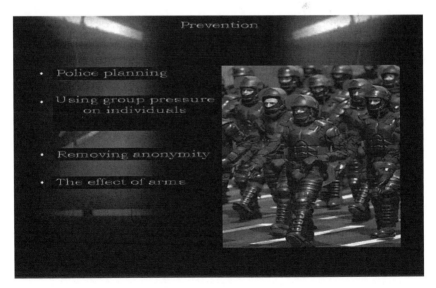

Prevention

WHEN IN A CROWD, people undergo a process of deindividualization where individual responsibility is gone. Reason, conscience, shame, common sense, caution, fear is completely in a crowd – conformist behaviour subdues the excitement of being 'like everyone else' and so one loses one's feeling of individual responsibility for one's own actions . It is exactly this anonymity that feeds aggressiveness in certain mass riot situations .

Police planning can help control, though once a riot is started fans become unpredictable . Therefore, it should be taken into consideration that the very fans are those who can prevent such accidents. Group pressure can curb unruly behaviour before it escalates . If the group says, 'Hey, don't do it! 'what you earn is the group's disapproval, which is vital for you .

The police response to a rioting mob is another decisive factor. Definitely , any mob member would not show the same aggro if driven out of the state of anonymity and addressed by name on a loudspeaker. On the other hand, tactics involving full gear riot police could make fans unite, develop group identity and become even more aggressive and violent – 'the weapons effect '.

The media also play an important role . TV channels never seem to stop broadcasting sensational videos of fans on a rampage, but they rarely cover the end of the story and viewers don't see the police intervention, arrests and any other actual consequences of such behaviour .

Young fans can be used in equally successful ways for both political and economic benefits since they are manipulated without much difficulty and they got easily stirred up in their constant search for adrenaline rush. For instance, the Barra Bravas in Argentina are often used to exert pressure and turn to violence for political purposes ."

Musical

AND SOME OTHER INFLUENCES

THE WORLD we live in these days is diverse and much more different than it used to be. Nowadays we enjoy freedom of speech and expression in many different ways and everyone is free to choose how to exercise it. Apart from football, music also had great impact on fans' lives in the 1970s, 1980s and 1990s its influence was of great significance for the development of youths in those times. Taking into account that life was rather hard and monotonous in socialist times, music was the only thing that could give people the much-cherished freedom to express themselves, to express what they had been keeping deep in to their hearts. In the beginning it was soul, blues and jazz and later rock'n'roll appeared. A real music revolution, a whole new world that changed the old concepts and ideas of music. When the system presses your back to the wall and you and to scream, when there's no one to understand, when your life is governed by rules you find everywhere around, then you start looking for something you can use to let off all of your emotions, pressure and problems. For example, some young Englishmen called 'The Beatles' hit the world of music really big time. They turned against anyone denying their right of opinion and expressed themselves in their creative style without paying attention to the society, government or any formal institutions. Those talented youths did not care what people would think of them and their only goal was to awaken young generations and show them they were not voiceless figures, but on the contrary, they were the pace of life. The energy in their tracks make you really feel alive. Later on, styles like Hard Rock and Heavy Metal appeared and they simply blow off fans' minds.

However, in Bulgaria, things were different back then due to the strict regime in which the absence of free access to information about the so called 'Western' music made people come up with a number of indirect ways to introduce modern music styles to a certain audience before the year of 1989. The first independent places such as local cafes emerged where fans would exchange information and swap audio cassettes, vinyl records (the predecessors of modern-day CDs or MP3s), and newspaper and magazine cutting long before the first rock clubs ever opened. Old-school lads know well what touchy issues John Lennon sang about in 'Imagine' and how and to what extent all of that, along with sexual revolution, was judged by the narrow-minded society with its distorting mirrors. In terms of music styles Bulgaria was back then nothing but a mixture of Balkan influences. In the 1960s and 1970s, the former so called in Bulgaria 'bourgeois grannies' wearing hats would fill the halls to listen to symphony orchestras and watch operas, the pre-war generation would hardly see any difference between jazz and swing, but they would readily dance tango. Clerks would sing old urban songs in choirs. The radio would mainly broadcast traditional folklore music. Army officers, having graduated Soviet military academies and married Russian women, would shed a tear over a glass of vodka listening to Russian popular military tunes like 'Berezi, Berezi' and 'Smuglianka Moldovanka', Vysotsky's songs and political tunes. However, intellectuals, students and school pupils, especially the so called 'rebels' studying in foreign language schools in Sofia and the other major Bulgarian towns, somehow unnoticeably got under the 'strong Western ideological influence and were simply hooked on Rock and Pop. After Elvis Presley the process gathered speed and after the famous Beatles, Rolling Stones, Deep Purple and Led Zeppelin it became absolutely irreversible and out of control. One of the most popular songs by the Liverpool quartet then was 'Girl' as it provided great opportunity to ask a bird for a dance at a house party. Accordingly, at those house parties (usually organised in flats owned by more frivolous mates) one could predominantly listen to the Western music in question. At those gatherings and house parties all the rebels branded by society would drink heavily contrary to the communist party's existing rules. Youngsters then would venture to let their hair grow, wear sideburns, tight jeans and badges instead of the customary then school uniforms and would downright refuse to sing songs in praise of the communist party and the Komsomol[1]. They would stay up all night recording music from tape recorders to cassette recorders. Cassette recorders were a luxury in those times and only those who were well-off used to have a National Panasonic (pronounced in Bulgarian in a very weird way) and listen for hours on end to tracks like 'Smoke on the Water' and 'Child in Time'. Songs like 'Catch the Rainbow' by the band Rainbow and 'Here I Go Again' by Whitesnake's David Coverdale used to give the feeling of freedom and rebellion. Similar rebellious spirit was conveyed by The Who's songs, the group becoming extremely popular in Bulgaria after the film McVicar (1980) shown in Bulgarian cinemas as an illustration of the way poor inmates suffered in UK prisons. But the film showed that inmate's lunch menu featured oranges on a daily basis, while in Bulgaria we could buy and have oranges only around New Year's Eve! In the late 1970s fell for Pink Floyd when some of their greatest hits like 'Another Brick in the Wall' and 'The Final Cut' were released. Those songs were illegally distributed in Bulgaria in the early 1980s since besides the Falklands War, the band would also sing about Afghanistan and the USSR, which was a taboo topic in our country. Uriah Heep is sometimes defined by critics as a poor imitation of Deep Purple and Led Zeppelin, but they got extremely popular in Bulgaria, which eventually changed the Bulgarian holiday calendar as each year on the first day of July thousands of people still meet up at the seaside for the so called July Morning fest, a ritual that directly resulted from Uriah Heep's song of the same name. Heavy music meant songs by Metallica, Iron Maiden, AC/DC, Helloween, etc., which at breakneck speed entered our lives in the mid 1980s and the early 1990s. Those bands had their loyal fans, especially among those who were more in the know, in terms of music.

Music was the soundtrack to our generation. If not to the entire generation, at least to, no matter how immodest it may sound, the more enlightened, more progressive parts of it. The lyrics of the songs we would listen to would often feature words like love, freedom & peace, which would make their way deeper and deeper into our minds.

1Communist youth organisation in some former Eastern Bloc countries

British invasion

The arrival of The Beatles in the US and their subsequent appearance on the Sullivan Show marked the beginning of the so called British invasion. The British invasion was a mid-1960s phenomenon. A number of British rock and pop stars and certain other British culture traits gained popularity in the US and became a leading factor in the rising counterculture on both sides of the Atlantic. Rock bands like The Beatles, The Dave Clark Five, The Kinks, Rolling Stones, Herman's Hermits and The Who stood in the forefront of this invasion.

In Bulgaria:

Protocol "A" № 255

From the meeting of the Bulgarian Communist Party central committee held on 14th May 1968

Attended by comrades Stanko Todorov, Boris Velchev, Kotsev, Stefan Vasilev, Angel Tsanev, Stoyan Karadzhov and Georgi Bokov.

...Industry Department instructor at the Bulgarian Communist Party central committee.

Hereby assigns to the Operational Board of the National Festival Committee to find the appropriate form of rejecting the Beatles' demand to take part in the IX World Festival of Youth and Students to be held in Sofia in July this year.

Prehistory

The rebellious sound and images of American rock'n'roll and blues musicians became vital for British youth in the late 1950s. The early commercial attempts to copycat American rock'n'roll failed, but the inspiration of traditional jazz through Skiffle and the 'do-it-yourself' attitude became the source of several British singles to appear in Billboard.

Some young British bands started mixing various British and American styles, e.g. 1962 Liverpool and its typical Mersey Beat and hence the Beat Boom. In the same year, the first three musicians of British origin reached the Hot 100 top.

Some observers say that American teens got sick and tired of pop groups like single oriented Fabian Fort and two English mid-1960s youth subcultures, Mods and Rockers, also influenced the British Invasion music. Mod oriented bands had the biggest number of fans, but balancing artists like The Beatles were also hugely successful.

Naturally, all those influences quite reasonably resulted in creating certain music styles and subcultures and entire movements, which undoubtedly had their effects on the formation of football firms.

Subculture

- A group of people sharing a culture (distinctive or covert) different from the dominant one

- Sense of belonging is shown by means of a distinctive and symbolic style, high level of group solidarity and their own ideas

- Provides individuals with opportunity for personal identification and behavioural security

- Counter-culture gives individuals the chance to be noticed, to gain distinction among the rest and to be somebody

Subcultures and countercultures

THE WORD 'SUBCULTURE' comes from the prefix sub- /sb/ (both Latin and English for 'under, beneath, subordinate, lower level') + culture. In sociology, anthropology and culturology it is a group of people (be it obvious, distinctive or covert) that differs from the greater culture they belong to. For example, if the relevant subculture is in systematical opposition to the dominant culture, it can also be defined as counterculture.

History of subcultures

The term 'subculture' was first introduced back in the 1940s, but the definition has changed a lot since then. Most authors have agreed that "Subcultures are groups of people that have something in common with each other ... which distinguishes them in a significant way from the members of other social groups" (Thornton) .

Many groups of people have similar things in common that set them apart from others, but we do not call them subcultures. The most obvious would include religious or political affiliation. Groups exist, according to Thornton, in communities, societies and cultures. So, what sets a subculture apart? It is helpful to define these three terms and then discuss a subculture in relation to them. "Community" is often defined as a permanent location built on ties of familial or neighbourly kinship. We all grew up in communities, whether in the country, the suburbs, the city or a hundred places in between. We understand that a community can be a block of flats in Sofia or a row of houses in the town of Gorna Oryahovitsa, for example. Inhabitants love to shop at the same markets, send their kids to the same schools and may even have similar interests about the quality of the water flowing through their taps. While some subcultures boast of offering a "family" to its members, (for example, the Harley Hogs motorcycle gang), the majority of subcultures are "apart from their families and in states of relative transience " (Thornton).

Paul Corrigan gives a good example of such a subculture in his essay on punks called "Doing Nothing". According to him, the second term we are discussing, i.e. 'society' also comprises of groups of people who share similar ideas. However, 'society' according to Corrigan implies officiality from bureaucracy. What sets a subculture apart from society is that it is generally informal, though some do require initiation as is apparent in the Punk subculture. The idea of 'the role in a community and society' is one of the cultural factors of the punks that we will be discussed further on. The third term that can be defined as a group of people who share something in common with each other is "culture." However, placing a "sub" prefix on the term culture implies that, while part of the culture, a subculture is subordinate to the parent culture, an idea that has been much discussed in the literature recently. A subculture, a smaller part of the dominant culture lives within the dominant parent culture. Before becoming members of a subculture, people utilise many of the same services, consume many of the same goods, operate within the same legal system (even though they may not believe in it) and walk the same streets. Even subcultures that rebel against the status-quo are not separate from it. Such rebellious subcultures "exist outside the main culture, while illuminating central features of it . For this reason, subcultures that rebel are often called reflective subcultures." (Levine and Stumpf). So, while there may be argument about whether or not a subculture is subordinate, it is agreed that a subculture is a part of the dominant culture and helps define its philosophy.

There is more to be said about a subculture than what Thornton offers in her three main definitions. Also useful in defining a subculture is its reliance on class distinction. Michael Brake, in the preface to his book "Comparative Youth Culture" says that "subcultures arise as attempts to resolve collectively experienced problems resulting in contradiction in the social structure ". Very often the problems that have to be solved are political or social. Youth subcultures often rise up out of the need for change and in reaction to the stresses of a down-spiralling economy or a bleak looking future. This would explain why many subcultures are comprised of low to middle class urban youths who are reacting to the stress of entering a workforce that has no jobs to offer. From the literature, we can say that subcultures have at least seven major determinants setting them apart or clarifying their differences from communities, societies or cultures. It has been shown through the writings of Thornton, Levine, Stumpf and Brake that subcultures are groups that have something in common, share different beliefs from the dominant culture and are often doomed or at least in the state of transience. They are usually youth oriented informal structures subordinate to the dominant culture and reliant on class distinction.

Subcultures are often defined via their opposition to the values of the larger culture to which they belong, although this definition is not universally agreed on by theorists. Members of a certain subculture usually show their belonging in a distinctively symbolic way, high level of group solidarity and their own ideology. They provide individuals with opportunities for personal identification (differentiating from the masses), and behavioural safety. That is why studying a subculture often involves studying the symbols in clothes, music or any other distinctive features of the members of a certain subculture, as well as the ways the members of the dominant culture understand and interpret such symbols. If a subculture can be described as systematically opposing the dominant culture values, it can be defined as counterculture.

Recently identification with a subculture has become more difficult due to the mass adoption of its style (particularly clothing and music) by mass culture for commercial purposes. Businesses often seek to capitalise on the subversive appeal of subcultures in search of what is 'cool', which remains valuable in the selling of any product. This process of cultural adoption can often lead to the demise or evolution of a certain subculture, if its members adopt new styles that are foreign to the dominant culture.

An example of such an adoption is the punk subculture in the UK whose distinctive (and initially shocking) style of dressing was quickly adopted by the mass market fashion once the media got interested in that subculture. This cyclic process ensures a constant flow of styles and ideas that could be adopted by the dominant culture for commercial purposes.

Subcultures can be classified as 'strong' and 'weak' according to whether its members remain loyal to the group until they get old or their behaviour is one of 'pretenders' dependant on fashion. A distinctive mark is also the group rigidness, i.e. how distinct the borders to the outside world are.

Subcultures may differ in age, ethnicity, class, location and/or gender. The qualities that determine a subculture as distinct may be linguistic (a specific slang), aesthetic, religious, political, sexual, geographical or a combination of factors.

Usually the choice of belonging to a certain subculture is made when an individual is between 13 and 18 years of age. Then an adolescent suffers a crisis as a result of the clash with the wide world when the dilemma is between personality development and social identity and when the individual still does not know who he or she is and in what he or she wants to develop. In such a situation, what helps a person define himself or herself in relation to the outside world is the feeling of belonging to a certain community or group. In this way youngsters internalise existing cultural patterns and norms, at the same time feeling protected by the collective nature of the group against the hostile world outside. Between 18 and 25 years of age this need of belonging is gone at the expense of the need of an individual style not attributable to group values, behaviour models and fashions. In other words, an individual either refuses to declare his or her belonging and breaks away or it drags him or her to deeper group identification. Then, men older than 25 once again tend to gradually return to certain more general group identifications that could serve as personal identification landmarks, but unlike the previous age groups, they are no more aimed at 'forming' the personality since that process has already been completed.

The more contradicting to the mass culture a subculture is, the greater the opportunity for an individual member to be noticed is. Appearance and notoriety make one visible, distinguish him or her from those lacking individuality and make him or her 'someone'.

A great example of a lasting subculture is the one of football hooligans to be discussed further on in this book.

Counterculture

Counterculture is a sociological term for subculture, where a group of individuals who do not share the established (nationally defined social and also other, different mainstream subcultures) culture and are situated in the so called prevailing cultural discourse, try to oppose, defy and change any traditional and widespread cultural practices, beliefs or established norms of behaviour in certain times, places and communities. A dictionary definition says that counterculture is 'culture of especially young people whose lifestyles and values are opposite the established culture'. Practically, counterculture can include a huge number of different and mutually incompatible beliefs and behaviours that vary in different historical periods.

The term was coined by Theodore Roszak in his book The Making of a Counterculture (1969).

Modern counterculture

Counterculture in modern days is most often related to the mass revolutionary youth wave going through parts of Central and Western Europe, North America, Japan, Australia and New Zealand in the second half of 20 century. In popular culture, thanks to the great number of artefacts that have been left, counterculture is mainly related to the Anglo-Saxon countercultural acts and the student anti-war movements in the 1960s. So, most often the highlighted movements are the Beat generation followed by the hippie subculture.

'Make love, not war' is an antimilitary slogan related to the 1960s counterculture and mostly to the hippie movement. First it was used by those who were against the Vietnam war and later by other anti-war movements. The slogan was promoted in various ways by a number of political activists. For instance, John Lennon used it in his song called 'Mind Games' in 1973. In the same year it was also used by Bob Marley in 'No More Trouble'. The phrase, considered to have been coined in 1967, was also used by Queen in 'We Will Rock You'.

Hippies, also called flower children, established a new way of dressing, experimented with a wide range of drugs as they thought they opened new doors to new perceptions and new experiences, and made interesting lively music. They also organised anti-war protests and music festivals such as Woodstock, Summer of Love, etc, and set up communes living in solitude far from the city and the surrounding environment.

The 1960s counterculture is a notion related mainly to certain cultural, but also indirectly to some political and social movements in the 1960s. The culture of that generation was shaped by the tensions in the American society, e.g. the war in Vietnam, race discrimination, women's rights, the breaking of sexual norms, hallucinogenic experimentation and the nuclear weapon tests. A number of young people in those times preferred an alternative way of life and refused to follow the generally accepted American dream pattern. They wanted to escape from the consumer society and longed for freedom of expression and freedom of creation, they did not want to recognise any authorities, but to develop their love for nature and music and most of all to be free and independent.

Sexual revolution

This period marks the start of the true revolution and protest against the established sexual norms and ways of behaviour in general. The young generation refused to follow the then existing moral rules. Those were the years of student protests, the psychedelic, audacious fashion and brilliant photography. It was then that the first scandalous miniskirts appeared. The Free Love movement and the cult of flowers and beauty emerged. And you can't imagine the 1960s sexual revolution without rock'n'roll, hippies and jeans.

Subculture and counterculture in Bulgaria in the 1970s and 1980s

Table No3

According to a SS report out a total of 39 groups featuring 233 participants, predominantly those created by Western music followers: Rockers, hippies, wild boars, punks, etc. 12 are built on pro-fascist grounds, but considering that almost all groups of the first category have the same orientation too, it becomes clear that these two categories of youths deserves more active and systematic attention by the State Security.

'Ideological diversion' and 'groups based on unsound foundations' are only some of the definitions used by the Bulgarian socialist governments in the 1980s to describe hippies, beats, punks, new waves and metalheads. Eventually, other labels like 'demoralised elements', 'informals' and 'degenerates' were also added. And all those youngsters wanted then was just freedom and free access to the Western music trends. 30 years later, those subcultural and countercultural groups and their relations with those in power then became the subject of a research and analysis with an exhibition and a book of the counterculture in Bulgaria in the 1970s and 1980s. Two years ago, two historians, associate professor Mihail Gruev and Boyan Gyuzelev, decided to start collecting artefacts and stories of the subcultural and countercultural movements in Bulgaria in the 1970s and 1980s. They found guys who belonged to those movements, i.e. hippies, metalheads, rockers, etc. and who were subject to repressions by the regime as a result of their belonging to such informal styles, groups and movements.

The organisers say that the aim of the exhibition and the book is to examine youth counterculture as a social phenomenon, as the result of the emerging in that period gap between Bulgarian young people and the regime and its ideology. The exhibition features emblematic cartoons denouncing the phenomenon from the Marxist and Leninist point of view and exemplary headlines from the specific genre called militia brochures giving the authorities a 'key' to the problem in order to understand and control it.

"We wanted to compare the youngsters' stories and photos with the files and records the police kept for them. Some of them had already had a look at their own records made and kept by the State Security (SS)", says Assoc. Prof. Gruev, who is a lecturer in Modern Bulgarian History and Ethnology of Ethnic Minorities at Sofia University.

SS 6th Directorate, 2nd Department was in charge of youth

"In those times Department II of SS 6th Directorate was generally in charge of youth. They also collected documents issued by the Komsomol, which in turn was appointed by the communist party to be in charge of the youth policy, monitor any newly arising phenomena and consider methods of their suppression . The aim was to keep the so-called 'monopoly over Bulgarian youths', continues his account of this project Assoc. Prof. Gruev. He says that what they would like to display in the exhibition and book is personal and emotional. *"We do not claim to cast some cold-blooded, reserved and strictly scientific look back at those times. We are convinced that the past should not be looked upon just for the sake of it, but instead we should take into consideration the emotional intensity those young people had then"*.

In its broadest sense the project covers the 1970s-1980s period though the organisers themselves admit that the major part of their material comes from 1980s. Prior to

1970s there were also some countercultural music related movements. 1950s and 1960s were the decades of jazz. This style of music was considered as decadent in Bulgaria. It was believed to be a kind of ideological diversion. That phenomenon could not become very popular in Bulgaria because the repressive machinery was much stronger then than it was in 1980s. On the other hand, the 1960s also witnessed some alternative formations and groups such as autonomous circles of hikers and mountaineer. The contact with nature was then considered as an alternative style of life. However, those were trends in the society, under its surface. According to Assoc. Prof. Gruev they became visible after 1968.

1968 – the emergence of counterculture in Bulgaria

"What happened after the Prague Spring and the IX Festival of Youth and Students held in Sofia in 1968 is a key milestone. It was after that year that those music tastes and trends shaped up in Bulgaria as countercultures and subcultures ", the historian says. / Assoc. Prof. Gruev says.

In the project he and his colleague Boyan Gyuzelev, in addition to the music trends, analyze those subcultures on grounds of the locations attributed to them. One of the key locations was the seaside, especially on 1st July when youngsters would go there to welcome the sunrise.

The July morning – the Bulgarian contribution to the hippie movement

"Talking about the so called 'July Morning', what lies in its foundation is the hippies' mentality. It first appeared in the town of Varna around 1 982. First it was just a group of young people from Varna that gradually grew larger and they started meeting up at the pier. What is unique in this case is that this fest is Bulgarian only . This is truly important since, generally speaking, this entire subculture was imitative, copycatting trends and lifestyles of the Western youth who had lived through all of that a little bit earlier . However, nowhere in the West there is a similar tradition to meet the first sun rays at the seashore on the first day of July" , the researcher says.

That is exactly why, according to Assoc. Prof. Gruev, the Bulgarian hippie culture cannot be considered as copycatting Western trends only. It had its specific features that could be observed nowhere else. It was in Bulgaria that Uriah Heep's July Morning got a special meaning as an expression of the youth's resistance against the communist regime and the drabness of that horrible system. "If we have to give an example of Bulgarian contribution to the world's subculture, well, this undoubtedly will be the July Morning fest ", Assoc. Prof. Gruev is positive.

In addition to the seaside meets for July Morning, the other countercultural locations were urban. The monument of Patriarch Evtimiy in Sofia was a popular gathering place of the underground in 1980s. Right beside it there was this Wall where people would write something and leave flowers in memory of John Lennon, founder of the legendary The Beatles. Another famous haunt was behind the Monument of the Red Soviet Army at the so called 'Baba Yaga²'s House'. Other legendary rally points in Sofia were 'Kravai', and 'The Hole' near the National

Palace of Culture and Peter Beron Cinema dominated by metalheads as in the 1980s it was the only public place in Sofia where one could legally listen to Heavy Metal, though on Thursdays only. "Youth counterculture was related to various music preferences and they were accompanied by other subculture signs like attire, hairstyles , and various discreet signs of different belonging . In addition, we thought it was very important not only to have a look at the background of those movements, but also at their consequences", Assoc. Prof. Gruev says.

New Flowers - the first punk rock band from the town of Kyustendil

"We have focused on several emblematic bands . A very interesting band was New Flowers as it is considered as the first punk band in Bulgaria . It was established in 1979 in a garage owned by Johnny, the band's frontman. They were evidence that those subcultural phenomena among Bulgarian youngsters were not only products of the capital. The hippie movement in the town of Plovdiv was also significant, with their gatherings at the Roman Theatre".

New Generation, Review and Kale - the beginning of New Wave

"Naturally, we have also paid attention to the first steps of New Wave in Bulgaria with bands like New Generation, Review and Kale . We have also considered Heavy Metal bands. However, it was kinda difficult to define which the first HM bands were as a number of them claim they were the pioneers. We think a band called Trotyl had the biggest impact on Bulgarian Heavy Metal scene ."

Drugs and counterculture

"As far as drugs and their connection to countercultural movements are concerned, no doubt they do exist. They are like ghosts. There is some interdependence, but I do not believe drugs play the leading part", says Assoc. Prof. Gruev.

"Drugs may be said to appear in Bulgaria after the Festival of Youth and Students held in 1968. Sofia was then visited by a lot of foreigners and they were actually let into our country as most of them were left-wing, i.e. hippies, beats, etc . But eventually the Bulgarian authorities understood that actually those left-wingers were very different from what the communist regime thought left-wing was. So, they were the guys who brought drugs to Bulgaria. Soon afterwards we had the first cases of drug addicts . But that's a different topic . It is present in some way in our research, but it is not its focus".

After 1990th. Where do we go now?

But what happened to the counterculture in Bulgaria after 1990? Did the bands that used to be the driving forces of those subculture movements disappear? Assoc. Prof. Gruev tries to answer this question.

"Subcultures did not disappear, they just changed . Those were the hardest times for the people who were against the communist system. The system collapsed but what also happened was that actually those changes left a number of those people jobless and with no prospects for the future. In fact, music is a global means of making a living and that was why a lot of them migrated in search of good fortune elsewhere. Some were lucky and others ... returned".

And isn't there nowadays a kind of revival of hippie values, of the longing for closeness to nature, which carries in itself the strife for freedom?

2In Slavic folklore Baba Yaga is a supernatural being who appears as a deformed and ferocious-looking witch.

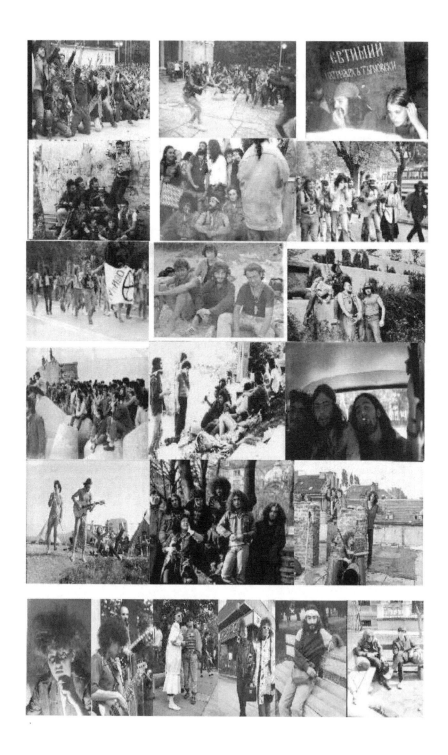

Skinheads' subculture, movement and style

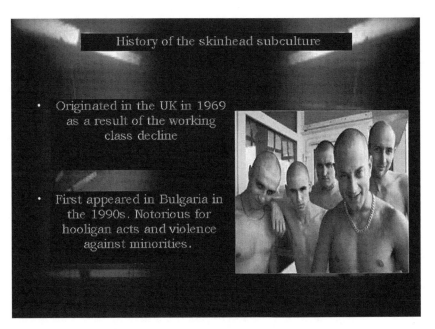

History of the skinhead subculture

- Originated in the UK in 1969 as a result of the working class decline

- First appeared in Bulgaria in the 1990s. Notorious for hooligan acts and violence against minorities.

Background

THE SKINHEAD SUBCULTURE appeared in the UK in 1969 as a response to the increasingly poor conditions the working class was living in. Generally speaking, it's a highly risky group taking into account their provocative and aggressive behaviour. The movement emerged in Bulgaria in the 1990s. What they were noticed for were their acts of hooliganism and violence against minorities. Like in most subcultures, this one was also represented mainly by teens."The sense of being oppressed by all those around: the rich bourgeoisie, the young yuppies , the antisocial hippies, the authorities represented by bosses, teachers and the Old Bill, the Pakis having better jobs, produced an intensified 'us-them' consciousness and an ever-increasing group solidarity" (Clarke). In those times England started to feel that it had been flooded with and conquered by foreigners and its citizens are left to the mercy of fate and would soon be 'uprooted' and literally left to die. "Strikes and letter-bombs at that time were all see n as concerted, even orchestrated assault by multitude of minorities that threatened to swamp the majority " (Savage). Such an approach to foreigners as enemies infiltrating England plunged the country into even more bitter social discontent. The huge mess and political deadlock, the ongoing recession and the other domestic problems UK faced in those times, along with all the emerging trends and movements, were considered as a bad omen.

The skinhead's movement is strictly political in its nature. As a result of the deteriorating economy and the influx of immigrants, they rebel with their racist and aggressive behaviour against everyone who does not fit in their world. Usually the ones who do not fit in are foreigners with whom the locals almost have to compete in order to find better jobs. Nationalists want to keep their country clean and simply discourage immigrants. Quite often such discouragement takes the form of violence.

Music as a means of group identification is a key aspect of this movement in general. It lies in its foundations and further development and expresses the ideology of the movement. When we talk about the biggest music influence on skinheads, we think of Ian Stuart Donaldson, a musician and member of the Screwdriver band and founder of Blood and Honour organisation. He was the first to sing political rock and thanks to him a new music style appeared, i.e. RAC (Rock against Communism). In his lyrics he promotes a dozen of messages regarding the problems white nations are to face.

The Bulgarian music scene also has a dozen of bands and projects, and some of them even played at different international events. The most famous are Brannik, Shame and Disgrace, Pure Blood, Tangra's Warriors, National Protection, Pride, Kubrat's Bundle, etc. Their lyrics are against democracy, the Roma problem, immigrants, Jews, politicians and the police. Their messages include ones of national unity and popularisation of the lives and causes of our national heroes.

Belonging to a certain group provides a kind of protection against the hostility of the outside world. Identification with skinheads, though giving notoriety makes a young man visible, makes him 'someone' and distinguishes him from the rest. In the so-called Skinhead Bible, the author George Marshall says,"There's a real sense of belonging, the sense of being special and being with someone of your own kind".

Fractions

- Traditional skinheads, Trojan skinheads
- S.H.A.R.P. (Skinheads Against Racial Prejudices)
- White Power Skinheads opposing migrants, drugs, homosexuals, etc. For instance, Blood and Honour, Combat 18, Hammer skins groups
- R.A.S.H. (Red and Anarchist Skinheads) – revolutionary anarchism and communism. For instance, A.N.A. (Anti-Nazi Front), Y.R.E. (Youth Against Racism in Europe), Antifa (Germany)
- G.S.M. (Gay Skinheads Movement)
- Straight Edge Skinheads - more fanatical followers of Hitler known for not smoking or using drugs

Fractions

A skinhead is not a homogeneous movement. It's got a lot of internal intolerance between different factions. Among those active in Bulgaria there are national socialists, the most numerous, either traditional or apolitical; SHARP (Skinheads Against Racial Prejudices), anarcho-communists and far-left. Also, there are skinhead factions that support different football clubs, which is also a kind of different belonging. With different factions there are different ways of identity formation.

What makes an impression is that collective self-awareness and group identification are better expressed with national socialists than with the other factions. This is partly due to the stronger presence of ideology, the strict hierarchy and the following of certain rules. Their group is known for excellent solidarity and cohesion between members. Among skinheads there are a lot of good students so there's no point in claiming that their social status is what determines their choice of the relevant subculture. Skinhead girls are even more aggressive than boys, probably because they want to prove their equality within the group.

All over the globe, including Bulgaria, there are different skinhead groups, the most popular being Blood and Honour, Combat 18 and Hammerskins.

Blood and Honour and Combat 18 have Bulgarian followers. Blood and Honour was founded in the UK by the above-mentioned Ian Stewart. Its members are white nationalists, including skinheads, and it supports music bands using national socialist and nationalistic themes. Its aim is to unite white nationalists all over the globe. Also, it organises different nationalistic events promoting national socialist and nationalistic ideas.

Combat 18 is sometimes defined as a terrorist organisation because it aims at spreading its ideas by using force. Established in the UK, nowadays it has branches in a lot of countries like the USA, Belgium, Holland, Germany, Northern Ireland, Scotland, Scandinavia and countries in Eastern Europe (in particular Russia, Ukraine, Serbia and Bulgaria). C18 members have been suspected of a number of killings of immigrants and people from ethnic minorities, as well as of bomb attacks based on racial prejudice. The National Resistance movement unites mainly skinheads and extreme nationalists. It has branches in many European countries. In Bulgaria, the organisation deals with manufacturing and distributing nationalistic books and merchandise and holding sports events. The media blame the organisation for a series of attacks against immigrants, gypsies, Turks, gays and communists. Its members have been trialled for murders and attempted murders on grounds of racial prejudice.

In different countries all over the globe there are different extremist right- wing organisations suspected of hundreds of racial and political killings. In Russia, for example, notorious are Dmitriy Borovikov and Alexey Voevodin's BTO, Iliya Goryachev's BORN, Nikola Karolev's SPAS and Maxim Bazilev's NSO. In Germany they have the National Socialist Underground led by Uwe Mundlos and Uwe Bohnhardt and in the US - The Order of David Lane and Robert Mathews.

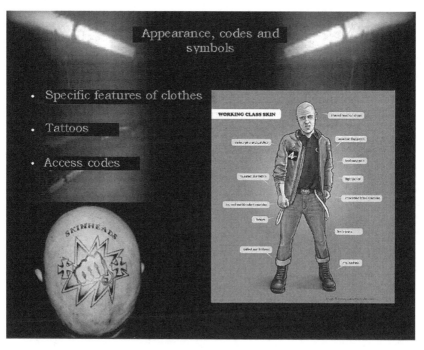

Appearance, symbols and codes of behaviour

THESE MAKE SKINHEADS most distinctive and recognisable. Their appearance is one of the most distinguishing features of their cultural belonging and is considerably loaded with symbolic meaning: boots, rolled up jeans, braces, shirts and Bomber jackets represent work outfit suitable for hard manual labour jobs. Afterwards those outfits became a fashion trend (for instance Doc Martens boots).

Other symbols inserted in their attire were, for example, the shoelaces of their military boots. With national socialists they show their place in the group hierarchy. So, white shoelaces are subject to special approval and are awarded for special merits only. They are also a symbol of the white race purity. With apolitical skinhead white shoelaces stand for the exact opposite, i.e. anti-racism, as they combine the two colours of black and white. Red shoelaces were usually worn by the so-called Redskins. There are also green, pink and blue laces that distinguish between different factions.

Typical signs of belonging to the skinhead movement are tattoos. The human body "turns into a source of social realities" (Godelier). Almost all skinheads have tattoos bonding them to the groups and making them recognisable as such. Tattoos often convey some information. For instance, having a spider web tattoo means you have been nicked by the Old Bill. Crosses are typical fist tattoos and they mean that faith is a source of great power. A swallow is a symbol of freedom and therefore a common tattoo. National socialist usually have different tattoos referring to national socialist ideas and are generally accepted as symbolic for the group, e.g. Celtic crosses, Nazi eagles, two crossed hammers, etc.

Also typical for national socialists are numerous codes used with the purpose of restricting access to the group by outsiders. The most widespread code was coined by David Lane: 14/88. 14 refers to Lane's 14-word famous quote "We must secure the existence of our people and a future for white children", and 88 is the numerical symbol of the letters HH standing for Heil Hitler.

A typical manifestation of collective solidarity is the demonstration of force that can be most often observed during different celebrations (most frequently national holidays or Hitler's birthday 20th April) or at football games. On such occasions, incidents or random attacks are very rare. National holidays are uses do boost cohesion within the group. Being patriots and nationalists, skinheads unite for such events, their collective self-awareness gets stronger and their propaganda has greater effects and it is then that they really stick out among the rest. That is also why during and after such celebrations there are more attacks on immigrants and people from different ethnic and religious minorities. The use of violence and the attacks against "the others" are the tools that boost the group self-awareness and solidarity. In this respect, their most obvious "enemy" is the Roma population, who, in addition to belonging to another ethnic group, 'don't work, but steal' and so they fall the most typical victim to the skinheads.

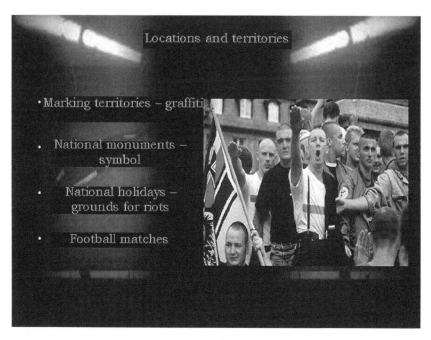

Locations and territories

TERRITORIES ARE USUALLY MARKED in order to make clear who rules them. All organisations have their own clubs where they meet up. The area around such clubs is also marked and organised. Most often it would be the graffiti.

As far as football is concerned, the places for pre-arranged fights are changed every time in order not to be sussed by the cops. In general, they do not like to stick out like a sore thumb and that's why they wear more common, daily clothes. Football grounds are the places they could be seen at as they are usually arenas of fights between rival groups and demonstrations of force. There one could hardly distinguish between hooligans, ultras and skinheads since they are mixed into one mass. At various other events, skinheads can be seen at monuments of national heroes or ones connected with national culture and history. In this way nationalism, which is the major idea behind the movement, is boosted.

Opinion

N.Y.G. (Blagoevgrad)

"Surely there's no way we can deny that the different subculture movements in Bulgaria were influenced by music styles. I'll mainly talk about the skinheads and their development. The skinhead movement had a huge impact both on terrace culture and Bulgarian nationalists. Everybody knows that a major part of the earliest Bulgarian hooligans were exactly skinheads . The main cores among Bulgarian ultras were boys with shaved heads wearing military boots . Among the white population, skinheads were initially a movement sharing nationalist and racist ideas. Such ideas were also followed by Bulgarian skinheads .

In the yearly 1990s, skinheads were key players on the terraces. Their ideas were spread among and adopted by the rest of the football fans. Having been well accepted on home soil, this subculture quickly grew to become a leading one on the Bulgarian scene . As the years went by, it became a way of life for those blokes who, in turn, passed it on to the next generations. Listening to different kind of nationalist music such as Rac, Oi, Punk, Metal, Hardcore , etc. used to be quite common. Also, it was almost obligatory to beat up blacks, gays, Turks, Jews and anyone else defined as racial or class enemy. It was a well-known fact that their political views were national socialist, which we simply consider as advanced nationalism . Some were even members of a political party known to be NS oriented . Skinheads are organised and active in their own different ways. They have different groups following their own different rules. Probably the most famous one was the gang that used to meet up at the place they called Kravai. They still exist, up to this day. Add to this going to concerts and beer drinking, and you'd get almost the complete picture of what skinheads used to do.

Nowadays it's kinda different . Going to football is still popular. Blokes still go to music event and they still beat up their enemies . The new generations also warmly welcomed those ideas . However, there's been a significant change in terms of social life . Quite a few skinheads and NS activists organise mass protest marches and events. They also have political claims they stand up for on leading nationwide TV channels and so they manage to give publicity to major problems our nation is facing currently . Some years ago, there was even an attempt to establish a new political nationalist party with its core being made up of skinheads and football ultras supporting different Bulgarian clubs . Unfortunately, the entire machinery of the government responded negatively and refused to register such a party . So those groups still do not have their formal political representation in our country .

In addition, I can positively state that for a few years now t here has been this trend for young people to turn to sports . The idea that a proper nationalist should be strong and physically fit is becoming increasingly popular. Different organisations set up gym 's and boxing clubs where their activists can train. In this way they shift the focus from their former drunk and disorderly behaviour to self-discipline and self-improvement because in their opinion Bulgaria needs disciplined fighters. Furthermore, there are even attempts to set up paramilitary camps training nationalists in military science. Straight Edge way of life is also promoted and adopted by dozens of nationalists .

Anyway, the history of Bulgarian skinhead movement is a rather rich one and it would not be easy to recreate it in detail".

Punk Rock subculture, movement and style

- Originated in the UK, USA and Australia in the late 1960s and early 1970s

- In Bulgaria, punk music developed later, though some bands were set up in the late 1970s

Background

Punk has been a youth trend, movement and subculture for the last three decades. It originated in the UK, US and Australia in the late 1960s and early 1970s. It includes the punk rock music style, punk fashion and its own ideology based on anti-conformism, individualism and anarchism. 'Punk' is a word (sometimes derogatory) mainly used with regard to the punk movement or to designate someone belonging to the punk subculture, or as a short name for the punk rock style. In the English language the word 'punk' is also used as an insult to someone so that the insulted one is represented and made to feel ugly, weak, insignificant and useless (trash).

It all started much earlier and, as in most cases, in Great Britain, which is traditionally the home of a number of youth subcultures. First it was the Teddy Boys with their Edwardian suits and short hair, looking like and making the impression of being well-behaved and respected young men. Their style resembled the 1930s popular fashion. The used to 'play' quite skilfully with stereotypes and the way they looked as being part of the English ideals in the 1950s and 1960s, but afterwards managed to surprise everybody resorting to street violence and even robberies. They fought against the system causing troubles, which is in direct contrast with their nice appearance. Then followed the Mods and Rockers of the 1960s. Those were now music and style dependent self-aware subcultures roaming the cities on their decorated scooters or ugly-looking bikes. Fractions from the two subcultures fight each other to gain territories where they could meet up. Mods appreciate the American consumer attitude and strive for the higher classes and strata though they also play quite well with the symbols of the dominant culture. Leather clad bike riding Rockers, however, were against that shocking type of consumerism. They did not share the same attitudes and tried to stick to the lower classes."The conventional insignia of the business world - the suit, collar and tie, short hair, etc. - were stripped of their original connotations - efficiency, ambition, compliance with authority - and transformed into 'empty' fetishes, objects to be desired, fondled and valued in their own right" (Hebdige). "In contrast, and the reason for the countless turf wars, the Rockers acted out an assertion of working class values" (Stratton).

Let's go back to some of the original motivators of British punk as it was politically and socially motivated by the crimes and injustices witnessed on the streets.The trends that shaped up punk in England were also present in the US in the 1970s. "Economically the 1970s ushered in an age of diminished opportunities, as the energy crunch and oil embargo of 1973 and early 1974 depressed industrial production and cut the real income of the American workforce" (Bindas). By 1980 it was clear recession was coming to the US, too. However, the American punk movement focused less on the working-class problems at the expense of the very punk music. America first heard the sounds of a fast, powerful and stylistically simplified music also in the early 1970s thanks to bands like New York Ramones and Blondie. Those bands would tend to attract subculture trends though the punk image, including the subculture symbols and beliefs like colourful hair, torn clothes, swastikas and crossed became popular in America not earlier than the late 1970s.

The movement has its roots in the early 1970s and it developed and advanced in several different forms. Its characteristic features were its own ideology, art works in the form of music, fashion, fiction and films and it also had its strong ideas and attitudes towards certain social problems in general. Criticism was the punk's driving force. A number of people involved in this subculture saw the world as corrupt and imbalanced and paid attention to the most sensitive topics in public life. Punk ideology was related to maintaining, supporting and expanding individual rights. The ideas of the punk subculture were in most cases referring to direct, drastic and sometimes even radical changes in society. The majority of punks had and still stick to their anarchist ideas. Anarchism was adopted as a means of building a utopia like society where there was no class separation, corruption, discrimination and human rights abuse. Some punks (in particular anarcho-punks) to some extent expressed endless criticism and denial of social ailments. But it was exactly that strong criticism in punk subculture that made the general and broad classification of its ideas almost impossible.

Punk subculture literally exceeded all concepts of that time and simply blew everyone's mind. The first real punks separated and became a spin-off from the skinheads in the mid-1970s due to their way of opposing to the system. Unlike the skinheads, they were against nationalism, which in turn was strongly represented in the governments and the executive authorities as a whole. Punks did not approve of racism, racial segregation and discrimination. And so, having at first sight absolutely opposite to the skinhead's viewpoints, they eventually followed their own way. There were a great number of other political, social and environmental that influenced the development of punk culture. In addition to their social identity, there were some determining cultural factors that contributed to the structuring of their world. One of them was the recession in England in the

34

mid-1970s. England's crisis had become what Stuart Hall calls 'the articulation of a fully-fledged capitalist recession, with extremely high rates of inflation, a toppling currency, a savaging of living standards, and of sacrificing of the working class to capital ". That recession brought disaster to the relatively stable British lifestyle. The cataclysm was particularly stressful for young people, who, upon seeing that their working-class parents were left jobless, were forced to look for jobs themselves no matter how young they were. "One only had to look at the decaying inner cities to realise that poverty and inequality, far from being eradicated, were visible as never before" (Savage).

In terms of music punk can be described as having a boisterous atmosphere, fast simple metre, melodiousness and predominance of the bass guitar over the solo guitar. Punk rock is closely related to Andy Warhol's art and the band he managed called The Velvet Underground. Since its very beginning punk music has been the major driving force of punk culture. Now we have different styles of punk, some of them still sticking to their original roots, others introducing heavier music items and still others even merge it with pop music. Some internationally popular punk artists were also: The Clash, Dead Boys, Pennywise, Sex Pistols, The Exploited, Rancid, Bad Religion, Black Flag, Dead Kennedys, Die Toten Hosen, Toy Dolls, Misfits, Millencolin, The Stranglers, Cockney Rejects, etc.

Punk music appeared in Bulgaria much later, though some bands were actually set up in the late 1970s. Representatives were bands with rather chocking names like Abortion, Household Terror, Hen's Head. Control, Milena, New Flowers (founded as early as the late 1970s and believed to be the first Bulgarian punk band), Review, Reformatory, Hypodile, Cholera, Cirrhosis, Repairs, Obstacle, Assault, Confront, Ignore, Ram, Ave Maria, Kale, No Exit, Debauchery and Corruption, Petrol, Regional Psychosis, Rascal, Fuse, The Pilots, Split, etc.

Fractions

Types

- Anarchist punks – largely influenced by the original anti-social and apolitical ideas of punk (absolute denial), a taste for vandalism and self-destruction
- Straight-edge punks – refrain from drugs, some leading healthy lifestyles as vegetarians, protecting the environment and animals
- Hardcore punks – the most aggressive and raw part of punk culture, where everything related to music and lifestyle is in the fast lane
- Ska-punks – the bright side of punk focused on the very music and entertainment
- Heavy Metal punks – probably the group that unites the most in terms of musical preferences, symbols and clothes

Fractions

TALKING about factions in this movement is almost pointless as one can hardly identify the particular differences since the punk image is a rather cumulative one and has its roots in other movements and styles. At the same time, its foundations are built on individualism, so definitely there are different outlooks and attitudes within this subculture. The very perception of the word 'anarchism' often leads to great corruption within the punk subculture itself. The main rule of anarchism states that everybody is free to do whatever they want, but at the same time not violate in any way the freedom of others. Conflicts with certain political and social ideas, as well as disagreements and criticism within and to the punk subculture make this movement integrally divisible. Unfortunately, the huge gaps in punk ideology are due mostly to the fashion, imagery and the wrong punk stereotypes imposed and supported by many. There is a huge number of internal differences, forced stereotypes and numerous damages made by the media and certain young enthusiasts that try to get inside punk culture defining themselves as punks, but at the same time unable to differentiate between good and bad according to punk ethics. An example of punk ethics corruption is the industrious maintenance of a particular shocking Mohawk hairstyle and stereotypical punk clothing with the aim of boosting one's self-confidence. Bands and individuals defining themselves as 'punk' make up a well-maintained image copycatting someone else and appearing in popular media without realising that such acts are ultimately contrary to punk culture, from which they have taken so much. A rather wrong approach in punk circles is the maintenance of a stereotype that punks considered as false seem to stick to. It is the building-up of an image of a callous punk who loves being photographed only smoking a fag and holding a bottle of beer. There are a number of punk rock bands maintaining such an image whose song lyrics usually contain no clearly expressed political or social messages. In the lyrics written by such punks, considered by many to be false ones, one could find verses dedicated on open sexual discrimination, paedophilia and promotion of drugs and alcohol, which is in full contrast to the original anarchistic ideas, freedom and equality. Punk dependent on tobacco, alcohol or drugs only helps greedy rich producers earn more money, which is also in direct conflict with anarchism. Most punks despise and are despised by the extreme right. Actually; their fight is exactly against the far-right political ideas such as class division, ill-treatment and exploitation on grounds of class, sex and ethnicity. Most punks are anti-Nazi both because of the strict discipline and order that the Nazi regime stands for and because of its extremely discriminatory nature, which makes the two movements' bitter enemies.

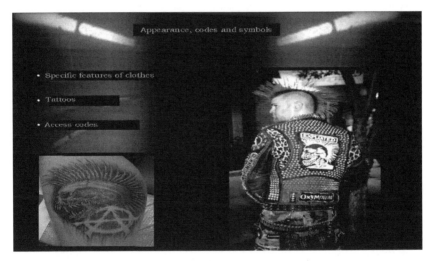

Appearance, symbols and codes of behaviour

TO UNDERSTAND punk is to know that its adherents are destructive, angry and anti-social, forming bonds only with each other which sometimes results in hostility toward others. The authentic idea of the multicoloured spiky hair was to symbolise something opposite the authoritative fashion symbols. The spiky hair was a means to successfully defy others. Its original idea was to stand for something unacceptable by people of high authority. Punk fashion is an expression of the desire to reject all symbols of power (authority, wealth, self-confidence) that seemed obligatory and replace them with their opposites. If a rich man would be proud of an expensive and universally acknowledged car or a shiny garment, a punk would do the exact opposite, i.e. tear up the garment and destroy the car. We can surely state that punk style stands in between Heavy Metal and Skinhead style.

Also typical for punks were the high military boots (skinhead style), torn up tight jeans, patched jeans vests (Heavy Metal style) and the numerous piercing's and jewels all over the body, and the aim of all those elements was to be different and, no matter how strange it may sound, to repel!"The well-ordered dress code of the punk might look like it is haphazard and dirty with no thought put into it to the general observer, but if one looks closer, one will realise that this first impression is deceptive: the seemingly tattered and shabby garb is carefully put together and arranged "(Soeffner). Soeffner continued his observations by stating that "Punk is the elaboration of a specific aesthetic of the ugly ." The idea of the ugly, or what some might consider obscene, also serves to explain why punks choose to wear offensive body jewellery, such as safety pins as earrings and face rings, swastikas and crosses as pins and painted emblems, etc. As we stated earlier, punk is a reflective subculture and it employs shock value in every aspect of life. The style of punk can also be viewed as taking the symbols of the dominant culture, mixing up their meanings and then applying these symbols to their way of dress. A typical example is the use of swastikas and crosses, which, while on the surface showing a loyalty to the neo-Nazi movement or some religious group, in reality serve only to offend the mainstream. In particular, for punks the swastika was a symbol of contempt used as a means of offending the traditional culture and actually devoid of any social or political significance.

Their clothing serves to set them apart from the dominant culture. Offending the mainstream, by their use of symbols in dress, seems to be the key motivation for the punks. "The punks wore clothes that were the sartorial equivalent of swear words, and they swore as they dressed - with calculated effect...Clothed in chaos, they produced Noise in the calmly orchestrated crisis of everyday life...a noise which made (no) sense in exactly the same way and to exactly the same extent as a piece of avant-garde music" (Hebdige). Many of the theorists who write about the look of the punks imply that it is a culture of style. The culture of style implies that it is devoid of any other cultural factor. Greil Marcus attempts to show the reader that the ugliness of punk is more than a fashion statement. He adds, "The punks were not just pretty people... who made themselves ugly. They were fat, anorexic, pockmarked, acned, stuttering, crippled, scarred, and damaged, and what their new decorations underlined was the failure already engraved in t heir faces". Today, this idea of ugliness is not quite so literal. Some punks may be physically attractive, but in attitude and dress they promote the "ugly and repulsive" quality.

The use of horrific symbols and jewellery speak to their philosophy. Naturally, there is an enormous symbol of anarchy, which is the first letter of the alphabet surrounded by a circle, on the back of the denim vest. Punks wear the sign of the anarchists not to necessarily say they are anarchists, but to imply that they hate the idea of organised government. Punk's symbols and style are meant to strike and shock onlookers. They hang and draw their symbols at all kinds of places like railway stations and bus stops so that "normal" people could see them. Their demonstrative statement is to be seen by as many people as possible and it is to stand against tradition in order to mock at it. Punks believed that if the economy could fall it was because it was based on a faulty foundation. They hated the government and thought the only way to live was to make your own rules on a personal level with no regard for the collective. They were anarchists who thought chaos would help to sort out the mess and put things in a natural order. Yet, for all of their concentration on chaos and the jumbling of symbols, punks had a culture and even ethics of their own!

Punk ethics covers a number of ideas that lay the foundations of punk culture. They include the idea of anti-conformism. The 'Do-It-Yourself' (DIY) idea calls for every punk to reject many products made, designed and processed by others. DIY is an inherent part of the punk movement strongly expressed through music, clothing and building up the punk image. According to the DIY-ethics, people should get rid of their role of consumers or a limitless number of goods, including clothes, food, ornaments, etc. and instead try to act as designers and creators of their environment so that they could adjust it to their inner selves. According to punk ethics, the stricter the laws and the more severe the regime, the more horrendous the behind the scenes abuses are and the stronger the discontent and resistance are. Punk ethics was also against any form of warfare.

Each of these ideas helps to define the Punk world view or philosophy. Each of the institutions and traditions they are against defines every other aspect of their lives. When you pick apart a punk, you don't find chaos, but a very well established and defined code that colours everything from their clothes and hair to their behaviour and social activity."The subculture was no thing if not consistent. There is a homological relation between the trashy cut-up clothes and spiky hair, the pogo and the amphetamines, the spitting, the vomiting, the format of fanzines, the insurrectionary poses and the 'soulless,' frantically driven music ". (Hebdige).

The language of punk gives meaning to the movement and the most visible sign of their language comes in the form of music. Punk music serves as a language to align their philosophies and give punks a place to rally in clubs and at punk functions. "If we were to write an epitaph for the punk subculture, we could do no better than say concisely: the forbidden is permitted" (Hebdige). Everything thought of as questionable or objectionable by the dominant culture, not just in music, is fair and preferable game for the punks. The music, while singing the belief of the irreverent punk band, the Sex Pistols, "No Future," also gives a purpose and a feeling of acceptance among youths who feel alone and unloved by the world. In the music there is hope and there is future. "What remains irreducible about this music is its desire to change the world...The desire begins with the demand to live not as an object but as a subject of history - to live as if something actually depended on one's actions - and that demand opens onto a free street" (Marcus Greil). The music seeks to prove that all of the popular institutions that punks are asked to accept by the dominant culture are false, ideological constructs. The style of punk music is reflective of the clothing. It is raucous, tattered and held together by a rhythm made up of as few as three chords. One might think that only the huge scandalous pins that hold together their tattered clothing that looks like rather hung than worn. The music is also offensive many times, as is illustrated by the story of the Sex Pistols' first television performance where they used the word "fuck" on air a thousand times. This was so obscene that the Sex Pistols were seen as a threat to the state and were denounced by the Queen. Even when one of their songs hit number one on the billboard charts, it was shown by a blank space at the number 1 spot. Some workers whose job it was to package the album in the factory refused to do so in order not to "get dirty" ...And here comes commercialisation... If we place punk culture even further than mass culture. It is interesting to note, however, that early punk music influenced society regardless of its inherent obscenity. Major record labels fought with each other in order to be the first to sign punk bands, the most popular being the Sex Pistols and the Clash. What is strange and surprising is that the music that inspired such revulsion could be such an inspiration for a label. Actually, it was a potential money maker. But what is equally surprising is that punk bands allowed themselves to be signed to major record labels at all, considering their severe distaste for the mainstream. Joel Schalit offers at least a partial explanation for this paradox when he writes: "Instead of advocating the overthrow of capitalist relations of production, punk insists on reverting to an early form of capitalist development which emphasises the necessity of the imagination, skills, and hard work of the entrepreneur as opposed to the blindness and stupidity of the corporation and the bureaucrat. In this light, punk appears as a critique of mass culture instead of a critique of capitalist culture. This paradox is important to understand, since even to this day it is considered selling out for punk bands to sign with a major record company. Knowing that punk is against mass culture, but promotes, or least accepts capitalist culture, helps one to understand that punk bands signing with major record labels or buying into the fashion of the punks are not really selling out when looked at from this perspective".

The style of clothing and the music remain two of the most obvious original influences on traditional culture... Folklore, too. Punk style remains as the defining music of not only a single subculture. In God Save the Queen, The Sex Pistols ranted their ideals for all of England to hear before being banned to do so. They released their single during the so-called Silver Jubilee, i.e. the Queen's 25th year on the throne. The lyrics define both how the punks viewed the world around them, as well as how they viewed themselves.

Here are some lines from this song: "God Save the Queen / The fascist regime / They made you a moron / A potential H-bomb / God save the Queen / She isn't no human being / There is no future / In England's Dream / God save the Queen / We mean it man / We love our Queen / God Saves / Don't be told what you want / Don't be told what you need / There's no future.../ When there's no future / How can there be sin / We're poison in your machine / We're the flowers in your dustbin / We're the future / Your future / God Save the Queen".

With no future as a major philosophy, there are also hints at no past. With no past comes no influence from outside sources because the outside sources simply do not exist for the punks. Therefore, their folklore is created internally by the musicians who believe and understand the idea of authenticity and the truth of the pure or primordial thought that inspired all other thought. Punks believe that since they have no inspiration, they are free to choose how to live, what to write, and what to believe. They are free to be authentic - to have their own ideas and thoughts without regard to the society around them. In her article on punk Widdicombe speaks directly to this idea of authenticity. She addresses how the Punk subculture defines itself in relation to other groups. "There are people who take to the subculture not only because it is fashionable or somehow cool. Punks admire those members who exhibit genuine commitment to certain values". According to Linda Andes, "An individual must be able to display expert knowledge of punk culture and especially of punk music to be perceived as authentic by members of the subculture".

"Within the punk subculture there exists a whole set of cultural factors that help to set it apart from the surrounding society. Even though punk is considered a reflective subculture, illuminating central features of the dominant culture" (Levine and Stumpf). Punks can still be viewed as a group of individuals with their own culture, values (or lack of values), structure and philosophy. Punk also exhibits other narrower cultural factors such as language and style (mainly through music). The punk culture shows signs of being socially active and in some ways have influenced the community. They have a definable philosophy further expressed by their art, symbolic objects and folklore. They have taboos, boundaries and a view of outsiders as "others", which further accentuate those cultural boundaries. In order to have a complete view of punks as a culture we should discuss each of the above-mentioned cultural factors (we already discussed some) as they pertain to the punk movement in general.

Generally speaking, Punk is anti-establishment, anti-status quo, anti-institutional and anti-religious. They believe in anarchy, freedom of the people, destruction of tradition and a basic truth that exists beneath all of these societal constraints. One of their major goals is to challenge, both actively and passively, what the dominant society sees as truth.

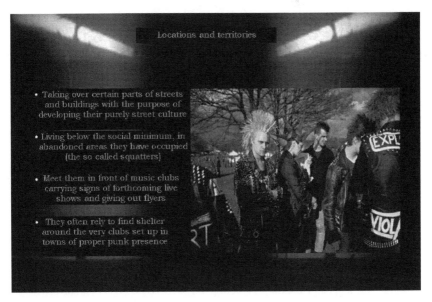

Locations and territories

SUBCULTURES INVARIABLY HAVE their own territories. For punks they are more often characterised as appropriating certain parts of the city with the purpose of developing their purely street culture.

You won't meet punks in the library, nor in front of it, though inside one could find quite a lot of books on their culture and movement, and a good number of them may be well educated and literate. You'd rather meet them in front of music clubs carrying big posters advertising a forthcoming gig and giving out flyers.

Real punks often live rough or rely on punk clubs established in cities with massive punk presence. They live in poverty, cramped in abandoned buildings with dozens of others. Their jobs are usually "outside the system" working as musicians in rock bands or artists, but, quite understandably, many are unemployed and live on the edge. Viewing this deprivation, popular culture has seen punk life as the same as a vagrant's life. For the punk, however, this view is not true at all.

Punk movement grew out of this drab and dark environment ready to challenge the status quo and show their contempt for government, society and tradition.

When asked, a punk said, "Punk left me penniless. However, it let me exit the system. I can roam the streets and do whatever I want instead of living within the system's requirements. When I roam the streets, I am a proud punk, not an asshole".

"Doing nothing" is a popular slogan in this subculture coined by youngsters who usually find it hard to get a job. The act of doing nothing begins with picking a place in the city like a street corner and then just waiting. To those around it looks to be a complete waste of time. However, punks see it as yet another case of standing their ground and protesting against the system.

The solidarity of punks is easily witnessed in any small town or large city that has a punk following. If another group of punks comes to town, they are quickly invited to stay with the local group. Punks are a family to each other, no matter how dysfunctional they may seem. If you are a punk, you always have a home, no matter where you go and no matter that it may often be … the street.

Nowadays, in this globalised world, it is even more difficult to understand one's motivation to be a punk. Those guys have travelled a long way from the rough times of "Doing Nothing". Punks today still create garage bands in which they write, perform and record their own music, and they often run away from the street life downtown to the suburbs and become more isolated than ever. Modern- day punks are a kind of paradox made up of past, present and future; they don't seem to be motivated by the same issues and aims of the original punk movement. As the writing on a wall says, "Punk is not dead; it lives in the suburbs with its parents ."

Opinion: C. N. C. (Bourgas)

"A lot can be said about subculture in the town of Bourgas Bulgaria, even a separate book can be written. By and large, just like everywhere else, it all started in the last years of the communist regime. One could already feel the rebellious atmosphere, the rock'n'roll and the aggro aimed at the Old Bill during football games . Rebels, hooligans, ordinary fans, all of them were skinheads , metalheads, punks, etc. in their daily lives.

In the beginning it was all mixed up . We'd all sit at a table and later on at night we'd all end up beating people from the minorities. Then we separated on grounds of politics and things got fucked up.

Punks were numerous and quite tough guys . At first, they didn't care about politics at all, they were just vandals and anarchists. Skinheads appeared years later and the fights between them became traditional at a later stage. The first signs of differences were to be seen in Sofia and it was there the fights began before gradually spreading across the country. Punks were dominant for years due to the weak skinhead organisation, especially in Bourgas.

As far as the strong HM wave and community is concerned, they were so big with us that they just didn't let any other trends to prevail and develop .

In 1982 Signal band were to play a gig in Bourgas having released their first rock album. Those were the times when Poland had seen the end of its anti-communist protests and so our militia was on the alert for that gig . The hall was packed. So, naturally, with just two songs played, trouble erupted, and it grew into such a huge melee that I think is still unparalleled on the Bulgarian scene! Both fans and coppers got injured . Naturally, after that incident, Signal were banned from playing live for some time by the communists and I think the police do not guard their gigs in Bourgas up to this date.

В спортна зала "Изгрев" настава страхотен бой между милиционери и публика. Мнозина са пребити, първите редове опустяват. Данчо Караджов хваща микрофона и извиква "Няма да свирим и да пеем под ударите на милиционерските палки."
Дни след инцидента в морския град плочите на рок групата са иззети от магазините. Певците негласно са изхвърлени от телевизия, радио и каквито и да било сценични изяви

През лятото на 1978 година на българската музикална сцена изгрява нова рок група. Тримата музиканти Йордан Караджов, Румен Спасов и Христо Ламбрев се отделят от група "Златни струни" и основават група "Сигнал". Барабанист е Георги Кокаланов, който през пролетта на 1979 год. е заменен от Владимир Захариев. Със създаването си групата работи като студийна формация в националното радио. През август 1978 година по радиото прозвучава и първата им песен "Любов", а на следващата година издават и първия си албум „Вечен кръстопът". Тогава е организиран и първият им концерт в столичната зала „Фестивална". Появяват се и първите им големи хитове "Може би" и "Спри се", които ги изпращат на върха на слушателския интерес. Печелят трета награда и на най-престижния тогава у нас международен музикален фестивал „Златния орфей". Вторият им албум излиза през 1980 год. и с "Попътен вятър" продължават и техните концерти и турнета у нас и в чужбина. На международния шлагерен фестивал в Дрезден печелят първа награда за изпълнение.

В годината, която България чества своята 1300 годишнина „Сигнал" издават първият двоен рок албум в историята на музиката у нас, от който излизат хитовете "Да те жадувам" и "Лодка ли е любовта". През същата година на „Златния Орфей", музикантите изнасят самостоятелен рецитал – своеобразен връх в кариерата на всеки български изпълнител, по онова време. С изключително силен старт започва и

международната им концертна дейност. Групата покорява сцените в СССР, Германия, Полша, Чехословакия, Румъния, Куба, като свири изключително свои песни на концертите си и изпълнява парчетата си само на български език. За краткия период от нейното създаване, бандата успява да набере изключителна популярност и многобройни почитатели. Концертният им живот върви с пълна сила, билетите се разграбват на секундата, групата заема челни позиции в музикалните класации в страната.

В началото на новата 1982 година им предстои поредния концерт в морския град Бургас. Афишите за събитието са разлепени из града, а билетите много преди обявената дата 10 февруари са разпродадени. В мразовития февруарски ден пред зала „Изгрев" (днес "Бойчо

Брънзов") се струпва тълпа от почитатели дошли да се насладят на музиката им. Напрежението е огромно и се усеща още преди началото на концерта. Феновете, които не са успели да се сдобият с билет за шоуто, търсят пропуски на черно и на двойна цена. Планираните от „Концертна дирекция" два концерта на групата са обединени в един. Залата няма необходимия капацитет за множеството дошло да види любимците си и се пука по шевовете. Групата едва си пробива път през публиката до сцената. Десет минути след обявения час на концерта, "Сигнал" се появяват на сцената на спортната зала. Шоуто започва. Пред сцената и отстрани нея има кордон от милиционери, които са натоварени с охраната на музикалното събитие.

Зала "Изгрев"

Заради полските събития тогава, (през 1980 г. Лех Валенса създава "Солидарност", а на 13.12.1981 г. в Полша е обявено военно положение) властите у нас са настръхнали някой да не наруши безметежното им управление.

Групата е изпяла първите си две песни. Същевременно милицията бди особено зорко за антикомунистически прояви в контекста на полските събития. На третата песен всички в изпълнената до краен предел зала пеят в един глас заедно с момчетата на сцената, няколко хилядната публиката е в екстаз. Феновете са на крака, веселят се и подскачат с ритъма на музиката. Милицията се разбеснява. Един от униформените превишава правата си, изважда палката и удря едно момиче, което се свлича пред сцената и припада. След това народната милиция устройва истински погром в залата, като започва да млати ожесточено ентусиазираната тълпа. Настава страхотен бой. Мнозина са пребити, първите редове опустяват. В този момент групата спира да свири. Данчо Караджов хваща микрофона и извиква "Няма да свирим и да пеем под ударите на милиционерските палки." Концертът е прекратен. Започва разследване, от което пострадват самите музиканти. Веднага след концерта от Комитета за култура последва моментална забрана да изнасят концерти. Негов председател по това време е Георги Йорданов, наследил поста след кончината на Людмила Живкова. Плочите им са иззети от магазините. Група "Сигнал" негласно са изхвърлени от телевизия, радио и каквито и да било сценични изяви. Това е и първата явна проява на дискриминация на български рок музиканти по времето на социализма. Многобройните им почитатели са бесни от случилото се. Те заставят категорично зад тях, пишат протестни писма до различни институции и това повлиява положително. Една година след злополучния концерт в Бургас забраната пада. Силният им дух и подкрепата на феновете им помагат отново да се качат на сцената.

По време на негласната забрана музикантите не стоят със скръстени ръце, а подготвят поредните си хитове, които публиката чува за първи път във Видин, където се състои първият им концерт след едногодишната им забрана за сценична дейност. През следващите години групата продължава да свири и издава хитове необезпокоявана от никой, печели много музикални награди и с много труд, упоритост и най-вече благодарение на любовта на своите фенове успява да се задържи на музикалния небосклон и до днес. През своята 35 годишна история рок групата има издадени 18 албума, над 7 000 концерта и участия, и повече от 500 000 продадени плочи.

IZGREV SPORTS HALL witnessed a brutal fight between the police and the crowd. A number of people got injured, the first rows were deserted. Dancho Karadzhov grabbed the microphone and shouted, "We won't play under the blows of police truncheons".

A few days after the incident, the rock band's records were withdrawn from the shops in Burgas. The artists were tacitly banned from television channels, radio stations and any other kinds of on-stage performances.

In the summer of 1978 the Bulgarian music scene saw the rising of a new rock band. Three artists, i.e. Dancho Karadzhov, Rumen Spasov and Hristo Lambrev separated from the Golden Strings band and set up the Signal band. Georgi Kokalanov started as a drummer to be replaced by Vladimir Zahariev in the spring of 1979. Initially, the band performed as a studio band at the National Radio. In August 1978 the radio broadcast their first song Love and the following year they released their debut album Eternal Crossroads. They also played their first gig in Festivalna Hall in Sofia. Their first smash Maybe and Stop appeared which sent them to the top of the charts. They finished third in the most prestigious then international music festival Golden Orpheus. Their second album Fair Wind was released in 1980 and they went on to play live both in Bulgaria and abroad. They won the first award for live performance at the international hit music festival in Dresden.

In 1981 Signal were the first in Bulgaria to release a double rock album featuring their absolute hits Craving You and Is Love a Boat . In the same year they played a one-man live show at the Golden Orpheus, which was considered as a climax of an artist's career in Bulgaria at that time. Their international live performances also saw a great start. The band hit stages in USSR, Germany, Poland, Czechoslovakia Romania and Cuba, where they played their own music and only in Bulgarian. Shortly after its foundation, the band managed to gain extreme popularity and attract numerous fans. Their live shows were sold out in seconds and the band hit the top in all Bulgarian charts.

At the beginning of 1982 they were to play two gigs in the seaside town of Bourgas. Posters were put all over the town and the tickets were sold out long before the date announced, 10th February. On that chilly day, a crowd of fans gathered in front of the venue waiting to enjoy their music. Tensions were high long before the live show. Those who did not have tickets were willing to play touts a double price to get in. The band was ordered to play one gig instead of the planned two. The venue did not have the capacity to host such a huge crowd and was literally bursting at its seams. The band barely forced its way through the audience. Ten minutes before the scheduled time Signal hit the stage. The gig started. A police cordon was lined up in front of the stage and in the very wings because of the events in Poland (in 1980 Lech Valesa founded Solidarity and on 13.12.1981 Poland introduced martial law) as the Bulgarian authorities were afraid of possible rioting.

The band had played their first two songs. Meanwhile the police were on the alert for any anti-communist acts in the context of the Polish events. During the third song everyone in the crowded hall was singing along with the band and the several thousand fans were delirious. The fans were on their feet entertaining themselves, bouncing to the rhythm. The police got mad. A police officer exceeded his rights by taking out his truncheon and hitting a girl, who immediately collapsed in front of the stage. After that the police started mercilessly beating everyone in the crowd. A number of people got injured, the first rows were deserted. At that point the band stopped playing. Dancho Karadzhov grabbed the microphone and shouted, "We won't play under the blows of police truncheons" . The gig was suspended. An investigation was started, and its victims were the very musicians. Right after the show, the Culture Committee banned them from performing live. Their records were withdrawn from shops. Signal was tacitly banned from television channels, radio stations and any other kinds of on-stage performances. That was the first act of discrimination against Bulgarian rock musicians in the years of socialism. Their numerous fans were outraged at what had happened. The categorically stood behind them and wrote letters of protest to different institutions and eventually succeeded. A year after that disastrous gig in Bourgas the banning order was cancelled. The band's strong spirit and their fans' support helped them hit the stage again.

During their implicit ban, the musicians did not remain idle, but worked on their next hits, which were first played in the town of Vidin at their first live show after their one-year stage performance ban. In the years to follow the band went on playing and making hits undisturbed and they won a number of music awards thanks to their strenuous efforts and perseverance, but most of all, thanks to the love and support they got from their devoted fans the band is still active and playing nowadays. In their 35-year history, the band has released 18 albums, played over 7000 gigs and performances and sold more than 500 000 records.

"Almost 10 years later, if I'm not mistaken, the first rock festival ever to be held in Bulgaria was organised at the seaside, in the town of Nesebar in 1991. The same riots and mayhem involving the OB just like what happened at the subsequent live shows of Sodom and Kreator. Water jets, injured people and torn up uniforms. Not just a rebellion, but a real little revolution that the youth of those times had been dreaming of . The Sodom and Kreator lives in questions turned into a display of chaos and disorder. I remember travelling by train for those gigs and upon entering t he loo I could see as far as the loo at the opposite end of the carriage... It was similar to the scene from the Czech film "Why?" portraying Sparta Prague fans, which by the way was the first film to open Bourgas fans' eye for vandalism. Not that they actually needed anything or anyone to open their eyes as they seemed to have it inborn in them (laughing). Burgas trains full of metalheads were traditionally intercepted by the police at Stara Zagora station and what usually followed were violent clashes and riots. Burgas in particular (besides HM fans) boasted of a good number of punks who'd go for English and Serbian punk mainly. Unfortunately, the early 1990s heroin craze hit those circles really bad . The places all those alternative groups used to hang around were well familiar and everyone knew where one could meet likeminded fellas, or buy a cassette or poster that one then had to take good care of since they could easily get 'nicked' in those times... When I say 'nicked' I remember that period in the early 1990s when it was a kind of craze going down the boulevard leading to the station with a couple of mates in summer and nick some poor tourists' denim safari jackets, badges and other fan items .

Emblematic rally points for years were places called 'The Holes', 'The Phonograph', 'The Blue Trap', 'The Mariner',' Voyage', 'Galatea', etc. Also, Satan disco club (legendary nationwide) hosted some unprecedented in Bulgaria events ...One of the first tattoo fests in Bulgaria was held there . Another exceptional event held for a few years in the town of Nesebar in early August was 'Port Royal', a convention rather than a festival, but it was a unique gathering of all types of weirdos like hippies, metalheads, punks, bikers, anarchists, etc. It would almost always end up in mass brawls with members of organised crime . On the whole, Bourgas was a hub for subculture and counterculture back in the dawn of democracy and even before that . Nowadays, folks from all corners of the country keep on going there for the underground metal fest traditionally held in the seaside garden just the way as it used to be back in the old days when people were not used to seeing M.A.V.O. (as we used to call them) hordes wearing military boots and tight jeans for days at temperatures over 40°C... Those were simply brutal times... Fellas from towns like Dupnitsa, Pernik, Sofia, Pazardzhik, etc. And naturally the usual never-ending fights between skinheads and metalheads, punks, skaters, etc. Each against all.

So, the status of Bourgas on the underground scene has long been absolutely top and the city even boasts of impressive hip-hop scene dating back to 1990."

Heavy Metal subculture, movement and style

- According to most specialists, its beginning can be traced back to 1964

- In Bulgaria Heavy Metal came in strong in the early 80s

Background

HEAVY METAL IS one of the most misunderstood and underestimated music genres of our times. Unfortunately, this is mostly due to the mass audience's gross ignorance caused by the media and public opinion. What is actually HM? Surely something more than just music, it's a way of life.

Traditional Heavy Metal, a.k.a. classic metal or just Heavy Metal is the rawest Heavy Metal style before the genre evolved to split into a number of types and subtypes. The brief, genuine and correct term for this style is Heavy Metal though the term can be used in different ways. It can be sued for the earliest style, but also for any subsequent type that appeared later. Therefore, classic or traditional Heavy Metal is used in order to avoid any confusion.

According to most specialised annals the beginning was in 1964 with the release of emblematic albums such as You Really Got Me by Kinks and My Generation by The Who. Alice Cooper, who started his career in 1965 in The Spiders but did not become famous before the early 1970s with the Love It to Death classic is considered by many as the first Heavy Metal artist. Between 1966 and 1970 bands like Golden Earring, Cream, The Jimi Hendrix Experience, Led Zeppelin, Vanilla Fudge, Iron Butterfly, Steppenwolf, Blue Cheer, Deep Purple, Grand Funk Railroad, Free, Uriah Heep, Mountain, Humble Pie, Bloodrock, Black Widow, Atomic Rooster, Cactus, and Black Sabbath appeared, each of them having a different impact on the further development of rock music. The very phrase "Heavy Metal Thunder" came from Steppenwolf's Born to Be Wild and as time went by it became an emblem of heavy music combining rock-and-roll and blues elements supplemented by brilliant guitars and unbelievable vocals.

The new genre was initially made popular mostly by bands like Cream and The Jimi Hendrix Experience. The former featured the legendary guitarist Eric Clapton and its most popular hits were Sunshine of Your Love and White Room. Cream's influence was the strongest with Rush, Van Halen, and later Blind Faith. Meanwhile, The Jimi Hendrix Experience was a music trio built around the guitar feats of another legend called Jimi Hendrix. The 'Are You Experienced' and 'Electric Ladyland' albums appealed to thousands of fanatics and were the reason for the band to become a legend among names like Janis Joplin and The Doors. Several new bands, including Savoy Brown, Foghat, Bad Company, Budgie and UFO appeared as a result of the growing HM explosion, but until 1973 the undisputed kings of heavy rock were Led Zeppelin, Deep Purple and Black Sabbath, still considered by many as the most influential bands ever in the history of Heavy Metal. All three bands were famous for technical prowess, compositional inventiveness and passion for music never seen before. Hard Rock live shows became an unforgettable experience and unique contact between bands and audiences. At the same time certain bands started introducing a satanic image to music. The first to dare do that were British bands like Black Sabbath and Led Zeppelin.

Led Zeppelin's guitarist Jimmy Page (a former member of the emblematic The Yardbirds that contributed to the rock world with names like Clapton and Jeff Beck) had a strong personal fascination with the occult, while many of Sabbath's lyrics also dealt with such themes. However, Black Sabbath never claimed to be satanic. On the contrary, Ozzy Osbourne, vocalist of the band in its early period, claims to have been scared off by Sabbath fans dressed in black robes and carrying candles.

Live shows were carried out by every heavy band, most notably by Led Zeppelin and Deep Purple. Alice Cooper put on unprecedented shows featuring boa constrictors, mutilated female mannequins and Cooper himself being beheaded. Bands introduced more and more visual effects, at the same time showing class through skilful performances in front of huge crowds of fans.

The first few years of Heavy Metal, called by many its classic period, created masterpieces like Led Zeppelin's Black Dog, Kashmir and Stairway to Heaven, though the band as more or less rock-oriented. In terms of music, "true" metal was made by Black Sabbath - gloomy, heavy and foreboding. Tony Iommi, Ozzy Osbourne, Bill Ward and Geezer Butler created classics like Black Sabbath, Paranoid and Master of Reality . Much later, bands like Corrosion of Conformity, Metallica and Nirvana were all influenced by the classic HM period. Meanwhile Deep Purple, after experimenting in the progressive rock field, shifted to a much heavier sound and for many years remained as the greatest innovators. Ritchie Blackmore's virtuous guitar, along with Jon Lord's synthesiser solid sounds and Ian Gillan's piercing shrieks turned into the prototype of classic Heavy Metal.

In the mid-1970s several new significant bands appeared, i.e. Thin Lizzy, Judas Priest, Queen, Aerosmith and Kiss. Judas Priest contributed to the popularisation of the two-guitar concept in HM bands and to a considerably heavier style. Aerosmith brought back the blues, sex and drugs. Thin Lizzy made a breakthrough due to aesthetics and their own musical style, and Queen reached a higher level of experimentation combining magnificent melodies with progressive shades. Kiss revolutionised the art of live shows presenting macabre theatrics reminiscent of Alice Cooper's.

While a number of bands established their reputation as founders of Heavy Metal, others turned to taking a popular genre like progressive rock to heavier dimensions. Bands like Pink Floyd and Genesis never really got into the heavy metal realms, while Jethro Tull, Yes and King Crimson often successfully flirted with heavy metal. Featuring complex song structures, old-school arrangements and the obligatory virtuous use of instruments, progressive metal was born with the emergence of Rush. On its debut album the band had not yet acquired tendency for that style but with the release of Fly by Night Rush developed their sound into the progressive direction to remain in history with their later albums A Farewell to Kings and Hemispheres. Other early progressive bands were Emerson, Lake, and Palmer, Focus, Asia, IQ and Marillion.

In the late Seventies the metal scene was in a state of stagnation. Aerosmith, Thin Lizzy and Black Sabbath were digging their own graves due to the mass consumption of alcohol and drugs. Kiss lost their charm because of over-commercialisation. Deep Purple suffered those never-ending personnel changes, Led Zeppelin ended after the demise of their drummer John Bonham. Only a few bands kept their former grandeur, among them Judas Priest, Queen and AC/DC. Rainbow was one of the last rock dinosaurs that made their music classic thanks to the unique pieces played by Blackmore and the legendary Ronnie James Dio's voice.

At the same time a new branch of rock music was appearing, i.e. punk rock. All of a sudden there were numerous new bands that could barely play their musical instruments, but protested against fascism, their governments and even everyday life. Bands like Iggy and the Stooges, MC5, New York Dolls, Sex Pistols, Ramones, The Clash hit the headlines. Punk's greatest contribution to the rock scene was the renaissance of energy in songs, the defiance of social norms and the fight against social injustice emphasised in their lyrics (originally hinted at by Black Sabbath in Children of the Grave and War Pigs). Iggy Pop made remarkably energetic live performances that he believed would only last for not more than 15 minutes. The Ramones laid the foundations on which bands like Red Hot Chilli Peppers and Nirvana would later appear. The Sex Pistols, still being the most famous punk rock band ever, destroyed all previous traditions. However, during one of their tours, bass guitarist Sid Vicious, under the influence of drugs, killed his girlfriend Nancy Spunge and then committed suicide, which was the end of not only The Sex Pistols, but of the entire punk movement, which was to remain underground for the most part until the 1990s.

While punk wave was taking over the youth, a quite different band called Motorhead set the beginning of a new mixture of styles that later on got known as thrash speed and power metal. The band's debut album On Parole was released in 1976 when they would only hint at the power unleashed in their later albums like Overkill, Bomber and Ace of Spades. Besides attracting huge crowds of Heavy Metal crowds, Motorhead were also extremely popular among punks and thus they marked the beginning of an interesting union that would eventually result in the creation of hardcore.

In the early 1980s classic HM returned thanks to Judas Priest, Accept, The Scorpions and the so-called phenomenon New Wave of British Heavy Metal. New

British bands like Diamond Head, Def Leppard, Holocaust, Iron Maiden, Saxon, Samson, Venom and Raven quickly gained popularity, though not all of them managed to survive through the years. Judas Priest popularised leather, studs and spikes attire that would characterise HM for years to come. Scorpions made both heavy songs and great ballads and the music made by Accept saw the first signs of power metal in their albums Breaker and Restless and Wild. Iron Maiden showed pure class creating some of the heaviest riffs until the advent of Metallica. While Maiden came up with harmonised riffs backed up by a thunderous bass, Venom actually started thrash metal (Welcome to Hell and Black Metal), out of which death and black metal originated later. Along with Judas Priest, Motorhead and Riot they made a wave known for playing fast aggressive metal joined by Metallica, Exodus, Slayer and Mantas (later known as Death). The NWOBHM to a large extent determined the development and the exciting success of Heavy Metal in the 1980s. The US responded to the British attack with a wave of glam metal bands. While Van Halen and Montrose released some legendary hits, and Angel and Foreigner additionally contributed to the development of the new genre, the real manifestation of glam was in two LA bands, i.e. Motley Crue and Ratt, who wrote accessible for the mass audience songs influenced by veterans like Sweet and T-Rex. The glam bands in question followed the example of Alice Cooper, David Bowie, The New York Dolls, Kiss, and began wearing women's makeup, tight outfits, headbands, spikes and whatever they could lay their hands on. Motley Crue and their album Shout at the Devil contributed to the commercialisation of metal in the States and to the consequent success of Ratt and even of older bands like Twisted Sister and Quiet Riot, at the same time paving the way for Bon Jovi. It was Bon Jovi's Slippery When Wet and New Jersey and Def Leppard's Pyromania and Hysteria that mixed heavy music with accessible pop, considerably influencing other commercialised rock/metal bands. A lot of talented American bands were left underestimated only because they refused to change their styles and turn to glam, while Kiss successfully adapted with songs like Heaven's on Fire. Later on, pop metal got too monotonous and needed some fresh air that came with the advent of Guns n' Roses, carrying over something from the Rolling Stones and Aerosmith and famous blues motifs. Dokken showed that even a commercialised style like glam can be a suitable environment for creating heavy and technically brilliant music and had their impact on the eventual transition of some bands (like Skid Row) from pop metal to heavier styles. The glam scene had its contribution to the appearance of female HM artists like Joan Jett & the Blackhearts, Lita Ford and Warlock's vocalist Doro Pesch.

Meanwhile some metal giants accepted a heavier and more classic approach to music. Black Sabbath with their new vocalist Ronnie James Dio returned with masterpieces like Heaven and Hell and Mob Rules, marking a stylistic change to a more melodic approach. Ozzy Osbourne released his solo albums Blizzard of Ozz and Diary of a Madman and together with Dio's later solo projects kept melodic alive through the Eighties. New bands like Savatage, Manowar, Cirith Ungol and Armored Saint emerged, each having its own style, but still united by the melodic and yet heavy sounds. Old-school HM fans were shocked by the fact that a number of bands would soften down their style in an attempt to get to broader audiences. The advent of thrash/speed metal was just the opposite, i.e. multiple heavy riffs, snarling vocals, and a wide use of double-pedal drumming, all being the factors that made thrash the heaviest music ever seen by then. Bands like Metallica, Exodus, Slayer and Anthrax pioneered the new wave. Shortly after Metallica threw out their guitarist Dave Mustaine, he founded one of the most successful thrash bands called Megadeth. Metallica experimented a lot in terms of music creating their masterpieces Ride the Lightning and Master of Puppets, which later on influenced bands like Sepultura, for example. Anthrax was the first metal band to start experimenting with rap vocals (featuring Public Enemy). Slayer created some incredibly heavy riffs combining them with satanic imagery and establishing as one of the Top 4 thrash bands thanks to their 1986 album Reign in Blood. Another particularly influential thrash band of the 1980s was Testament, who after releasing the classic Practice What You Preach and Souls of Black simply faded away. In addition to the American monsters, the German thrash scene was also quite successful due to big names like Destruction, Kreator, Tankard, and Sodom.

Thrash's response to the commercial glam scene was brutal and uncompromising, though a number of good bands like Flotsam & Jetsam, Sacred Reich and the early Anvil never got the recognition they deserved.

Another crucial trend of the mid-1980s was power metal. It was a style that took the speed and heaviness of speed/thrash metal bands and combined them with the epic sounds of classic Heavy Metal. Some power bands made more standard, American-style power metal like Metal Church, Savatage, Jag Panzer and Manowar, retaining the harshness of their sounds to the greatest degree. Unlike them, the representatives of German power metal like Helloween, Running Wild and Rage combined melodic, strong guitar speed with classic elements. Helloween's Keeper of the Seven Keys epic albums were the height of this trend. Unbelievable compositions, unique guitar parts played by Hansen and Weikath, plus the astounding voice of Michael Kiske made the two albums the most influential power albums, along with Manowar's Kings of Metal. New talented bands like Blind Guardian and Iced Earth emerged on the scene, forcing old veterans like Riot to adjust to their style.

Thrash gave birth to another branch of extreme music that later on became the most brutal one, i.e. death metal. Albums like Hellhammer's Apocalyptic Raid, Death's Scream Bloody Gore and Possessed's The Seven Churches marked the beginning of the new style. Guitars became as heavy and down tuned as possible, tempo changes varied from breakneck speeds to slow aggression, double pedalling became a rule and vocalists switched from screaming to uttering creepy growls that were barely intelligible. Afterwards, some brutal bands like Obituary, Morbid Angel, Malevolent Creation, Cannibal Corpse and Fudge Tunnel made history resurrecting death metal. The genre was extremely popular in Sweden, where one could find some melodic elements in the albums by Entombed, Dismember, Edge of Sanity, Pan-Thy-Monium and Hypocrisy. Despite the achievements of Morbid Angel and Deicide and the new approach of Death, the style became a boring repetition of sounds. In the late Eighties, the most radical form of punk was born, i.e. grindcore, whose founders were Napalm Death, Carcass and Godflesh. Their sound was so extreme and soon some grind bands turned to some not so radical forms of death metal.

In the early 1990s bands like Tiamat, Therion, Sentenced and Cemetary moved away from their death metal roots in search of new musical forms, including progressive, doom and classic metal. The album Heartwork by Carcass laid the foundations of a melodic wave in Swedish death metal, further developed by At the Gates, Dark Tranquility and In Flames, who combined the harsh death metal sound with melodic approaches reminding of Iron Maiden's style. On the other hand, black metal appeared as a branch of death metal and though Slayer and Venom would sometimes be called black bands due to their satanic imagery, the actual beginning of the style was marked by Bathory in 1984, mixing barbarian and satanic imagery with blast-beat drumming and extreme guitar distortion. The Norwegian bands Immortal, Darkthrone, Burzum, and Mayhem took the lead and until the mid-1990s remained among the most influential in the genre. The expanding underground movement involving church burnings, incarcerations and even murders, quickly turned into a leading metal style. In the Nineties, bands like Satyricon, Dark Funeral, Emperor, Dimmu Borgir, and the English Cradle of Filth brought in new melodic elements like keyboards and female vocals. Those later bands did not share the extremes in the fight against religion, but their sound remained savage and uncompromising, though a bit more appealing.

While thrash metal revolutionised the concepts of speed and technical skills, some musicians decided to go for slow doom metal, a style that had practically died out after Ozzy Osbourne left Black Sabbath. Witchfinder General, Trouble and Saint Vitus played heavy riffs and occasional bluesy influence, continuing the approach once taken by the early Sabbath. Later on, a more operatic style was brought in by bands like Candlemass with their innovative Epicus Doomicus Metallicus, but doom metal was not to really flourish until the coming of Paradise Lost and Cathedral. The former incorporated haunting keyboards and death metal-oriented vocals. Cathedral, in turn, created revived a modern Black Sabbath sound adding lots of emotion. The gothic wave originated in doom but was to include more operatic elements and touching female vocals taking turns with growling male parts. Crematory, Theatre of Tragedy and Tristania are representatives of this new approach, while others like Tiamat would experiment with acoustic guitars, creating broad musical themes somewhat reminiscent of Pink Floyd.

Heavy Metal diversified itself even more and some artists decided to leave vocals in the background or to completely eliminate them. That was what guitar virtuosos like Joe Satriani, Steve Vai, and Yngwie Malmsteen did. Satriani created masterworks like Surfing with the Alien and The Extremist , and his student Vai worked with Frank Zappa and Whitesnake. Maestro Malmsteen is recognised for mixing metal elements with classical music influence and for his unparalleled guitar skills but was often criticised for having a huge ego and extroverted persona. Guitarists like Jason Becker and Steve Morse also proved the prominence of the instrumental versions of metal.

Meanwhile bands like Queensryche and Fates Warning kept progressive metal alive. With Rush turning to softer sounds in the early 1980s, progressive metal lost a lot of its popularity, but Queensryche's Operation: Mindcrime and Empire revived the style. Crimson Glory offered a melodic and at the same time strictly instrumental sound and the trend culminated in the 1993 release of Rush's Counterparts.

While Queensryche, Fates Warning and Rush created complex music backed up by lyrics varying from philosophy to fantasy, some new bands mixed punk and metal elements and so created hardcore. Their approach was a simple and direct one and their lyrics covered socially important topics. Bad Brains mixed punk, rock, jazz and reggae in their albums I against I and Rock for Light. Other influential hardcore bands were Circle Jerks, D.O.A., Husker Du, Murphy's Law, Reagan Youth, Antidote, Agnostic Front, War Zone, the Cro-Mags, Youth of Today, Sick of It All, Madball etc. Meanwhile some bands took hardcore even further into heavy metal domains, thus creating the so called metalcore or crossover. D.R.I. (Dirty Rotten Imbeciles) released their albums Crossover and Definition, and Corrosion of Conformity created Eye for an Eye and Animosity to pave the way for S.O.D (Stormtroopers of Death), whose debut Speak English Or Die is the most representative of crossover yet.

In the late Eighties, a branch of electronic music called industrial left its underground background to attract wider audiences. Based on the use of electronic instruments (like synthesisers) and drum machines, industrial rose to fame thanks to The Swans and Killing Joke to be further developed by Skinny Puppy, Controlled Bleeding, KMFDM, Cop Shoot Cop and Godflesh. The final breakthrough came with Ministry's Twitch and The Mind Is a Terrible Thing to Taste, who, together with Nine Inch Nails, started mixing the originally electronic style with HM themes.

Come the end of the 1980s, HM was slowly dying running out of ideas. A number of great bands were simply repeating old stuff while newcomers were just copying the old legends. Slayer, Megadeth and Metallica had all softened up to a different extent and taken to new directions. Metallica's Black album brought them global fame beyond the extreme scene and marked their further total commercialisation. Thrash was somewhat relived thanks to Pantera (originally a glam band), who left behind previous speed and death influences to create unusually heavy riffs accompanied by a mixture of sharp screams and snarls.

Glam saw its end with the advent of alternative rock/metal created by bands like Crazy Horse, Ventures, Living Colour, Jane's Addiction and Faith No More. Living Colour mixed Heavy Metal, jazz, blues and rap, and Faith No More combined even more musical influences fusing them with the hysterical screams of their vocalist Mike Patton. Not before long Nirvana shook the music world by releasing their smash hit Smells like Teen Spirit that marked the beginning of the grunge craze. The mixture of accessible punk and depressed lyrics appealed to millions of teenagers and until the death of their frontman Kurt Cobain in 1994 Nirvana grew to become one of the most popular and commercially successful band worldwide. Due to the unstoppable commercialisation of alternative music, new bands began springing out, actually over saturating the scene. Few remained loyal to their original styles and Black Crowes and The Four Horsemen revived the spirit of 1960s. The media would largely promote bands like Alice In Chains, Soundgarden and Pearl Jam at the expense of real metal bands.

Meanwhile, progressive metal reached new heights thanks to albums like Images and Words and Awake by Dream Theater, who established their reputation as one of the most brilliant modern bands. Under their influence, a number of bands started experimenting with the style, the most prominent being Threshold, Shadow Gallery, Damn the Machine, Ayreon, Symphony X, the unbelievably technical progressive thrash act Watchtower, ultra complex Spastic Ink, the original Pain of Salvation, etc.

Probably the most important sub-genre to emerge from the alternative chaos was stoner rock. Initially not bearing such label, acquired later due to the obvious hallucinogenic influences, this style was led by bands like Monster Magnet and Kyuss. The style strongly reminded of Black Sabbath but was far away from doom though more energetic and exploiting elements like low tunings, thick distortion, and riffs that could have been written by Tony Iommi himself. Unfortunately, stoner bands remained underground for the major part of the 1990s.

Alternative music slowly faded away in the mid-1990s. Nirvana ceased existing after Kurt Cobain's demise, Pearl Jam stopped playing live and Alice in Chains slowly became less popular due to the deepened drug addiction of their vocalist Layne Staley. Bands like Offspring, Bad Religion and NOFX took the lead in the genre for a while only to be replaced eventually by relatively unoriginal acts like Blink 182.

Since the second half of the 1990s Heavy Metal has enjoyed its triumphant comeback. Initially, the reunions of rock giants like Kiss, Black Sabbath, Riot and Motley Crue turned out to be nothing but pure business tricks devoid of the old enthusiasm and great achievements. On the other hand, Europe and Japan saw great interest in melodic heavy/power bands. Blind Guardian, Gamma Ray and Helloween were as strong as before, while new power heroes like Rhapsody, influenced by legendary Yngwie Malmsteen, successfully mixed elements of classical music with fast and powerful power metal. Swedish HammerFall, German Edguy and Finnish Stratovarius and Sonata Arctica proudly continued the HM tradition and contributed to the revival of classical metal. Kamelot and Labyrinth added some progressive elements to the emotional power and neoclassic Children of Bodom mixed virtuoso guitars and keyboards with thrash riffs and aggressive black metal vocals.

An undisputed phenomenon in rock music was the emergence of the so-called rap metal, an experimental style created by Anthrax and The Bad Brains that in the late 1990s had huge commercial success. Body Count, Dog Eat Dog, Downset and Rage Against the Machine had their contribution to the genre. Biohazard has 'legalised' it with songs such as "How It Is" (with Cypress Hill) and "Judgment Night" (with "Onyx"), which comes from the so-called soundtrack for the 1993 film. Bands, styles and tracks like Just Another Victim by House of Pain & Helmet, I, myself and my microphone by Run-DMC & Living Colour, Disorder by Ice-T & Slayer, Another Body Murdered by Faith No More & Boo-Yaa TRIBE, I Love You Mary Jane by Cypress Hill & Sonic Youth etc. Later on, it all gave birth to the Nu metal wave that truly hit it big. Style pioneers were Korn and Deftones, and eventually the scene was taken by bands that one way or the other just copied their sound. Down tuned guitars, the occasional lack of solos, the insertion of samples and scratches and vocals that borrowed from rap became a successful mixture and so bands like Limp Bizkit, Coal Chamber, Linkin Park, Papa Roach and P.O.D. soon became genre leaders, while Hatebreed and Slipknot experimented with Nu metal in a more brutal direction following "try everything" bands in metal genre like Prong, Machine Head and Soulfly (of Max Cavalera from Sepultura). System of a Down brought lyrical deviations and somewhat of their own distinctive style. Similar formations are coming out today with projects such as Powerflo and Prophets of Rage mixing former and current members of Public Enemy, Cypress Hill, Rage Against the Machine, Biohazard and even Fear Factory.

What lies in the future for heavy metal? One could hardly say for sure, but undoubtedly it will remain the music style that can inspire millions all over the globe, urge numerous talented artists to create beautiful eternal masterpieces, rejecting all limitations in its strive for new discoveries and innovations. Apathetic commercial performers come and go, but the works of HM bands, though largely underestimated, forever remain in the hearts of the fans of this eternal genre, comparable only to the immortal classical music.

Fractions

Styles

- This style originated in the late 1960s and early 1970s in the USA and UK
- In the 1980s glam metal got commercialized thanks to bands like Motley Crue and Poison
- Thrash metal developed in the early 1980s influenced by hardcore punk and New Wave of British Heavy Metal
- Thrash metal soon advanced and split up in more extreme metal styles such as Death and Black Metal
- Death Metal uses the speed of Thrash and Hardcore mixed with violence and Satanism oriented lyrics
- The first wave of Black Metal originated in Europe in the early and mid-1980s thanks to the British band Venom

Fractions

Metalheads, or the so called 'metal brotherhood' do not like talking about factions as all the fans, no matter what kind of metal they listen to, belong to that brotherhood. Although they differ in their musical preferences, they are all united under the common classical term Heavy Metal, and even those who listen to extreme genres like death, thrash, black, grindcore, etc., do not mind being classified and defined as metalheads. Since HM fans with no exceptions have the self-confidence of people who understand music and hear things the others (who do not understand and love this kind of music) simply can't hear, the majority of fans defining themselves as metalheads not only listen to that music, but take a live interest in its development, style diversity, band personnel changes, tours, personal lives of their beloved stars and in even the promoters and labels of their albums. And they do not do it for a year or two only, while a band is at the top of its popularity, but they follow their favourite bands from beginning to end. What we trying to say is that real fans never betray their favourite bands and music, don't feel ashamed of them and go on listening to (and even perform) them to a very old age. Examples are Rolling Stones, Motorhead, Iggy Pop, Ozzy Osbourne and hundreds of others. This entire huge audience of millions of fans and artists (who also tend to be fans) worldwide, have an unwritten convention that all sub genres originate from the classical Heavy Metal that emerged in the Sixties and developed through the Seventies and Eighties and that's why even fans of new styles such as metalcore and nu metal pay due respect to the pioneers and never try to denounce them. We are talking of generation gaps of 50-60 years, which is unique for a music genre, apart from probably classical music, since you can easily listen to a HM band that your grandfather used to listen to without anyone saying it is out-of-fashion, obsolete, ridiculous, etc. that is why, just like in classical music, the pioneers of metal are also defined as classics. Examples are Deep Purple, Black Sabbath, Led Zeppelin and many others.

And yet, if we do try to specify some factions, movements or rather style differences among the types of metal and their followers, we should only name them because if we make an attempt to describe them as briefly as we can, we will end up writing an entire book on them and fortunately, there are a number of books on this particular topic. Therefore, we'll just list in a non-alphabetical order the different styles and trends in Heavy Metal, hoping that we will arouse the interest of our readers and they will look for further information in order to expand their knowledge and in this way, we could attract more fans of this rich and diverse music coming from deep within our souls.

SO HERE THEY ARE:

Avant-garde metal, alternative metal, black metal, Viking metal, glam metal, gore grind, Gothic metal, grindcore, groove metal, grunge, dark metal, death doom metal, death metal, death grind, death core, drone metal, doom metal, extreme metal, industrial metal, Celtic metal, cyber metal, crust punk, crossover thrash, melodic black metal, melodic death metal, melodic metal core, metal opera, metal core, Neo classical metal, New Wave of British Heavy Metal, Nu metal, power metal, post-metal (or post-rock), progressive metal, rapcore, symphonic black metal, symphonic metal, sludge metal, speed metal, stoner rock, thrash metal ,folk metal (or Pagan), funk metal, hardcore, hard rock, Heavy Metal, Christian metal, cello rock, etc.

Appearance, symbols and codes of behaviour

The great variety of Heavy Metal styles, as well as the natural desire all young people share to look different from the rest, to be unique, noticeable and recognisable results in their different type of attire, symbols and accessories according to the genre they go for. If you have ever attended some big international 3-4-day festival, you must have noticed that no matter how many different fans of the aforesaid metal sub styles were present, there is no way for them to have been mistaken for the 'ordinary' people from the neighbouring town or for the usual impartial onlookers. Naturally, we'll start again with classical Heavy Metal, characteristic of which are the Rob Halford-style clothes and accessories. Black leather jackets and trousers, numerous studs and spike bands, chains, silver skull rings, crosses, etc. Shoes must be some kind of military boots, knee-high rocker boots, etc., but they have to be heavy, strong and menacing. This type of apparel in general applies to the rest of styles, only certain accessories are replaced by genre-specific others, but by and large leather jackets, military boots and the respective band T-shirt are mandatory for the metal brotherhood way of dressing. The black colour prevails along with silver in the form of rings, earrings and piercings, numerous buckles, chrome plated elements and pendants on jackets and shoes. Glam metal fans, for example, wear some women's accessories on men's garments. They also like to wear bright colours like red or yellow, tight glossy pants, shiny shirts unbuttoned down to the waist, women's makeup and lipstick, long teased hair and bangs, scarves, colourful bands hanging down from their clothes, etc. And since fans are said to copycat the way of dressing and behaviour of their idols, imagine them dressed like the artists from Ratt, Poison, Motley Crue, Kiss, Twisted Sisters, Aerosmith, etc.

Power metal representatives, for instance, dress and even behave like medieval warriors. Leather wear, strong muscles, leather vests on bare skin, chains hanging down from belts, elbow-high leather bands, heavy high-heel boots, spurs, etc. It is them who most often use the term 'metal brotherhood' since they think of themselves as an army of heroes fighting the evil, riding armour-clad horses, killing dragons, wielding swords and saving beauties. Imagine that, eh? If you can't, simply have a look at bands like Manowar, Sabaton, Hammerfall, etc. Their behaviour is markedly manly, uncouth, disciplined as if following strict military orders. They like drinking mostly beer and wine, they would greet each other with a fist or elbow bump or with a strong hug and shoulder taps. They emphasise their heterosexuality and would do their best not to let any gays inside their circles since homosexuals are considered as a disgrace for the brotherhood.

Thrash and death metal fans must have at least 4 or 5 T-shirts of their favourite bands to underline their belonging to the relevant style. They wear military boots in winter and high-top leather trainers in summer. Stretch jeans and camouflage trousers with multiple side pockets are other almost mandatory elements. Another typical garment is the denim vest featuring images of their favourite bands displayed on badges and pins. According to preferences, one could also wear studded leather bands and belts. Long hair is another must for men, though recently things are getting up-to-date with fashion and besides, not everyone can wear their hair long taking into account their jobs and positions. And mind you, the height of that style was way back in 1980s. If you'd like to imagine in more details thrash metal fans, just look at the most famous artists playing that style, namely the German trio Kreator, Sodom and Destruction. Overseas there is the big four, i.e. Metallica, Megadeth, Slayer and Anthrax, we well as the undeservedly underestimated Overkill and Testament. Thrash metal fans meet up in parks and gardens and underground boozers where they can listen to their favourite music. They'd go for beer and sometimes mix it with spirits like vodka. Generally speaking, alcohol is particularly enjoyed in thrash metal circles and as a rule, by all fans of hard and heavy music. At the same time, drugs are things metalheads would generally stay away from. Of course, there are sub styles like punk and grunge where drugs seem to belong. We may be disproved by their fans, but our grounds for saying that are mainly the lifestyle of bands they tend to identify themselves with, like Sex Pistols, Exploited, Nirvana, and Alice In Chains.

We'd like to address mostly our younger readers and point out that the alcohol and drug abuse does not make a metalhead out of you, nor does it make you some kind of separate group of unappreciated and rejected by the society individuals. What make you a metalhead is only the music power, influence and mentality, along with the lyrics and messages, the bands' attitude towards their fans and the relations between the very members of the metal brotherhood.

Other interesting representatives of extreme music are black metal fans. They usually copycat their idols in every single aspect, i.e. every move they make, every new accessory and extravagant garment they wear. Their makeup is ghastly; their appearance is raw and uncompromising. Black and white is their makeup predominant colours and the way their faces are made up originates in the German folklore. In Nordic mythology it is related to the appearance of a member of the legion of lost souls resembling a ghost or a vampire. To a large extent, black metal makeup resembles the one worn by the members of KISS, Alice Cooper, and King Diamond in the past and Immortal, Dimmu Borgir, Emperor, and Marduk nowadays. The prevailing black colour in the black metalheads' clothing does not simply refer to the name of the style, nor as an attempt to attract attention or as an inferiority complex manifestation as shrinks could interpret it but contains a much deeper symbolic meaning. Black is the colour of the occult, of the unknown, mysterious and infinite. It's the colour of death and funerals. They wear accessories like elbow-high wristbands and collars with long nails or spikes, pentagram rings and necklaces, inverted crosses, ancient pagan symbols, etc., unjustifiably declared by the Christian Church as Satanic, while they are rather ancient occult and mysterious symbols of knowledge and secret societies, but that's a vast topic that goes right into mythology, philosophy and religion and we are certainly not experts in these fields.

Gothic metal fans resemble black metal ones in terms of clothes and accessories, though they are softer and more elegant. Representatives and fans of this particular style are to be found mostly among females. They'd wear long and stylish dark-coloured dresses, Medieval cloth or leather corsets with numerous laces, large pieces of jewellery with plenty of details and strange shapes. They like wearing pendants, rings, necklaces and bracelets depicting snakes, dragons, spiders, wolves, owls, bats and other creatures of the night. Also present are Gothic crosses, crucifixions, Runes, pentagrams and other ancient signs. We can also see leather collars and wristbands, but without the nails and spikes so typical of black metal. Sometimes they'll wear tunics, cloaks, veils, gloves, fishnet stockings, and whatever accessories worn by Medieval princesses one could think of, but always in dark colours. Their makeup also has to be dark, black eyeliners, long and emphasised eyelashes, sometimes black lipstick and nail polish, and raven-black dyed hair. Ladies would sometimes wear lenses in order to change their colour of eyes into green or blue. The outfit is finished with knee-high black leather pointed high-heels like the ones worn by witches in movies, but occasionally they'd go for heavy, knee-high military boots with unusually thick platforms and a number of metal clasps. To get a better picture you can have a look at bands like Nightwish, Epica, Sirenia, Tristania, Moonspell, Within Temptation, Lacuna Coil, etc. which usually have female vocalists.

Hardcore, crossover and rap metal representatives can be mistaken for ordinary guys, though if one has a closer look, one will also see some distinctive features. Those are the guys who most resemble modern-day football fans. Long hair is no longer a must and it is even not particularly liked. Prevailing piece of clothing is the white, yellow or other colour T-shirt with a band's logo, usually some kind of a three-letter abbreviation like D.R.I., S.D.I., S.O.D., M.O.D., or cartoon characters from the Simpsons and South Park, etc. They'd put on white sneakers, preferably Converse All Stars, a baseball cap with the logo of an American city, baseball or basketball team, or a black-and-white bandana. Sometimes the T-shirt could be replaced with a white undershirt. Then we could see them wearing multi-coloured shorts or 2-3 sizes wider baggy trousers with their legs sweeping the ground. They don't wear wristbands, rings or other accessories, but they have lots of tattoos, usually black and grey. Generally speaking the style can be described as Latino Gangsta. For a quick reference, look at bands like Cypress Hill, House of Pain and the definitely more guitar-oriented Body Count, as well as at all Hard-Core New York reps led by Agnostic Front and Madball, of course.

Other reps we'd like to draw your attention to, are grunge fans, which seem to stand somewhat outside the metal wave. They prefer to think of themselves as an alternative, underground and independent and so they keep on staying clear from the mainstream both in terms of music and clothes. So, though their background is a metal one, they in a way do not fit into this paradigm. On the one hand their music is hard, guitar-oriented and raw, but on the other hand it is melancholic, slow and depressing. The most prominent artists here are the Seattle ones, i.e. Nirvana, Pearl Jam, Soundgarden and Alice in Chains. Grunge fans prefer solitude, they are introvert, go on their own, avoid noisy parties, look thoughtful, gloomy, romantic and disheartened, just the way their favourite music sounds. The same goes for their lyrics that deal with social isolation, suicides, anger, fear and sorrow, i.e. themes typical of teenagers. Grunge fans wear ordinary, daily, simple clothes comprising of jeans, sneakers and T-shirts. In cold weather they'd put on yellow or brown work (safety) shoes with thick soles, and a checked woollen shirt typical of Canadian woodcutters. In this way they seem to focus on social inequality and the humble origin of grunge followers, who believe they come from low and middle-class working strata of American society. In support of this idea, artists try to avoid the glitter and vanity of show-biz, wealth and fame. They look for independent labels to release their albums and stay away from the big stage as they prefer small clubs and underground joints. For the same reason grunge fans tend to avoid noise and loud parties, they withdraw into themselves and, at times intentionally copycatting the artists and sometimes unconsciously led by inner psychological factors, they turn to drugs. Well, this should not be misunderstood as a statement saying that all grunge fans use drugs, but our personal observations show that this was a usual practice back in the 1990s.

Finally, we'll take a look at Nu metal or metalcore fans, who are influenced and inspired by bands like Korn, Disturbed, Linkin Park, Limp Bizkit, Slipknot and the latest, also called Emo artists, like Asking Aleksandria, Bring me the Horizon, Papa Roach, Evanescence, etc. Their appearance features short fashionable male hairstyles; they look almost like yuppies who sometimes wear their hair short but with a long fringe or tied up in a small ponytail (bun) on top, or with the so common nowadays African rastas or dreadlocks. Their clobber is fashionable and stylish designer labels. Designer jeans, shirts, jackets, fashionable pointed men's shoes, and sometimes ties casually loosened or untied. Generally, Nu metal representatives seem to try to stay clear from the underground so typical of classical HM in terms of style and behaviour and instead go to a higher level of perception by the society. They are involved in causes such as environmental protection, ethical treatment of animals and other fashionable trends. Metrosexuality and the different types of mixed sexual orientation are also allowable. The so called "third gender" can also be observed in their circles. Ladies following this style are not much distinctive as they'd go for simple T-shirts and backpacks with the logo of their favourite band, but men would sometimes wear those long well groomed Muslim style beards, combined with short hair, just the opposite of the classical Heavy Metal style. The lyrics also cover modern themes like urbanisation, social isolation, space technologies, life on other planets, space travels, man-computer symbiosis, biomechanics, aliens, etc. In recent years there has been a kind of dormant conflict, a silent war and considerable differences in the points of view shared by Nu metal classical old-school HM. Classical HM fans accuse new bands of profaning the music. Nu metal uses easy to play heavy riffs, bellowing or hysterically screaming vocalists; not very skilful compositions and so its fans are not that choosy about what they are presented with as metal music. However, the songs are recognisable, easy to remember and play. On the whole, representatives of the classical school seem to not welcome the very word 'metal' into the name of the new style. In turn, Nu metal fans accuse the old school of 'frigidity, retrograde beliefs, lack of development and ignorance of new technologies such as computers, digital processing of recordings, software apps, compositional programming, etc. Also, Nu metal fans claim that old school metalheads are nothing but pissheads, drug addicts, simpletons and degenerates. They do not want to be part of the metal brotherhood. On the contrary, they try to stay as far away from it as possible. They believe they are a brand-new generation of artists and fans having appeared all of a sudden and as a matter of course and are not willing to admit that they follow the well-paved path of classical Heavy Metal that has been developing for 5 decades now. We do hope that this hidden war, which is actually a natural opposition between younger and older generations in all spheres of culture, will end up with a kind of agreement and Nu metal fans will join the enormous metal brotherhood army instead of gravitating more and more towards pop music and MTV's plastic industry. If you ask us, they're more than welcome!

Locations and territories

HM FANS, no matter which trend they are followers of, generally meet up at one and the same locations. Those are mostly parks, gardens, squares and other open spaces that can be used as music event venues, bars purpose special rock clubs. There they feel at home, sure that they will meet like-minded mates and won't be ridiculed or criticised by other for the music they like, the clothes they wear and the way they behave. Because metalheads share a common feature, i.e. they don't think of themselves as a part of the "standard" society, though they cannot do much to escape from it in their daily routines. The extreme representatives of the different styles who literally adopt their favourite music as a way of life usually get in trouble with their employers since they like to wear their hair, clobber and accessories on a daily basis, even at their workplace, which is rather often frowned upon by both colleagues and bosses. Also, like the true fans they are, they have to attend gigs and fests that are not always held at weekends and unfortunately far away from the place they live or work, sometimes even abroad. For that purpose, fans have to travel, go on a leave, and take a few days off and, in addition, upon coming back from a fest, they still need to have a rest as what they did there was get pissed and totally knackered. But those are just parts of the fascination and the romantic side of HM culture, as such fests are long talked about and stay forever in the memories of those who attended them. Usually every city has at least 1 or 2 boozers, frequented by rock and metal fans. There they go on the piss with beer and spirits. No one expects you to order coffee there, but if you do, the coffee machine will be switched off and while waiting for it to warm up, the bartender will most probably ask you if you'd like to have a beer instead. It's good if it also a diner so that those who have drunk too much can have something to eat as some guys tend to stay in such boozers for days. It is also good if it a 24-hour bar for smokers, though its' hard to find such boozers now due to the new anti-smoking requirements so most of them have separated smoking areas that are usually packed unlike the rest of the pub or bar. Unfortunately, metalheads in their majority smoke and drink alcohol, or at least that goes for those who lived through the Eighties. In terms of territories, there is no such thing as territorial division. Fans of different genres, factions and styles usually go to one and the same places in towns and may change or merge companies resulting in much bigger groups. Fights over territories and boozers are rare, but conflicts over birds are quite usual. Apart from betrayal, only on such occasions members of the metal brotherhood can become bitter enemies. Metalheads find betrayal as one of the greatest sins. A traitor, an apostate, one who has betrayed and let down a fellow metalhead, is subject to immediate condemnation and, if not ostracised at once, one is made to understand the rest no longer want one's company. With regard to this, metal fans follow the military logic and when confronted by a common threat they tend to join forces and face it, rather than argue and eventually retreat. Common enemies may be the skinheads, though some of them are in contact with HM fans, different right-wing paramilitary organisations, the Roma minority and of course, the Old Bill, as no counterculture reps seem to like and have anything to do with coppers. Almost every town has a park, garden, boozer or at least a couple of benches considered to be the "metalheads' meeting place", so you can easily get an idea of the places and areas you can see them. Of course, there are also house parties, but they usually involve loud music that neighbours never seem to like, damaging property, vomiting in washbasins and toilets, smashing bottles and glasses, carrying stoned guys down the stairs, which ultimately ends up in yet another encounter with the police. After such events, unfortunate hosts will be chased away or forced to run away from home themselves as parents tend to be rather displeased with the fact that their children have invited their mates to an innocent house party.

Opinion: M.N. (Gorna Oryahovitsa)

Counterculture and the Heavy Metal trend in G.O

"My first introduction to Heavy Metal and its fans in general was thanks to rumours . I must have been 6 or 7 when one evening my older cousin came back from school and started telling a scary story of some youngsters who roamed the streets usually at night. They'd carry chains and knuckledusters and wear leather wristbands with razor-blades. They'd roam the city in groups, call themselves metalheads and beat up anyone who would dare to stand in their way . She didn't say anything about music then . Metalheads sank into my child's mind as bad and dangerous guys and I secretly hoped I would not encounter them on my way back from school in the evening (especially in winter when it would get dark early) out of fear they'd beat me up with their chains or slash me with their razor-blades. Of course, I was later to find out that those myths about metalheads and heavy metal music were just parts of the communist propaganda aimed at keeping the youth away from Western culture and influence , which had already started penetrating thanks to those trends depicted as vicious and decadent.

Afterward I forgot about metalheads and my fears eventually subsided . A few years later, when I was 11-12 years old, I took up wrestling. Those were the times when everybody used to do some kind of sports. During that regime it was kinda obligatory for youngsters to take part in out-of-class activities, be it sports, choirs or workshops . Since I was a good student I did not need to stay after school, so I took up sports . Besides, birds (that I had just begun to take interest in more seriously) used to find strong and muscular boys attractive, you know the story.. . The sports hall we used to train in was located near a park , where after trainings we'd go and smoke a cigarette or two that we used to steal from our parents back home . We started smoking not because we found it pleasant (on the contrary, it was rather unpleasant, taking into account the poor-quality tobacco they used to sell in Bulgaria then) but because it was forbidden! Especially for athletes like us, this made smoking even more attractive. First, you'd hide from your coaches (who were in the habit of passing through the park in search of smoker athletes), then from your parents and teachers , who in those times were also obliged to wander the parks and pubs in town in order to catch "bad" students . I knew the story well cause my mother was a teacher, so I had to hide from her, too . She also used to wander the town. They'd do it in couples, in shifts, following a schedule worked out by their headmaster. Such were those dark times of discipline and fear. So, we used to hang around the park smoking inside those circular metal bench structures they had just built . It was there that I first got in touch with heavy metal culture and its representatives . It must have been either 1986 or 1987. The best years of HM that continued until the Nineties when grunge took off. So those benches were the place where some older boys would gather, some wearing jeans and denim jackets (quite rare in those times and as a result sticking out like a sore thumb), others dressed in black, some wearing military boots (army boots taken from a friend serving in one of the several military units in town), some with forelocks and some with ponytails (being their first attempt sat wearing their hair long as long hair was strictly forbidden then). Now I'll make a digression and tell you how every single morning at the school entrance there would be that teacher on duty, scissors in hand, checking boys' haircuts and if they were longer than permitted, he'd warn the poor boys to have their hair cut by the end of the day and if anyone did not do what he was told, he'd cut their hair right there, on the spot, the next morning and they'd look more than ridiculous and have no other option but visit the local hairdresser. So, on the park benches, there were those older boys smoking, drinking homemade raki or wine, passing bottles to one another and listening to music on battery-run cassette recorders. Heavy Metal, naturally. Among them there were blokes I knew from school. One evening, as we were hanging around there, they called us, searched our pockets, took our fags (anyway, we didn't have any money on us as in those times kids used to take homemade breakfast to school instead of money), and then they let us light up a cigarette and stay with them. Someone spoke up for us since one of my classmates was a neighbour of his, so we got introduced and were offered to have a drink from a bottle of homemade red wine, we listened to some music and that was my initiation in HM circles. I must admit I felt scared during that first encounter, though. No matter that there were several of us, no matter that we were athletes, wrestlers in particular, those older boys looked powerful and one could feel they were united and they belonged to a kind of community that united them and at the same time distinguished them from the rest . The look in their eyes was brave, cocky, and bad if you like, and they did have self-confidence. They'd meet up in the park so that they could stay away from the disapproving eyes of teachers, parents, the society in general, and the cops as we were to find out later. And the police in those times were omnipotent and awe-inspiring. It was a machinery of state that was allowed anything. They were allowed to frisk you, nick you, beat you up , shave your hair, what not, for no obvious reason. Only because you might look different . Nothing to do with the current state of affairs .

After that first encounter I started hanging around the park after school more often. I'd go there after trainings, be it alone or with some mates. I wanted to be accepted in those circles, become part of them, be audacious and cocky like them, laugh out loud and cry out without giving a fuck that people in the park would turn around and look at me scornfully, scream and shout at the top of my voice, wear different clothes , wear pins and badges of different forbidden bands and generally feel free. I was immediately hooked on that style of dressing, music and behaviour. I felt I had liked them all my life . I can't remember exactly the first time I ever listened to HM, but I think it was in our street where we used to play as kids. A mate's older brother was studying in the ports school in the town of Veliko Tarnovo. I think he brought some cassettes from there and he started 'educating' us, younger kids. First thing he played was Accept's Russian Roulette. We listened to it with mouths opened wide . Never before had we heard anything like that . Not that we were so behind our time. We did have our Bulgarian rock bands . We had Shturcite, Signal, and Konkurent... but they were rather pop-rock and not the thing we were looking for. The early Era and Control were closer to heavy metal. They were downright hard, you know... I mean hard for Bulgarian bands, but still they were Bulgarian, singing in Bulgarian and, you know what I mean ... and that was heavy metal, you know, something coming from the West , a forbidden music. It felt quite different, it sounded quite different . In addition, the geezer went on to tell us that the music was forbidden and if the cops caught us they'd lift us, throw us out of school, send us to a reformatory, etc . I recently came across an article from those times which truthfully illustrates how the communist regime was trying to 'push us into the right path' by persuading us that this kind of music was bad for adolescents' health and mentality, bad for all of us... By the way, the article was written by one of the most famous Bulgarian female pop singers , but that was part of the policy the communist would follow then, imposing their opinion using the voices and images of young and popular celebrities who one would find easier to believe in. "

Here it is:

„Моля, разкажете ни нещо повече за хеви метъл музиката" — писах ни много пионери, между които и Галя Иванова от село Главан, Силистренско, Сия Динкова от град Тополово, Магдена Илиева от София, Ивайло Динов от Варна.

РУБРИКАТА СЕ ВОДИ ОТ РОСИЦА КИРИЛОВА

Скъпи приятели, мисля, че ще ви бъде полезно и приятно да изучите повече за някой стилове в музиката, защото и към нея, както към всички неща в живота, трябва да се отнасяме сериозно и с разбиране, да я харесваме не само защото е модерна.

Днес заедно с музиковедката Розмари Стателова ще ви разкажем за хеви метъл и в следващите ни срещи ще продължим разговора ни за музиката, политиката и идеологията.

РИКОШЕТЪТ НА „ГРЪМОТЕВИЦИТЕ"

Терминът „хеви метъл тъндър" в превод означава „гръмотевица от тежък метал".

Най-напред този стил се представя от съставите на така наречения „твърд рок" — „Лед цепелин", „Блек сабат", „Дийп пърпъл". Въпреки че в началото на 70-те години редица в западните класации попадаха техни песни, и че съвременните хеви метъл групи като „Венъм", „Металика", „Мотърхед", „Айрън Мейдън" са с по-малко мелодични песни, те се харесват главно от възраст от 12 до 18-годишна възраст.

За музиката и сценичната изява на хеви метъл съставите са характерни примамки от съзнанието, взаимствувани от митологията, различни образи на насилието и ужаса. Например: чудовищно Еди — огромни рисунки в ярки цветове на едно ужасяващо същество — нещо между мускулите на оголен труп и робот убиец — винаги въоръжен с автомати или ножове. Самото име „Айрън Мейдън" — един от хеви метъл съставите — означава в превод „джелязната девица" — това е средновековно английско средство за изтезания и бавна мъчителна смърт. Певецът Ози Озбърн от състава „Блек сабат" в момента е подсъдим — срещу него е заведено дело от родителите на самоубило се 13-годишно момче, което не прекъснато слушало песните от самостоятелния му албум. В тях Озбърн призовава към „вечна младост" чрез самоубийство.

Чудовищно безвкусните измислици на хеви метъл съвсем не са безобидни. „Гръмотевиците" на този стил не случайно се изсипват върху главите на младите хора, които имат лабилна психика или чувство за малоценност. Полудетското съзнание, мечтите за героя ви подвизи и благородно рицарство се манипулират по много умел начин и се насочват в ясно определена цел — към човеко ненавист и насилие. При казаното се съчетава с уж сияещото, към него се прибавят свръхусилените, кънтящи звуци на китарите и барабаните, а към всичко това и завладяващите ритми на рока и ритъм енд блуса. Ето какво представлява стилът хеви метъл — този осквернител на рока.

РОСИЦА КИРИЛОВА

The Echoes of Thunders

The Heavy Metal Thunder style is represented by hard rock bands like Led Zeppelin, Black Sabbath and Deep Purple. Although their songs would rarely hit the top charts in the early 1970s and modern heavy metal bands like Venom, Metallica, Motorhead and Iron Maiden have even less melodious songs, they are favourites mostly with youths aged between 12 and 18.

The music style and performance of heavy metal bands are typically known for their lures of perception taken from mythology and various images of violence and horror. For example, the Eddie monster, i.e. huge bright coloured pictures of a hideous creature, a mixture of a skinless corpse and a killer robot always armed with knives or machine guns. The very name Iron Maiden of one of the heavy metal bands means a medieval English torture and slow and painful execution device. The Black Sabbath leading singer Ozzy Osbourne is currently standing trial. The court case was brought against him by the parents of a 13-year-old boy who committed a suicide after listening continuously to his solo album. In its songs Osbourne calls for 'eternal youth' through ... suicide.

The monstrously tasteless trumped-up stories of heavy metal bands are far from innocent. The thunders of this style intentionally fall down on youths, who have unstable mentality or inferiority complex. The half-childish attitude, the dreams of heroic deeds and noble knighthood are skilfully manipulated and directed to a clearly defined goal, i.e. hatred and violence. The fantastic meets the creepy and you add to them the super amplified and thundering sounds of guitars and drums to supplement the entrancing rhythms of rock and rhythm and blues. That's what heavy metal is all about, the violator of rock.

Rositsa Kirilova

WELL, tell me now, how could you NOT listen to such music? How could you NOT feel the thrill when it was forbidden and even dangerous? You know that if you want to make sure a kid does something, then you forbid him to do it. This was exactly our case. And to make things even more interesting and mysterious, the geezer went on to tell us (he was making it all up, of course) that the lyrics were anti-Russian, they sang about waging war on the Russians and so on and so forth. And since our command of English was not good at all and the only thing we knew was the album's title, Russian Roulette, we simply took his word for granted.

On another cassette he played Manowar's Fighting the World. Fucking hell! Just imagine what it was like to hear that for the first time . For the very first time! Then we listened to Running Wild, AC/DC, Metallica's Master of Puppets and in a week, we were all metalheads. The years of 1986 and 1987, apart from giving us the best HM albums of all times (see the top charts in all leading magazines), also marked the beginning of the wind of change . I'm not a 100% sure, but I think it was back then that people started talking about "perestroika". The USSR announced a new, shall we call it more democratic policy, and seemed to loosen the reins in the East-

European states. The Bulgarian communist government must have also been confused and so it also loosened its grip on us youngsters. That was exactly what we had been waiting for. Well, not that we had dreamed of it consciously, but we did feel it and want it. So, the more rebellious and more progressive kids immediately took advantage of it. We began to declare and express ourselves as different. We started wearing different clothes, behaving in a different way, be it like metalheads, like hooligans, like louts (as the elderly used to call us). We wanted to be at the same time a part of something and different from that something. That was HM music and movement meant to us . And all of a sudden everyone became a metalhead. Or at least all the boys did. My street mates, my classmates, students from other schools we'd meet downtown or at some school events . It became the norm. Occasionally we'd see photos of some HM band being sold at funfair shooting galleries and we'd buy them, collect and swap them. They had some long haired muscular guys on them wearing chains, leather clothes , wristbands, belts, bandoliers , spikes and carrying hammers, axes, circular saws and other weapons and tools . We as teenagers just fell in love with that stuff as it was the exact opposite of the good student norm, i.e. an outstanding bespectacled well-groomed student wearing a white knitted sweater , black trousers and a leather school bag full of books. We didn't want to look that way. We despised that kind of classmates we had (to top it all, they were respected by both our teachers and parents), so we'd take advantage of any opportunity to harass them and mock at them . We'd do any kind of tricks to them . I even don't want to remember what we did to them, especially when we were on school outings or summer camps where discipline was not that strict . It's not something to be proud of, but that was the way it was. Everybody did it. So, what I was telling you was that suddenly all my mates and half of my schoolmates became metalheads . Girls would listen to Madonna and Michael Jackson, but we'd forgive them, you know girls will be girls . Now I recall a funny incident. We were on a 14-day trip in the Rhodope Mountains . Beautiful and exciting stuff . We'd sleep in chalets between two hikings. Of course, we had a cassette recorder with us . It was a must then, wherever you went, no matter what music you listened to, every time someone would bring a cassette recorder. So, there we metalheads were arriving for lunch in a chalet after 5 hours of hiking . Knackered, nervous, hot...Everybody sat down to have lunch in the form of canned food and stale bread . And just as we were sitting their clattering forks and plates in the canteen, we heard that greatly agitated and slightly aggressive female voice, "Well, isn't anyone going to play some Manowar so that I can boost my digestion?!" We all got silent and turned around in the direction the voice was coming from. A girl from the other class belonging to the caste of diligent students I described above, slightly plump and not so popular amongst boys, was looking at us persistently expecting us to fulfil her wish . We were dumbstruck. We just stood there staring at her in surprise for a few seconds and then we all burst out laughing, "Wow, is that you, G.? Do you really listen to such kind of music? Why haven't you spoken about that before?" Of course, we immediately played on Manowar and after that this previously humble person became a great friend of ours . She never dressed or showed in any other way she was a HM fan, but as we already knew she liked our kind of music we started respecting her and we'd greet her every time we'd meet her at school and... we even got to like her . She sensed or change of attitude and one could tell she really liked it . She wouldn't hang around with us, but she felt us closer to her and she knew we'd protect her if anyone harassed her like they used to do before. When our gang would walk down a school corridor we'd greet her, and she would respond by modestly nodding her head and blushing . I haven't seen her for 20 years, but I still remember that story. I'm sure the rest of us also remember her. G., if you ever happen to read this, take my best regards. I hope you still listen occasionally to our favourite music…

It was damn hard to find records . I'm talking of the 1980s and I'm talking of our small town . It must have been different in the capital Sofia, but in the country, it was almost impossible to find cassettes to make records . Bookstores would sell Bulgarian audio cassettes, but they were real shit in terms of quality . The sound would deteriorate and in a year's time they were already useless. Every self-respectful HM fan had to have cassettes from the special stores called Corecom where they sold goods imported from outside the Iron Curtain and prices were in foreign currencies. They sold mainly high quality Japanese cassettes of the TDK and Sony brands, which were the most preferred and wanted . Having such an empty brand-new cassette, unsealing its package, feeling its smell… it was magic . Anyone who has ever unsealed a TDK cassette and felt its smell knows what I'm talking about. They smelt really good. I never knew why. On the whole, Corecom stores smelt fine, they smelt of luxury, of the West, of a cherished and forbidden world beyond the Iron Curtain . But we didn't have a Corecom in Gorna Oryahovitsa. Nor did we have foreign currency. Unless your father was a TIR truck driver or worked in Libya where people got paid in US dollars. But one way or another, semi-legally or downright illegally, Bulgarians would find their own ways of getting foreign currencies from the black market and then go shopping in Corecom stores. The government did not seem to care much … what they cared about was the profits they made . Prices were far from low, but luxury is costly you know. It still is. So, in some mysterious ways I also became a proud owner of a whole box containing 10 brand new TDK tapes, two of them being 90-minute. How about that, eh ? So, I started collecting records. It wasn't easy, but mind you, nothing was easy in those days . At least I had tapes now. 90-minute ones would also have 2 albums recorded on, one per side. Well. It was just fine if the album was about 45 minutes long. You could even skip a beat from the last song or the entire song, but you had to save space. However, if the album was longer than 50 minutes, you had to record on the other side and then you had to add half an album or a few songs by another band at your discretion. The important thing was to have a good number of bands in your record library . And how did you make records? Most often it would be by using the microphones of two cassette recorders. A mate of yours would come and bring his cassette recorder, then you'd put them opposite each other, play the music and sit there silent for an hour until the recording is finished while making sure you did not make any noise. And then either your grandma would open the door calling you for lunch while Kreator's Pleasure to kill was being recorded, or the phone in the corridor would ring… and all you could possibly do would be to start all over again, if you had the time, or you'd simply leave the song with the intruding noise or voice in the background. Few people used to have dual cassette recorders as they were expensive, so if you had one, you'd have the biggest number of friends around. Anyway, there were substitutes, i.e. some Polish Finesia and Unitra cassette decks that made recordings via cable, but the quality was not that good. However, that did not bother us much . What really mattered was variety and more and more bands listened to . We thought of ourselves as music researchers, not just fans . A few years later some enterprising fellas saw the increasing demand and the business opportunity and bought high quality equipment to start making semi-professional recordings. Cassettes were sold at flea markets and cost a real fortune . But I dare say they were good . We'd make loud and clear recordings and make the cassette case cover design ourselves writing down the name of the band and the year their album was released. Afterwards we started copying and printing them so covers were sold in their almost genuine design, even featuring the lyrics and the musicians' names inside. Things started looking more Western, more professional. Soon after the fall of socialism in 1989 the first record shops were opened. First it was the big cities and then smaller towns like ours. They didn't offer a great variety, but it was better than nothing . I made special trips to towns like Plovdiv and Varna to buy cassettes. Bourgas also had such a shop and when I'd go on a seaside holiday I used to stay in that shop all day long. I would spend all the money I had on music. I simply wouldn't buy anything else apart from cassettes and posters . The entire wall opposite my bed was covered in posters of my favourite bands and each evening as I was going to bed I'd look at them and feel strong, peaceful and part of something big, mysterious and heroic, i.e. the global metal brotherhood . I didn't know a single foreign HM fan, but I felt their presence and I knew there were millions of them out there . You know, we'd occasionally pick up and watch videos from big live shows across the globe, massive torus and crowds of tens of thousands of fans. Back in those days shows of monsters like Kiss, Iron Maiden, Accept, Manowar, Metallica, etc. were held at stadia, not in clubs and halls like nowadays. And we could see the seas of fans at those venues . The musicians in those bands were real rock stars – rich and famous, surrounded by hot birds, they'd do whatever they wanted to, e.g. smashing hotel rooms and any other acts of misbehaviour. Well, how could you NOT like them ? How could you NOT want to be like them after living all those years of restriction and suppression?

Once we had settled the issue with records, we started to look for ways of finding HM attire and accessories. We just had to look like our idols . So first it was T-shirts with bands' logos and prints. There was this guy in Gorna Oryahovitsa, a HM fan older than me . And there was another one in the town of Tarnovo. Both of them would travel to Hungary (the country had got rid of communism earlier and was almost like 'the west ') and bring from there T-shirts, pins, badges, wristbands and anything else pre-ordered by Bulgarian metalheads. For example, you want a Kreator or Sodom T-shirt, so you order, pre-pay it and have it delivered. The blokes were honest and reliable and upon returning from Hungary they'd take the train and travel all across the country to make deliveries . They did not work together, but actually were doing the same thing and they were even competitors at some point . I don't know the details but they're friends now and they're also friends of mine . Afterwards the geezer from Tarnovo expanded his business. He opened a shop, probably the first of its kind in our region. It would sell anything: T-shirts, pins, badges, denim jackets, wristbands, studded belts, bandannas , military boots, what not... Anything a metalhead could possible need. He'd even sell records of rare bands that had not been officially released, like ones by the Canadian industrial metal band Malhavoc. I still can't find an original CD of theirs with their 1990 and 1991 albums .

I'd buy stuff from both guys and I'd be really pleased. I still have in my wardrobe an Obituary T-shirt and a few pins and badges on my old sleeveless denim jacket. They are more than 20 years old, but I don't throw them away. Nor do I wear them, but they remind me of olden times and all the fun we used to have. So, thank you guys and full respect. You two were the pioneers in our region and helped a lot of young metalheads become "old metal bastard "(laughing). Then HM shops sprang up in most major cities like Sofia , Plovdiv, Varna, Bourgas, etc. Now there are HM chain stores all over the country . It's easy to be a metalhead nowadays. Actually, it's easy to be whatever you like, there is everything for everyone out there on the market . At some point another guy appeared in Tarnovo, a biker, and he started making biker wear, i.e. leather jackets with numerous pockets, zippers and metal buttons; leather trousers and vests, etc. they were expensive, but nice and strong. He's still into that business nowadays and he's doing fine . His stuff is first class . It was from him that I bought a wonderful leather biker jacket made of calf skin. It must have weighed at least 15 kilos. I could barely wear it, but I did it in pride . After I did my military service I reluctantly sold it though it was still new because it was too big for me. Had I known that years later I'd be 30 kilos heavier like the guy I am now, I would have kept it. It would fit me fine now. I still feel sorry for it …

In the late 1980s and the early 1990s, I and my mates would mainly listen to thrash. The German trio Sodom, Kreator and Destruction were in their prime.

Everybody would listen to them. Tankard were fast on their heels as another extremely popular band in our circles. Naturally, the big American four would finish the thrash picture . Everyone had the albums of Metallica, Megadeth, Slayer and Anthrax. In addition, we'd go for Testament, Exodus and Overkill. Brazilian giants Sepultura with their 1987, 1989 and 1991 albums took over half of the world . Brilliant! Now they're not that popular, but it's all a question of taste . American hardcore, a mixture of punk and thrash, also took off . Graffiti of three-letter bands like D.R.I., S.O.D., and M.O.D. could be seen written on walls all over our town . What followed were Suicidal Tendencies, Cro-Mags and Agnostic Front. Later some of us turned to heavier styles like death and grind that were also quite influential in 1990s. Bands like Death, Pestilence and Morbid Angel were everybody's favourites. Then we'd reach the metal extremities like Napalm Death, Cannibal Corpse, Autopsy, Suffocation, Mortification, Brutal Truth , etc. Naturally, different people like different things and HM fans are no exception. After the first wave when we'd all listen to the same bands, the music market got over - crowded and some mates started separating on grounds of music preferences . I'm talking about the group that use d the gather in front of the town cinema. We studied in different schools, but we were almost the same age, 2 or 3 years of age difference only. Some of us fell for industrial bands like Ministry, Malhavoc, Godflesh, G.G.F.H. etc. Others turned to grunge, which in the 1990s almost killed Heavy Metal , though not at war with it . The Seattle sounds of Nirvana, Alice in Chains, Pearl Jam and Soundgarden just blew the minds of hard music fans, including me for some time. Then I just erased or gave away half of my death and grind records and replaced them with softer rock forms like the above mentioned grunge and Heavy Metalbands like Guns N' Roses, Iron Maiden and Helloween. Not that I didn't listen to them before, but I just started liking them more than the others. I guessed something was wrong with me, was I getting old and wise, or was it my girlfriend's influence... how I could tell.

Metalheads and their mates in town used to meet up in the centre, on some stairs in front of the cinema. It was our territory . The walls were all painted in bands names and logos; we'd drink beers, smoke fags and watch the passersby. They'd watch us, too, sometimes with criticism, sometimes in fright, sometimes with respect and even admiration, especially the birds . It was probably because of our long hair and free spirits, but quite a few girls wanted to join us, and they did. No doubt we were popular, and we were hot shots. That was one of the advantages of being a metalhead in those times . We were numerous, we were strong, and we were united. A real brotherhood. No one dared say a word against us or harass us . However, we were the ones to harass people from the minorities, so they'd do anything to avoid us. I remember we had an open confrontation once, right in the centre of our town, but I knew we were much stronger . It's completely different nowadays, but now these topics are rather touchy, and I'd rather not discuss them. Once we'd met up downtown in the early afternoon, especially in summer, by the evening we had chosen a boozer to have some beer. We'd sometimes hang around in the parks and gardens as I already said . We'd listen to HM, we'd drink beer and we'd talk about music mostly. And with the authors of this book we'd talk about football also . Sometime all of us would talk about women. But no topic ever stood in the way of others. I can't remember any fierce disputes, but there must have been a few . Especially in pubs at night . There were several pubs, but none of them was particularly meant for fans. And we'd change our favourite pub every summer. We'd choose one and start meeting up there until the owners' patience would wear thin and they'd throw us out. Then we'd change boozers. And even if no one sent us away, we might simply decide it was time for a change so the whole bunch would just go somewhere else . We'd also have house parties, but there we felt the resistance of both parents and neighbours . That was until our 'second home', the legendary Domino boozer, opened. We'd also go partying in cottages, we'd put up tents near Kapinovski Monastery, on reservoir banks, at the seaside, etc..., but we'd stick together the whole bunch, or the majority of us, bringing our girlfriends, of course . We used to bring them everywhere apart from football games and concerts, where things were likely to get rough.

Now as I said 'concerts', the first metal live show in Bulgaria was held at Academic Stadium in Sofia on 15.09.1991, Sodom in the main act . I was there, of course! Unbelievable experience. Instead of attending the first day of the school year, I went to watch Sodom live. The level of rebellion against the system. Though socialism had collapsed a year or two earlier, practically it was still there and some even claim that its consequences are still felt nowadays, which in itself an utterly sad conclusion is taking into account all that rebellion then!"

Here are some anonymously taken photos that could be used to describe this memorable event

That was the official poster for the gig

And here is the official opinion of the authorities about the event, the headline reads "Following Sodom's gig things looked like in ancient Sodom".

After Sodom's gig, a Sodom like situation

Chains, knuckledusters, 3-4-kg belts, studded bracelets, horned helmets, etc. are among the sinister items captured by the police after the rock concert by a band called Sodom on Sunday. Metalheads seem not to care that their idols do not preach violence, they just report it.

Drunken and stoned mobs went on rampage hours before the gig. Its overture included screaming, teasing female passers by and smashing bottles all along Vitosha Boulevard, around the Central Railway Station and Academic Stadium. A huge mob broke into a construction site and started having fun by throwing bottles at the people passing by. The police intervened resolutely and spoiled their fun. Two heavy metal units were engaged in a security breach operation. While some of them were throwing bottles, their brothers-in-arms stormed the ground fencing. There are reports of casualties, including a police officer. Other policemen got punched and kicked. However, the music then kept the attention of the fans for a while.

The thrash metalheads from Sofia and the country went on rioting after the gig. While fighting, they seriously damaged two cafes. It is not reported whether the brawl started for music related reasons. Exalted youths are reported to have laid on the tramway tracks along Trakia Boulevard, risking their lives. A number of them have hooligan records. Among them is a fellow-villager of the cannibal from the village of Usoika, aged 41. More than 200 police officers were involved in ensuring the concert security. Their opinion is that Academic Stadium is unsuitable for holding such events.

"And truth to tell, they were right to some extent. It was mayhem . Bulgarian metalheads, dying for Western music and having no concert culture and experience, showed their most violent and brutal Balkan nature during the gig . Along with their most dedicated and passionate support and cheers for the band, of course. Sodom themselves admit up to this day (recently I listened to an interview with Tom Angelripper) that this was their most attended and in general their best gig ever. And they mean it. According to records, the band never attracted such a big audience as headliners. 15 thousand fans at Academic ground having come from all corners of Bulgaria to see their German idols, wild, drunken, aggressive, and ready to fight the police and each other. In his interview Tom says that backstage, w hen they heard the crowds roar, they just couldn't believe it was meant to welcome THEM. They even hesitated whether to hit the stage . What if they did not meet the crowd's expectations, those wild hordes would eat them alive...

Tickets were sold in Sofia only. A family friend working as a pilot, who often travelled to the capital, bought three tickets for me and two mates of mine . My old folks wouldn't let me go on my own. And they had good reasons. I knew it the moment I set foot in Sofia . Actually, I realised it back at the station in Gorna Oryahovitsa. The three of us went there to catch the train to find it occupied by metalheads. I didn't know all of them then, but I'd seen some of them downtown . Our number was about 30. There was this big and tall and most intimidating bloke who became the leader of our group. All of us youngsters just followed him . And he, standing on the pedestal of well recognised high esteem, would scream at us, "Stick around, your assholes!", and we'd go laughing out loud, our voices hoarse and guttural, like real metalheads . I had just turned 16 . So, the train arrived. We heard it before it entered the station. Fucking pandemonium . Screams and shouts, Sodom flags and scarves flying out of the windows . At least 5 long-haired guys sticking their heads out of the windows, headbanging . Bottles flying out of the train smashing down on the platform . It looked as if the Huns, the Tatars, the Vandals and a few XII-century Viking tribes had been loaded onto that train . "What the fucking hell?!", we'd go . The train was coming from Varna and was packed with metalheads. I can't remember if there were any ordinary people travelling or did they simply refused to board the train upon seeing us . And those who'd get off at the stations before Sofia we re happy to get off lightly. It went on until we reached Sofia, screaming, shouting, drinking, running along corridors, pushing, and hell on Earth! We arrived in Sofia to be met by at least 100 cops. There were at least 1000 of us aggressive guys booing them, but they insisted on escorting us from the station all the way to the stadium . It's a hell of a distance, mind you. It turned out to be a wise decision, though . Sofia skinhead shad gone out on a manhunt and this time their targets were people arriving from the country . Simply because they had no one else to attack . We were the only different ones they could recognise. No gypsies, no other minorities. So, they identified people from the country as aliens and were about to unleash their aggression against us. The OB was well aware of that and pretended to guard us, but when we reached the venue they stepped aside and stood only around the entrances . So, the skinheads were stood on a hill on the opposite side of the road. There were some 200 of them and the y started hurling stones, bottles, rocks, bits of wood and anything else they could find . They'd send their missiles right amidst the crowd so there were a lot of cracked heads and faces covered in blood. The crowd sent a mighty roar and was ready to lynch them. There were at least 5000 people outside the ground and no force would have been able to stop them . However, there was no one to lead the charge. It was getting tenser; the clash was a matter of minutes. The cops realised the impending catastrophe an d intervened. They set the warring groups apart and stood in between. The skins went on throwing missiles over the police line. Mounted riot police arrived . The skinheads got even more enraged. So, did the metalheads. Word went out that separate mobs of skinheads had had a go at smaller groups of metalheads on their way to the stadium and had robbed them of their trainers, jackets, money and tickets. Things were starting to get nasty . Angry shouts and battle cries could be heard from both sides. I plucked up courage and asked a nearby mounted policeman "Officer, why are the locals so hostile and willing to fight us?" The copper's reply was like, "Well, who the fuck invited you here? It wasn't me for sure"... Would you believe that?! Anyway, after about half an hour, in which anything could have happened, the doors of the venue opened, and people started getting in . We had come to a concert, hadn't we? The tension subsided as the skinheads were denied entry. The cops kept them outside for the entire gig. And I'm glad they did. The show went fine though the sound was not that good. One could hardly distinguish between songs and almost all of them sounded the same way, but we did manage to listen to 'Agent Orange' and 'Remember the Fallen'. It was more than enough for us. The experience was thrilling, unique and all those who attended it will hardly ever forget it . Sodom also remembers it well. We had no problems on our way back. We walked in a huge mob looking around for skinheads, but no one had a go at us. We got on 2 or 3 trams and reached the station where we stayed till dawn to wait for our train back. There was some minor trouble at the station, but we had a police escort all through the night and nothing worth mentioning happened. We came back home safe and sound and proudly told our friends and classmates what we'd been through. I'm glad I was part of it...

On 29.03.1992 the second big HM concert was held in Bulgaria. Another German thrash band called Tankard. The venue was Festivalna Hall. I went there again . It was the same old situation as with the case of Sodom, i.e. crowded trains, lots of booze, bottles flying , Sofia skinheads willing to fight and mounted police . Poor sound quality and songs hard to tell apart . But we were hungry for live shows and would bear anything, so nobody criticised the organisations like they do now. We were simply happy that finally there were such shows in our God-forsaken motherland . Tickets for the Sodom gig cost 22 BGN, which was quite a significant amount for times when monthly salaries were still 100-120 BGN. Just 6 months later, Tankard's show cost 55 BGN. No doubt, it was expensive . Thanks God, my parents were over-indulging and would allow me anything, or else, I wouldn't be able to tell you such stories now. God knows what they did without, poor old folks, so that I could buy those tickets. Truth to tell, we were not well-off.

The third big and memorable gig was Kreator. November 1993. They did two shows then - in Sofia and in Varna. Due to the trouble anticipated in Sofia after the two similar shows, this time I and a mate of mine decided to go to Varna. And we were not the only ones . Word went out that the show in Sofia was attended by some 2000 people, mainly locals , while the one in Varna had at least a 5000-strong crowd, guys from all over the country . Besides, the Varna gig was much better in terms of organisation, sound quality and everything else . And no trouble erupted at any time. We returned satisfied and happy, feeling like some kind of veterans since in three years we had attended the three biggest shows held in Bulgaria .

In the years that followed professional promoters appeared and now a good number of security guards make sure there is order across stadia and halls. They do their job quite well . No pissed, stoned and aggressive people are allowed entry. No bottles, knives, knuckledusters, baseball bats or other tools are allowed, either. And metalheads finally acquired some concert culture and no longer get pissed as a newt on route to venues because they won' t be let in even if they have tickets. Skinheads no longer turn up at HM shows because they've got their own bands now singing their own stuff . We haven't had any encounters and problems with them ever since. And it is no longer the police that are in charge of security. The events are guarded by bouncers. Nowadays one could see an increasing number of women and even kids at big concerts and festivals. The atmosphere is much more peaceful and pleasant, and everyone can have their fair share of fun, which is actually everybody's intention . I keep on attending live shows up to this day. I try to attend big events at least once or twice a year, but now the choice is wide, and one has to go to work, you know the story…You can't get fucked up at a, let's say Slayer's gig, and go to work at 8 am on the next day and, most of all, be able to work all day. But anyway, sometimes we do it. We are still fans, aren't we?!

As I'm coming to the end now, I'd like to finish with something football related, or rather give further ground for the main topic, by telling the story of the summer of 1994. The football summer of 1994. For those who don't remember, Bulgarian national team finished fourth at the USA World Cup. We, the metalheads from Gorna Oryahovitsa, naturally followed this memorable feat. We'd meet up at various pubs that had TV sets, and everybody watched the games and cheered for our team. I'd go with some mates to a hunting lodge or the "Lodge" as we used to call it. They used to serve cold beer, deep-fired sprats, French fries and they had a big TV set on the verandah. What else could you possibly need? My hair was as long as it could be, I had a girlfriend, lots of mates and I knew every single metalhead in town and the area, we'd go wherever we wanted and do what ever we liked, I was already 18 years of age and felt the happiest person on Earth . After each great victory of our football team , all metalheads, no matter where we were, would dash downtown and would jump right into the town fountain . There we'd splash around, throw water at each other, pour in dish soap so that the water gets foamy, drink beer and shout out loud like mad. And all of these we'd do just for fun. It was great euphoria . Beating Argentina, Mexico, Germany…, way to go! After we did Germany, there were more people than water in the fountain. Absolute mayhem ! It was a brilliant summer . Maybe the last happy summer that united Bulgarians in such a way . The same went for the metalheads too as it was the last summer I felt I was really living a full life and I really had the feeling of belonging. In September I joined the army (military service was still obligatory back then), had my hair cut and turned the page as they say . The same happened to most of the metalheads my age . We were in different units, so we could meet on much rarer occasions . And when we did, we talked of things so different from music like company and platoon commanders, discharge and similar bullshit. While in the army I met other people, completely different one, and we listened to music completely different from what I was used to listening before . And since everything was weird in the army, I began to listen to weird music . In addition to the grunge I was telling you about, I also fell for bands like Dead Can Dance, Skunk Anansie, Filter, Tool…, as well as Bristol trip-hop reps like Portishead, Massive Attack, Tricky, Morcheeba , etc. For a while I abandoned thrash and death metal. I even almost dumped Heavy Metal as those bands could hardly be defined as belonging to it .

After I was discharged I started studying Psychology in university and I met even more weird blokes. My main contacts were students from the town of Ruse and they had quite an impact on my music tastes. Besides, hardly any of my colleague's psychologists listened t o HM. To compensate, in their company and at student parties I rediscovered bands like Morphine, Orbital, Prodigy, Therapy…, we'd listen to soundtracks to different films (there were plenty of them then) like The Raven, The Matrix, Judgment Day, etc ., featuring Pantera, Marylin Manson, Rollins Band, Body Count, etc. So, while being a student and afterwards, I expanded the range of my music preferences. I'd listen to a lot of jazz , Louis Armstrong, Annie Lennox , PJ Harvey, Amy Winehouse and other oddn balls…

…Nowadays, especially during the last 5 years I did a kind of comeback to the roots . I started going out with some metalheads from Tarnovo, all of them old-school thrash metal fans from olden times. I knew some of them from times gone by and I made some new friends recently. Together we started going to live shows and we did Slayer twice, Anthrax, Destruction, Kreator, Behemoth, Meshuggah, Soulfly, S.D.I., Annihilator, what not . We all have different jobs but somehow, we manage to find free time . Besides, we have worked out a plan. We hire a van from a licensed transportation company . They drive us while we drink and listen to the corresponding band to get ready for the gig . The driver waits for us in the van, we attend the show and, on our way, back, usually at night, we go on drinking, though in a more modest manner, and we listen to any kind of metal, though not so loud, while some of us doze off as we have to go to work in the morning. The plan works fine, and we have followed it several times now . Thus, we can attend shows not only at weekends, but on weekdays too . So, what I'm trying to say is that I once again listen to death and thrash, go to shows with my old-school mates, I've bought a few HM T - shirts and I wear them at weekends . I have my camo trousers and military boots and by and large, Rock is not dead. In addition, I also see t hat old-school giants do not give up and have no intention of quitting . Slayer have a relatively recent album, Megadeth have a relatively recent album. Kreator and Destruction have very powerful brand-new albums. Tankard are getting ready to release one, if they haven't already. Metallica have a new, extremely powerful album that can also be described as going back to their roots . Sepulture also have new albums, though they are not what they used to be . Even Venom and Napalm Death released albums 2 years ago. So, this is it! Thrash till Death & Old School Forever (laughing).

I still feel proud I belong to the metal brotherhood. Consciously or subconsciously, we, metalheads, often address each other using the word 'brother', which is meaningful for shrinks like me. I keep on listening to my favourite music , which these days is more accessible than ever in any ways as one could find virtually anything on the Internet. I mean high quality sound, covers, info, lyrics, translations, anything one could possibly need . We no longer need to use cassette recorder microphones for the recordings . I don't buy cassettes from Corecom or elsewhere. I don't even buy CDs as they take up too much space at home. It's all digital, you know, memory sticks, EHDs and laptops and carry them with me and listen to music everywhere I go. Even now, as I'm writing these lines, I'm listening to some stuff on YouTube and searching the web for info about past events . Clothes and accessories are now sold everywhere. In general, being a metalhead is easy these days. Being anyone and anything you like is easy, but I made my choice long ago. I've been through a lot in my life. Everyone has. But I dare say this kind of music is what helped me not lose heart and mind in hard times and for that I'd like to thank musicians, bands, producers and fans for that music as so many folks have been involved in its development so that it can still be listened to and appeal to more and more new fans ready to join the global metal brotherhood. I also thank the authors of this book for inviting me to participate in it and for making sure my words will be read".

Counterculture in Gorna Oryahovitsa, 1994

QUOTES from Beyond the Hatred book:

"It all started in the era of hard rock and heavy metal , when we used to have long hair and wear tight jeans, military boots and badges. We would spend all day listening to our favourite style of music and having a good time in the company of young ladies and lots of booze. In a few words – a picture portraying a kind of mild debauchery. I think there was the same phenomenon in England, when in the ecstasy pills era, the most notorious English hooligans replaced football grounds with music clubs for quite a long period of time. It was a "Make love, not war" between the violet and black-and-white fans. Gorna Oryahovitsa lads would fuck the rivals' birds , on much rarer occasions some of the m would chat up our local girls. Apart from some drunken rows, both camps would get off lightly, being involved in minor accidents only, something like a fist or two from the one side or the other. Things were even more different and peaceful back in the hippie years. Then the black-and-whites used to be friends with the "Boyars" (the nickname of the citizens of Veliko Tarnovo, our rival). There were joint trips to the Black Sea beaches and music concerts, so generally it was a period of blissful peace between the two towns. Maybe the seven miles of picturesque scenery separating the two towns facilitated such meetings. The area between our two towns is called Arbanasi, a small tourist village and practically no man's land. In terms of geography, these areas are all hills area, and, believe me, it is one of the most beautiful and enchanting places in our country! It was there where the house of my best mates was situated and in that house some of the parties in questions were thrown. The very structure looked like a castle and was quite spacious. Inside I would meet crowds of people, not only from the two towns, but also from the nearby towns of Gabrovo and Lovech."

Using this quote from our first book, we are now moving to the climax of the present one. Having provided definitions of a number of concepts and phenomena and having introduced you to three prominent representatives (from different parts of our country) of the three global major subcultures and countercultures that had their impact on the formation of the collective image of the 'old-school' hardcore football fan (hool) in Bulgaria... As authors of this book, we find it sensible and appropriate to give you another example by introducing you to another representative of HM culture who comes from a region including neighbouring towns like Gorna Oryahovitsa, Tarnovo, Gabrovo, Lovech and Pleven. We find this as our primordial right since we ourselves are representatives of this trend and we define ourselves as hoolies, and besides it's not a secret that this region used to be and probably still is the 'capital' of this subculture and its derivatives.

Opinion: S.R. (Gabrovo)

"Brothers ... I'll make a statement ...

I'd like to make it quite clear that I'm writing these lines after coordinating opinions and events with a few mates. It's kinda several of us writing this. Because I am well aware that whatever I say there will be those who'll disagree and challenge my words ...

Gabrovo

What can I tell you about my native town? I can't ... I just can't help beginning this way... You know I come from a town known as 'the town of humour and satire'... (laughing).

In 1903 Bourmov[3] wrote that in Gabrovo "One who does not drink raki is not considered an intelligent person" ...Now, more than a century later, it's the same old situation ... Now I won't waste my time writing about intelligence , entrepreneurship, hospitality, etc. as those are qualities we are quite famous or notorious for . But, do you know why I agreed to help you with this book ? And I'll do it with pleasure! Because estimating Gabrovo through the prism of the activity of this town and its self-expression through the support for its local football club is an amazingly clever idea, and especially with regard to this topic ... Gabrovo has a lot to say about it ...Honestly ... Take my word!

My first memories of that generation of metalheads, respectively football mob, and of the ways and manners of that time include the packed 'Chicken' (a legendary HM boozer) in Gabrovo and the garden in front and I, in front of more than 100 witnesses, dared to slash the tyres of two police cars that used to bother us on a regular basis with their very presence, not to speak of their constant questions what kind of aliens we exactly were and what our cause was . They didn't like us... Our appearance was not to their liking . Naturally, afterwards the rabid coppers sniffed around trying to find who committed that offence (literally considered as violation against the governmental authorities), but no one snitched on me. So, it was around that incident that this strange mixture of glammers, bikers, metalheads and any limbs of Satan as t he society would call us back then was formed.

There was hatred but not for the rival mobs. It was genuine, sincere hatred for the cops . A separate book has to be written about the purest and never-ending hatred between Yantra[4] mob and the police... Hell of a story! Fat angry bastards in uniforms who, instead of staying in the shade all day smoking fags, had to deal all week long with the same dishevelled brats and when Saturdays came, had to handle the same urchins, this time wearing green-and-white scarves and throwing crackers at them! We always thought of them as obese neurotic individuals looking for trouble, suffering from different disorders, who could never catch us no matter how long they would chase us... A hell of a story! I am damn sure that in those times there were more arrests for blokes from Yantra firm than there are nowadays for the leading Bulgarian mobs! By saying arrests, I do not mean staying in the nick, being sentenced or any other forms of formal detention. What I mean is getting lifted, thrown out of the ground, punched in the kidneys a few times and finally being kicked in the arse ... Anyone whose old school knows what I'm talking about. I don't know a single soul who's ever been a part of Yantra mob and has not been subject to such treatment. But all this when time comes I'll pay special attention to the mob later.

Quite often my house would turn into an open inn for non-stop parties involving a countless number of guys coming from different towns . Occasionally I and a few mates would go to the 'Chicken' for a change leaving behind my home full of strangers . Nothing valuable ever went missing for all those years. We had complete mutual trust and we loved helping each other.

The title "Gabrovo – Bulgarian Heavy Metal capital" does not originate in Gabrovo at all. The company I used to hang around while in Sofia was not consisting people I got to know in Sofia. They were guys I met at binges in Gabrovo and not only there... A small town in the country that had two downtown parks with hundreds of drinking youngsters dressed in denim vests , three all-metalhead pubs, i.e. the legendary 'Chicken' , 'Experiment', 'Bros' bar and a metalhead den called 'Black Hole' night club. Oh, I almost forgot... At the same time there were two HM shops in town ! Our friendship with long-haired pissheads from all over the country did not begin at the Goldfish Campsite in the town of Sozopol only . For a number of years Gabrovo had become something like a meeting point for metalheads coming from all corners of the country. I can definitely say that this variety and the constant presence of visitors had their impact on Yantra mob.

We never had real enemies. We never went somewhere or hosted some team with the intention of having a go at our opponents ! That does not mean that we ever refused to take up a gauntlet thrown down by a rival mob or that we did not earn respect thanks to our fists. No fucking way!

But we never started up a fight and by 'we' I mean the mob and the metalheads as part of the mob. There was another group of people who have nothing to do with this topic. They can write down their own memories if they like . The only reason for us to fight side by side with them was that we all supported Yantra Gabrovo and whenever trouble flared it was the entire t own getting involved! But as a whole we had different opinions and we never kept close contacts with those blokes... What is more, they even didn't like our appearance and the way we dressed ... They didn't like our style in general as it was the opposite of theirs. So, there were those fellas (men in their 30s and 40s), who had nothing in common with us . They used to hang around in a café by the market hall and they were known as V.'s crew . They were never part of the mob, they never wore scarves, they never carried flags and we never kept in touch with them . They would take their seats in the fenced VIP sector and they used to have lots of dough. When, under the sponsorship of TAURUS, Yantra FC was the first club in Bulgaria to sell season tickets, they were the first to buy them . They never missed an away game, but they organised their away days in their own way and in each town, they'd meet like-minded folks, but unlike us they were not sworn brothers with Tarnovo metalheads and did not meet up a rival mob from Gorna Oryahovitsa at half times. Generally speaking, they were diehard Yantra supporters, but not a part of the mob as you'll find out further in my story .

When I say that actually we did not really hate anyone..., maybe I exaggerate things a bit ... Gorna Oryahovitsa, Tarnovo, Lovech, Ruse, Svishtov, Beroe ... There was the banter and there were skirmishes, but we had not hatred . The urge to protect the honour of your native town – yes, but deep and genuine hatred for our opponents - never. How could you hate a crew of, let's say 100 fellas, when some of them had been guests at your home and with others you had been on the piss all night long on several occasions?! We used to wonder at the mentality of Tarnovo lads, who'd pay us a visit and we'd join forces as early as the night before Lokomotiv G.O. would come to play in Gabrovo. Now their hatred was (and still is) deep and genuine. An extreme hatred though both sets would also come together at times for parties in the region or at the seaside .

We were predominantly a home mob. We wouldn't take big numbers anywhere we didn't have friends among the local metalheads . Those who went everywhere were the group of middle-aged blokes. We were all for the parties and we fought rival mobs only on few occasions, which I'm going to tell you about . Well, there are individual incidents, like the one in the town of Svishtov, where two lads, P. and K. decided to stay for another day after the game so that they could finish their binge, but ended up being chased by a whole neighbourhood... We were a friendly lot, yes, we were! Who were you supposed to have a go at or who was supposed to have a go at you, J. from Tarnovo or P. from Lovech?! Well, it's true that in Gabrovo we'd retaliate if they didn't come in peace... In a few words, it was come to Gabrovo to have fun and party and you'll be having the time of your life but come to bring a sword and you'll die by the sword, you bastards.

Anyway, I've got lots of memories to share about particular clubs such as Etar, Osum, Spartak Pleven... loads and loads of them ... and all of them good memories, all of them off the pitch . At half times mobs would often meet up to arrange ... parties and not fights ... Heavy Metal all the way!

---

3 A BULGARIAN CULTURAL FIGURE AND POLITICIAN OF THE LATE XIX CENTURY, BORN IN THE TOWN OF GABROVO

---

4 YANTRA FC IS THE FOOTBALL CLUB FROM THE TOWN OF GABROVO

The Crowd

I know a lot about it, mainly thanks to my deceased grandfather , who was a devoted Yantra supporter. He was the man who took my hand and brought me to the stadium for the first time . He was several years older than the football club and in general was a living football encyclopaedia. I am much obliged to him for sparking my interest in football.

Yantra was a privileged (in terms of geographical location) club. The close vicinity of towns like Dryanovo, Sevlievo and Tryavna and the numerous quarters where people had no opportunity to watch their own club playing in the top flight, made Yantra FC quite popular in the region, especially in its best period . My memories of it date back to a time between the mid-1980s and the late 1990s. The 12,500-capacity ground would always burst at the seams and there were even crowds on the nearby hills so those who could not find tickets could cheer their beloved club from there. We also travelled to away games, especially in our region. I asked my father about his memories and he recalled how he went with my Grandpa on a motorbike to watch games in the towns of Lovech, Vratsa, Tarnovo... No matter how little entertainment people in Gabrovo had in those years, Yantra FC somehow managed to provide a little fun. Even now, when you start talking to some fella from Gabrovo , he's quite likely to recollect "that promotion game" in Gorna Oryahovitsa ... On that momentous day, fans from Gabrovo jammed the roads and up to this day they still argue whether they took 2 or 3 thousand to that away game ! There was always something for us to boast about in those times, and though our club was a lower-league one, we would put up a resistance against much stronger mobs. .. We always tried to bring numbers, not only as a mob, but as a crowd.

In those years even, bigger clubs had no craze of going on all away days. Not to speak of Yantra FC! Yes, we were a markedly home mob, I admit to that . Anyway, there were a few exceptions as we'd always travel to Tarnovo and Gorna Oryahovitsa. As far as Gabrovo is concerned, I am absolutely positive that only the two Sofia giants5, Lokomotiv G.O. and Etar were the only ones to regularly bring good numbers here. On some rare occasions we were visited by Botev, Lokomotiv Plovdiv, Dunav, Spartak Varna, Dobrudza and... a small club called Olympic from a mountainous village of Galata brought three coach loads of Pomaks6 steamed in, I swear to God!

The Mob

The first and most important thing I have to strongly emphasise is that there was a considerable difference between Yantra FC ordinary supporters and its mob. These are completely different and even contradictory definitions. Their only common ground is attending a football ground at one and the same time to support their beloved football club because of their love for one and the same town... This division is probably the only reason for the current total lack of interest in what is going on at Yantra FC ground, Hristo Botev Stadium . It's just that the football club has long stopped deserving attention and being the representative of a town that otherwise deserves attention. Cause there is marked interest in the town's volleyball and handball teams ...

Three years ago, I went to Gabrovo during my leave. Even before I boarded the plane in Manchester (where I live) I knew that while I was staying in my hometown, there would be a football game Yantra vs Sevlievo. I had no illusions and great expectations , but still, after so many years I had the opportunity to go to Hristo Botev and watch my club. So, I went out to have a few pre-match drinks at the town square just like we used to do in the olden days. That was where my series of disappointment started. The same people that used to keep me company once at Yantra FC games just laughed in my face upon hearing my intention to attend a game, "Haha, what game? Does this club still exist? You must have gone really mad in that England of yours!" and so on and so forth . I had shared my intention to buy a bottle of rum and drink it with my mates, but I was joined only by some complete stranger, an alcoholic who swore he knew me. So, it all became a 'let's see how bad it can get' thing. Little did I know! I bought two bottles of rum so that I did not share one with that filthy pisshead. We got to the ground ... to find... nothing. Just nothing, not a single living soul, no players, no game! Nothing... My first reaction was to think I was a fucking moron who had misunderstood everything. I checked my mobile to find out that I was not wrong and that at that very moment the two line-ups were supposed to be warming up... I got the shock of my life... I called Yantra's coach and he told me that the two clubs had agreed to postpone the game for two days as a Sevlievo player was getting married! And I was standing at the main stand with a bottle of rum and a damned babbling alcoholic beside me... So, I just sat down speechless , oblivious of everything around me. If I have ever been on the verge of having a heart attack that was the time. The fella next to me would not stop jabbering but I was not listening. At some point I just turned my head to look at him, but I just stared blankly at him as if he was not there at all. I looked at the seats, the fencing, the club's building... memories, memories, memories… sadness, grief and sorrow got hold of me … I didn't recover until the sot poked me and asked me if I was OK … I was sitting there staring at him, and in about a minute I just managed to say, " Mate..., it's all fucked up...and this time it's for good ..." I stood up and left … forever .

The fear of discrediting ourselves is innate in us, the ones born in Gabrovo, and it is what we hate the most. .. During our first stay in the top flight in the 1970s we beat CSKA 1-0 and the mayor ordered all churches in town to ring their bells. When we agreed to let one of our best players play in Levski FC and they didn't do their best, so we peacefully drew 1-1, giving us a point out of gratitude for that successful transfer , two days after that our players did not go training as there was an angry crowd waiting at the ground to lynch them … Pride! I know people who after that point were given to Yantra FC as a gift never set foot inside the ground as their pride was hurt … And there was a scandal when the united Gabrovo club was named Chardafon-Orlovets! Some wanted to name it Gabrovo, but they were told that" The name of the town should not be used in any situations that could result in its disgrace !" I am far from thinking that this trait in the mentality of my fellow citizens makes me proud of them because there's something more to that, in Gabrovo nothing is considered "too good" ...

By the mid-1980s Yantra FC did not have the support of a united crew, separated from the rest of the crowd (a mob), who'd persistently stand all game long wearing scarves, flying flags and singing out loud. I think that in general no club in Bulgaria had such groups of supporters in those times and everybody was a part of one whole , i.e. of a crowd.

We were not free in those times. Everything in our and in our parents', lives was just norms, rules and stereotypes. Each and every minute we were prompted and reminded of what would happen to us if we didn't stay away from those blokes belonging to 'football mobs' . We were also shown a particular, purely geographic line that we should never dare cross! I think that if the so called 'scaly caps' (the rank-and-file fans in those times) had pondered upon the maxim that "forbidden fruit is the sweetest" , the system would surely not have done away with them so easily . The great Bulgarian dissident author Markov explains that wonderfully in his 'In Absentia Reports', giving as an example Levski FC: "If the 'scaly caps' had not ostentatiously established their own club to symbolise their party invincibility and at the same time unambiguously pointed a finger at their 'fascist' enemy Levski FC, the latter would have surely remained an ordinary club and would have never become a cause and the unrestricted love of almost everyone in this country who does not agree with the regime ". For the very same reasons I became part of a generation that was quite keen on the forbidden "rotten Western" things like porno films, HM music and going mental across stadia. Porno films and HM music were scanty. Your daily allowance was 0.20 BGN and a HM band pin cost 10 BGN. But any given Saturday no one could stop you from attending a football game for 0.50 BGN (the cost of tickets then) and letting off anything inside that had been tormenting you! So, it was stadia that my generation let off the angry and tormented adrenaline they had built up inside.

In general, Yantra mob appeared at Hristo Botev ground when mobs appeared across the other stadia in the country . It was long shaped, but simply all the metalheads, punks, skinheads, etc. moved to the football ground making it a really lively place . The same faces you'd see on a daily basis drinking in parks, streets, tunnels, etc. They started sewing flags, making bombs and smoke bombs and demonstrating their quality at the ground . Someone might get angry with my conclusion (surely there will be such fellas), but Bulgarian mobs in the late 1980s and the early 1990s were almost 100% made of metalheads plus a few punks to add a little colour ... Gabrovo, Tarnovo, Gorna Oryahovitsa, Dobrudzha and Spartak Varna were good examples of that and up to this day I have never seen more drunken mobs than theirs . And I'm not the only one to share such an opinion... Lokomotiv G.O. for example would bring good numbers, including lads who had run away from hospital in their pyjamas after being hospitalised for alcohol intoxication! I'll never forget one of them having lined up a dozen of 'quarter bottles' of grape raki along the curb on the railway station pavement, watching them as if they were his children, and there we came and blew up a few bombs that knocked them down like bowling pins...Strike...(laughing). I felt sorry for the lad, but anyway, I'll tell about their mob further down .

At Yantra FC first home game after November 10th 19897 the coppers just stood there helpless and had absolutely no idea what was going in and which master to kneel before. So totally confused the police were that they seemed to have turned into kind, friendly and helpful fellas . We were teasing them ahead of kick-off and one of them (obviously their chief) called this lad K. To have a word with him in private ... On his return K. was grinning and giggling like mad and he told us the Old Bill had explained they were aware that we were 'hot-blooded young boys' and could easily get away with blowing up bombs if we just threw them at a predefined spot on the racetrack ...In just a few seconds probably 10 bombs went off right in front of the cops, but their response was not the one we were used to, i.e. charging at us wielding truncheons ! They simply split apart in two groups and stood at a considerable distance on both our sides . No one that day could believe their eyes and all we could say was, "Hey, so finally we made it, didn't we?'

Yantra was promoted to the top flight after an away 1-0 victory over Lokomotiv Gorna Oryahovitsa... It was a game that we should have lost by at least 0 -3 in view of the chances both teams had, but we ... won . A couple of thousands blokes from Gabrovo made the trip to Gorna Oryahovitsa. I was pretty young, so I went with my Dad and Grandpa as I didn't know any metalheads from our mob. Truth to tell, even Levski and CSKA can't take such numbers on away days even nowadays... Well, probably they could, but they won't be all Sofia fans. So, if I have to describe Yantra FC mob in just a few words it would be something like this: Yes. was famous and recognised nationwide for the bombs he'd make the size of pumpkins and then , standing on the roof of the Yantra Hotel, throw them at away fans arriving at the station ... And believe it or not, Lokomotiv G.O. had something to write about us in their first book !

Interview

Tosh, Gilly and Milen, the first and most important thing for me altogether regarding my participation in that brilliant project of yours is that I would like to explicitly emphasise that I have never been one of the leaders of Yantra mob, nor a top face among metalheads ! I was not a prominent figure on either scene, it was just that destiny placed me somewhere between football and Heavy Metal. I might have taken up this hobby of mine to collect memories of different events through the years and I will be extremely happy to share them with you so that I can warm up the readers in view of what they have coming on the next pages, i.e. meeting the real hard-core faces of the Bulgarian scene.

Since I was asked by the authors of this book to share my personal opinion I must kinda introduce myself so that you, readers, know who's writing the lines that you'll be reading ...

My Mum is a lawyer and Dad is a civil engineer. My family friends... well, I'd better not talk about them as it might sound as swagger ... By and large, I had the best background possible for bringing up a good boy and making him a good man.

In a two-boy family, the older brother almost always follows the path his parents have been dreaming of while the younger one in most cases, if born under a lucky star, can be whatever he wants to be, in my case a ... metalhead (laughing)... There are loads of examples, me being one of the most vivid ones . The first thing of significance that ever happened in my life and I remember it crystal clear is becoming a football fan . Lots of people do not have distinct memories, but I do, and they seem like yesterday...

As I said before, my Grandpa (may he rest in peace) was a man totally and unconditionally devoted to his native Yantra FC. He went to away games even before World War II . Later he got the problems with his legs, but two hours ahead of kick-off he'd go out and nothing could stop him, slowly limping and with the help of his cane, from going to Hristo Botev Stadium . In the end, when he was almost out of energy, I used to order him a taxi so that he could watch his beloved club again, poor old man. He used to live with us, but most of the time he'd take care of his native home and keep bees in the small village of Lesicharka. I remember going to his village once. I can't remember the date, but it was in the summer of 1985. I was 8 years old and Grandpa was waiting for me as he always used to do. He had baked a stuffed carp and while I was eating, he was reading the Balkan Flag newspaper. He'd always read the back page only, the football things . The rest he'd refuse to even look at, saying "If I wanna know what the communists have to say, I'll personally ask someone I know !" At one-point Grandpa popped out his eyes! I asked him what the matter was ... and saw tears brim his eyes! He was sitting there, staring blankly, eyes in tears, as if he'd seen a ghost and I was already freaking out, "Come on, Grandpa, what is it, what's happened?!"... He uttered only a few words, "Gundi's son started playing for Levski FC" ... Well, how about that? Who was Gundi[8] and who the hell was his son?! Obviously, there were still things that an 8-year-old boy had not been told yet. A greater shock followed when, upon returning to Gabrovo, I told my mother what had happened. Good Heavens! She also burst in tears ! I immediately started asking her questions and then she said, "Well, we were all in love with Gundi ..." That's it! End of story!

At that very moment the number of Levski FC fans increased with one ! And since then Levski FC has not stopped being for me what Yantra FC also is. It was some kind of supernatural and strange phenomenon for me. Like a force of nature, like an avalanche... and the first thing I got to know about it was that it could bring tears to anybody's eyes even after years, even up to this day!

Exactly three years passed from my 'blue' [9] christening. Gabrovo had no team to play Levski in the foreseeable future . And I already knew well all Levski current and former stars . I was totally obsessed with the colour blue! While still a little boy, I had already nicked (after a nasty beating) my first scarf only to be caught by my parents and made to go and take it back to the poor boy ... So, it was around that point that my childhood ended, and I started taking an active part in such events some of which I am going to tell you about ... naturally, events involving my native Yantra FC.

Dunav Ruse

I already said that we've always been nice to nice guys, but we'd never ignore a gauntlet thrown down on us. Not to speak of any insult ! Not to speak of it happening at home ground, in our native Gabrovo!

We played Dunav a decisive game for avoiding relegation, we beat them 3-1, they didn't bring a mob and so we all forgot about them. a year or two passed . Once again, we played them, so I went to that game just like I did on any routine home game, but ... WOW !!! Not only were than more than a hundred, but the OB had stood them in the main stand ! Blimey! OK, we could forget about it, but... they had come all tooled up like ninjas, carrying chains and knives, one of them even smuggling a machete... Never before had I seen such a sight . Needless to say, that the news of a visiting mob's presence in town had spread everywhere. The game finished. We won 1:0. No one cared about the result and no one left the ground. The entire home crowd stood in the shape of a crescent around the away fans throwing at them stones, bottles, etc . It was a day to remember, oh, yes it was ! The cops did a great job as they managed to escort them out of the ground… but that was it. No police escort along the street. And what followed was Armageddon! Gabrovo is nothing more than two parallel boulevards . The travelling supporters were ambushed at both the bus and the railway station. Those who were still in town were also given a good hiding. And there was this poor small crew that got separated and lost heading for the bridge … The poor fellas jumped into the river to find rescue …

There was no animosity between us and them . And there still isn't. I have absolutely no idea why they decided to take liberties in Gabrovo on that day! Years later, in Sofia, I met a lad who happened to be there. His words were, "Mate, it was my mother who saved my life on that day!" What he meant was that his mother (knowing he was heading for Gabrovo) made him take in his biker jacket a note with the address and phone of some relatives of theirs living in Gabrovo, just in case… That's what you call a life -saving decision…So right here I'd better finish with the words of a fella who's long gone now (RIP Boza), "In the of Gabrovo you can get a free drink from a fierce stray dog and you can get beaten up by a flower grown in the garden in front of the town theatre!".

Botev Plovdiv

Yantra FC was to play Botev Plovdiv. The Botev squad featured my childhood Gibby Iskrenov[10]. I remember I had been looking forward to this game for days . Never before had I seen him in the flesh, so I was strongly determined not to miss the opportunity to ask him for an autograph. Loaded with a newspaper cutting with his picture and a blue marker I set off to Hristo Botev ground. Back in the first half Gibby was brutally fouled and taken out on a stretcher . After a while he appeared with his foot bandaged and started watching the game le ant against the fencing by the dressing rooms. I said to myself, "Now it's the time ! "I walked across the stands to be stopped by the cops, but after explaining my case to them they let me go. I will never forget that moment… I was shaking all over … I came from behind Gibby, approached him and somehow managed to utter, "Mr. Iskrenov, can I have your autograph? " He was in a bad mood, to say the least. He nervously turned around, grasped my notebook with the picture glued inside and he was about to sign it… In the picture he was playing for Levski, wearing their blue kit… NEVER shall I forget that … The man saw the photo I wanted him to sign, hung his head for a while, then raised it again, looked at the sky as if he wanted to say "Fuck it! Was this the right moment to remind me?!", then smiled, ruffled my hair and signed the picture , the smile still there on his face .

I started going back and as I was walking between the fence and the first row of seats I saw two weirdly looking blokes. Bikers whom I didn't know… They were sitting all alone in the metal enclosure next to the dressing rooms . Passing by them I noticed a bag and a yellow-and-black[11] rag sticking out of it. I got it! I went back to our mob to report … The lads livened up… How dare some fuckers come to Gabrovo incognito?! In just two minutes I was standing in front of them, while a few other lads had sneaked behind in case those two tried to run away. Then said, "Hi there, boys! What have we got here, eh? Fucking rags to put on while on the train and have some pictures taken with them, eh? " Upon hearing this, the two offered their flag themselves in return of a promise for a safe retreat ... It was yellow-and-black checkered, and I think it's still kept as a trophy. And I still can't believe there were only two of them as Botev had quite a good reputation then . I guess more of them had set off, but they must have been taken off the train by the cops, as it usually happened. I have never had any Botev friends to ask them about the nicked flag and probably this book will help to throw light upon that incident. Just to make a comparison, later on Lokomotiv Plovdiv turned up and they were three blokes carrying four flags, but they did not arrive incognito! Our entire crowd laughed at them, but truth to tell, it was the first time we'd seen Bulgarian fans flying Italian style flags, huge ones on long poles . You may wonder what happened to those lads. Well, they got an invitation to a party ! As people say, "Respect where respect is due"

Septemvri Sofia

One of the most interesting stories involving our mob dates back to the late 1990s.

Yantra FC was actually existing on paper only then . They were literally picking up guys from the street to complete the squad for some games . Even Gabrovo Today Newspaper had stopped writing about Yantra FC! I'd try to find out when and where they were about to play and ... nothing, there was no info ...

I was having a drink with several other Levski fans from Gabrovo following a Levski FC game in Sofia. Someone brought the topic of our native club . Another one picked up the phone and a mate of his in Gabrovo informed us that the following week Yantra was playing Septemvri FC in Sofia. So immediately we had the idea of attending the game . By word of mouth and through more phone calls, more lads got involved and we arranged to meet up at three rally points ... Nobody had any Yantra fan articles so L. stole ... a Passport Scotch green flag from a pub! The Gabrovo diaspora in Sofia went into a state of total hysteria and so many of us turned up at the ground on match day that we started asking ourselves for a quarter of an hour, "Wow ... what the fuck?!" I won't lie when I say that there were more than a hundred of us, all drunk as hell ... We entered the ground during warm-up and both teams just stopped warming up. We stood in the away end drinking and singing out loud and the players on the pitch just stood and stared . The home supporters were at the opposite end, their total number not exceeding 15. Two coppers on duty came up to us and said, "No one told us you lot would be coming !" Someone replied, "Mr. officer, you have no reason to worry. We come from the town of humour and satire and we are not here to cause trouble. " The cop said, "Blimey! I always start worrying when I hear such an answer..." Then one of Yantra players plucked up courage and also came up to us, "Hey, lads, where do you come from?" Our mate L. replied, "What do you mean where we come from... We are Yantra support, are you deaf or blind or what ?!"... "What support? We don't have any home support in Gabrovo and you're telling me all those guys have come to Sofia to support us?! Get a grip! Are you sure this is not a hidden camera?" Next thing we saw was L. throwing up . D. started tapping him on the back and said to the player, "Hey, what about this? Do you think this is also a part of the hidden camera prank?" (laughing). At that point I saw a guy I knew from high school warming up in his green kit. He was a CSKA fan and was used to being harassed by me during school break times. I called him by name, but he didn't come. I called him again but … no, he wouldn't come!!! Finally, I made a mate guarantee that I was not going to do him any harm and so approached us timidly. "Well, how long have YOU been playing for Yantra, eh?!" And he goes, "No, I'm just a sub, I probably won't play a minute !" - "OK then, tell me the name of the guy who came to us a while ago! " - "You mean the goalkeeper... Mitkov, why?" – "Go on warming up now!" So, from then on, all through the game, we went chanting the name of Mitkov in any versions we could think of. We simply didn't know any other names playing for Yantra!

Then a penalty was awarded for Septemvri, but Mitkov saved it, the game finished 0-0 and that was the first point Yantra FC won away from home that season! Playing in front of a crowd that probably no third division club has ever had at home!

5 Levski and CSKA

6 Minority group known officially as Bulgarian Muslims, inhabiting mainly mountainous regions in South Bulgaria

7 The day the communists officially fell from power in Bulgaria

8 Gundi was the nickname of Georgi Asparouhov, Levski FC best player ever, who died tragically in a car crash at the height of his fame in 1971

9 Levski FC colour

10 One of the biggest Levski FC stars of the 1980s, the fans' favourite called "The people's joy"

11 The colours of Botev Plovdiv

Part II

Interviews

Meet the Bulgarian scene Top Faces from the past (old school) and our special guests from abroad

Tosh and Gilly

PART OF THE INTERVIEW THE AUTHORS
GAVE FOR 'VICE ' MAGAZINE

"YOU SAID that the name of your firm JRF (Jolly Roger Firm) was borrowed from a song (Under Jolly Roger) by a German Heavy Metal band (Running Wild). Were this music style and its different versions popular among hooligans in Bulgaria and how closely was music related to subculture?

Yes, it's true that in those times we got so much inspiration from music and it was so closely related to our movement that we took it over to the terraces.It was peaceful back in the olden times and the hippie years, but when the music became more aggressive, fans (quite naturally moving with the times) got more aggressive too. So, all of a sudden everything changed so fast and in the early 1990s (when the communist regime collapsed) the floodgates got opened and the rock music from 1980s was transformed into different subtypes like punk, heavy, speed, thrash, death, black metal, crossover, hardcore, grindcore, etc. Movements were getting bigger and then they also split to make different subcultures, but they all seemed to take over stadia across Bulgaria.

Nowadays it seems that fewer and fewer football fans are interested in this type of music. For us extreme music was always the driving force, a great part of our activities and it used to go along with the aggro we'd take to football grounds."

In Bulgaria there are several firms of football fans that could be openly defined as hooligan or ultras. organised groups of fans of Sofia giants Levski and CSKA, Plovdiv clubs Lokomotiv and Botev, Varna clubs Spartak and Cherno More, Burgas clubs Neftochimic and Chernomorets, as well as Beroe, Lokomotiv G.O., Etar and a number of other clubs identify themselves as followers of hooligan and ultras ideas.

In recent years, firms grew in numbers in inverse proportion to crowds of ordinary supporters (which for one reason or another are almost extinct across Bulgarian football grounds) dominated by younger fans who are interested in this subculture and willing to continue the 'old school' traditions .In the second part of our book we'll introduce you to those real men from the past, describing their lives and personal experience across Bulgaria stadia. They will tell stories you won't hear anywhere else since such topics are still taboo beyond their immediate circles and for our society in general. In defiance of those who still dream of the long gone communist regime and have already dared to warn us not to glorify football related hooliganism (which is obviously in direct contrast to their outdated views), we will go back in time and introduce you to those men of honour. A lot of those lads were and some still are Bulgarian terrace legends. Unfortunately, we couldn't interview some of them as they left this world too soon, but they will be the subjects of our next book. Most of them enjoyed and still enjoy the status of heroes and were popular with both their names and nicknames (which we will deliberately keep confidential) not only on the terraces, but in football circles in general.

Naturally, we can't, we wouldn't like, and we don't have the right to put everyone on a par since we do believe in everyone's inherent right to determine their own status and decide what to say, believe in, listen to and wear, or how to behave... Generally speaking, everyone has the right to determine the limits and boundaries for their individual images... All of them have long been completed individuals different in their minds, hearts and souls. They have chosen their paths in life and one way or another have found their places in society. All we are trying to do here is simply portray a common image and convey a common idea of Bulgarian football fans from the past.

Meet the Bulgarian Hardcore lads, the Old School Top Faces, and Terrace Legends in the following interviews with representatives of different football firms/mobs, ex-athletes (boxers) and blokes who used to be part of subcultures (music/ fashion movements and trends), and participated in the wave of discontent (rallies, protests, marches, demonstrations and riots) during the last years of the much hated communist regime and after its collapse. The time has come for those men to break the silence now!

Profile - fighters

V. M. - (Gabrovo)

Meet and greet

- **Where and when were you born?**

I was born in the town of Gabrovo on 25th October 1965 to working class parents, in what we used to call a working-class family.

- **Would you tell us something more about yourself, something about your childhood like childhood hobbies and dreams?**

I grew up in the hard and severe environment so typical of those times. We used to live in a council house, 15 families on one floor. Back then communism was praised to the skies, and some people still dream of it today, but I'll tell you what, it was downright misery! I don't know why some people forgot all those things or maybe they wouldn't like to remember them on purpose. I was quite a studious kid, I loved reading books (mostly history books), some of them defined as taboo and included in the banned books list. I used to read a lot. I could easily read 5 or 6 books a week, but afterwards my fiery temper made me take up sports, boxing in particular, so I became a fighter and like in most cases, the physical overpowered the spiritual. In complete contrast to the partial image you may already have of me, I was a rather hot-tempered kid and a bully. I used to fight kids back in primary school. In most cases I would have a go at kids of darker colour of their skin, but I'd also intimidate others. I remember those older guys arranging fights in the school backyard and in return of a snack or some sweets (as a reward) I'd simply beat the shit out of some poor lad... So as time went by my reputation of a ruffian improved beyond belief.

- **What sports did you do when you were young?**

I already told you about boxing and those inclinations of mine. I was pretty strong and tall for my age and I just stuck out. Back in the days there were the so-called school class commanders (during the Komsomol times) and they knew everything about everyone of us. Scouts in different sports used to go around schools looking for talents and when some boxing scouts arrived at my school, my class commander pointed at me, as she was well aware of my reputation, and told them, "Here's the boy you're looking for"and so I took up boxing. I trained for 12 years, 7 of them professionally. Back then professional boxing meant fighting for 15 rounds without being paid! By and large, sports give youngsters a lot, build up discipline, develop a number of qualities, but at the same time sports can also take a lot. For example, boxing can take away your good health, though it depends on the particular individual of course. My first coach's name was Stoyan Karnakov. In those times strength and power sports were much valued and though training facilities were not very good (not that they are much better now, on the contrary), and as I said before one could hardly make a living out of them, people used to love them and wanted to do them.

In 1983 I became champion of Bulgaria, I also finished in the top 3 several times and competition back then were quite tough, and it was not easy at all. There were no financial incentives, but only a great deal of urge! And somewhere at this point the iron hand of the much-detested regime would intervene. One could not find realisation abroad (we were not allowed to travel abroad), and I have already become part of the punk rock, heavy metal and skinhead movements (to be more precise I'd follow the trends of changes in our society subcultures). As I said before, each of us had a personal file and the police knew everything about everyone.

My file, in particular, just kept on expanding in the negative sense, of course. I already had that image of a rebel, a man who was an opponent of the regime and afterwards it all escalated to being classified as a right-wing radical! I remember being punished simply for making the sign of the cross in the ring!

- **How would you define yourself in those times?**

There was this period when it was difficult to find prohibited books, but somehow, I just managed to read some stuff from which I became convinced that the communists' biggest enemy was Adolf Hitler, respectively the Nazi party in Germany. Naturally, as a man who renounced communism as ideology, I'd turn to the opposite side. For such reasons I took up those 'anti-social' activities and started to express my different opinion in public. I'd do it by painting swastikas across bus stops, subways, etc. So, after all that's been said, I would say I'd rather defined myself as an anti-communist first and, quite naturally, as a skinhead. Though I had not shaved my head yet as a typical skinhead would do. On the contrary, I was trying to do the opposite out from love for rock music and the emerging heavy metal movement. I mean, grow long hair, but as a matter of fact those subcultures and movements had not made their way through our society yet... Maybe, if I was born an Anglo-Saxon then and not 'another shade of white' nationality (laughing ironically) I would have also looked like a real skinhead, something that anyway happened later in my life. So, to sum up, I used to define myself as an extreme right-wing rock fan and in my opinion, there was a very thin, almost invisible line between all those styles and movements, a line that I used to step across bravely and easily move from one trend to another... I can boldly claim I've been everything and everywhere with everybody who shared the same or similar ideas. Or like The Beatles used to say, "One has to try everything in order to die happy."

- **When did you first get acquainted with punk rock, heavy metal and skinhead culture and the movements in general?**

I think it was around 1981, but I'm not a hundred per cent sure. I came across some 'pirate' records of AC/DC, Black Sabbath, Dio... In addition, I'd read articles on English skinheads, who, naturally, used to be defamed by the communist press and I, in turn, just loved everything the commies would renounce. Also, I followed the biker's 'thread' in stories about the Hells Angels, etc. At some point, there was that, let's say craze, to collect heavy metal pins, T-shirts, backs, and badges that we'd sew on denim vests, etc. That was everything a metalhead could possibly value greatly in his life. Accordingly, it became fashionable to nick such items (just like football scarves and flags), and I, as one of the first prominent fighters, would often be called upon to restore order and justice by returning someone's belongings.

- **Would you tell us something about the setting up of your gang (firm/ mob), movement in your town and your experience when partying in other towns (in your region and at the seaside)?**

I'll find it hard to answer the first part of your question for the simple reason that I am a natural born loner. I don't know, it is probably in my very nature and I wouldn't like to make a self-appraisal here, but I really find it hard to identify myself with a certain group. I've been asked a number of questions like that all through the years and possibly that was one of the reasons I didn't join a particular football firm as I guess you are about to ask me about that later in this interview! I can't find the exact words... because I'm not anti-social; I have my own views and ideas. I see that even nowadays there are nice guys sharing similar ideas, but let me put it straight again, that's the kind of guy I am and I'm not gonna change because I

106

don't see anything wrong with that and that's the way I like it. As far as incidents in my region and partying at the seaside are concerned, well, one can write a whole new book about them and I really did take an active part in most of them.

In the beginning I, being an athlete, kept some kind of regime and tried to avoid things like that. Moreover, alcohol seems to unleash my evil demons within. After 1990 there was some really incredible stuff going on, but I cannot use first-person narrative as during that very period I used to live in Germany. When I did go partying, I'd usually go on the piss and have a blackout and then my mates would tell me what actually happened (laughing). Also, at the first heavy metal fests held in Gabrovo and other towns, we'd always kick or punch our way in ticketless. When we'd go to Sofia to watch live shows, we'd certainly go after and beat up members of different minorities. There was this time when motorcycle rallies would welcome me with standing ovations as they knew that their evening fun was guaranteed and during the night alcohol was sure to uncover my artistic skills. So, during that period, every time you'd go to the seaside, especially south of Bourgas, there was not a single cop you'd see patrolling. Absolute abuse of freedom... Guys from towns in our region (traditionally famous for its strong heavy metal movement) like Gorna Oryahovitsa, Veliko Tarnovo, Lovech would flock in large numbers and form a real army meeting up at pre-arranged places. Our let's call it heavy metal crew also contributed to the Black Sea coast invasion and one might as well say we stormed over the entire coast. Pub owners were horrified of us and would not let us in. I recall some crazy stories like steaming in a local disco club and throwing the DJ out of a window just because he refused to play some song... In general scenes reminding one of the Mad Max film... Even before organised crime groups took over the Bulgarian coastline, major camping sites were totally under our control and their owners would come and plead us to show some consideration for the other holidaymakers. For example, I'd walk about bare-naked and I remember a funny occasion when another guy ran after me, towel in hand, as he must have thought I would like to cover up and he had absolutely no idea that what I was trying to do was simply roam the beach in my birthday suit (laughing). It sounds funny now (for some of you at least), but come to think of it, probably it was not the right thing to do back then. It was just that we considered such stupid acts as rebellion and as an expression of our aspiration for freedom, of our intention to show the world we were different. Those were the times...

- **Which is your favourite football club and how important it is in your life?**

My favourite club is Levski, and though I'm not a die-hard supporter, I used to be quite active after my return from Germany in 1993. And once again my blackout years of drinking would prevent me from going into details... Quite often I'd end up nicked in a cell or squad car with no memories of what I'd done. In contrast to my football affiliations, I admired CSKA skinhead Crew and in particular K. is a great friend of mine. I simply like them, I like their organisation and ideas and we've had a number of good parties together. I dare say they are great guys and we've always enjoyed perfect relationships. I've never been indifferent to my native town club Yantra, either! Although I trained as a Trakia Plovdiv boxer for 2 years and as an Academic fighter for another year and I don't share that kind of pure fandom and affinity with the native. As a Yantra athlete I got to know a number of their football players, coaches and managers and I could go wherever I liked.

- **What is your wildest favourite club related dream?**

Well, I wouldn't call it a dream exactly as it is easily achievable, and it's happened so many times, and that is … always defeating CSKA! When we lose to them I get really annoyed and sick. The 'pigs' start nagging at me and I go really mad. And when we defeat them (then and only then) I feel really happy and over the moon.

- **Which is your favourite football match of all times?**

I've no doubt about it; it's CSKA vs. Liverpool in 1982. I am a Levski fan, but we have to admit that what the reds did then was pure class! Against all expectations and all odds, they won 2-0 in a very brave game. I was 16 back then and I found the atmosphere at the ground truly magnificent. It was an unforgettable experience for me. To some extent it resembled my experience at the derby we crushed the red pigs 7-1... That's another vivid memory I'll have until my dying day!

- **Favourite players (Bulgaria, Europe, worldwide)?**

The only Bulgarian player I put on a pedestal is Georgi Asparuhov. In spite of being constantly provoked on and off the pitch, he remained the true gentleman he was. Some players from his time are still alive and I'm damn sure they still have nightmares involving Asparuhov's football skills! They used to feel so helpless playing against him that in addition to kicking him, they would also resort to pinching, biting and insulting him in every way imaginable, to which he actually never responded. I am convinced that even nowadays those people recognising Asparuhov feel ashamed to tell the true story how they used to play against him. Unfortunately, fate was also merciless towards him! When he crashed his car and died I was only 6 years old, but I do remember the national mourning and I realised how much everybody loved him, I mean everybody, not only football fans, but our entire nation... And if a can slightly paraphrase a popular Levski fans' chant, "Both women and children dream of him and old men would even take their hats off when they see Gundy, the true Bulgarian son!"

As far as foreign players are concerned, I like the so called tough men. Manchester United had a whole galaxy of such players, starting from Bryan Robson and Cantona, going through Roy Keane and Paul Scholes, and ending nowadays with a guy like Ibrahimovic. Real warriors and gladiators on the pitch fear no foe. Naturally, I cannot skip the hilarious Paul Gascoigne (Gazza) and the funny accidents he was involved in both on and off the pitch.

- **Which are the best and the worst football grounds you've ever been to and why?**

I'm not into comfort when I think of football grounds. I go there to cheer, shout, jump, go mental, and hurl insults… so what comfort does a man need at football grounds, eh?! A ground is a ground… OK, it's not bad if you can enjoy the modern facilities and I have been to such stadiums, but there is no such thing as a bad football ground as even the ugliest one imaginable is home sweet home for some fans. When I lived in Germany I went to watch Hamburger SV play Juventus, well it was modern, and it was posh for those times. By the way, I shall now go off the point and tell you a story of how I met then a gang of German skinheads among which there was this guy whose grandfather was an army officer and fought in World War II. What I found really exciting was that he had this separate elevator back at his house and a secret chamber, something like a cellar, where he kept uniforms, medals, pictures of Göring, etc. Generally, the Germans were so respectful to me as if I was one of their own and for me it was a great honour to see and touch those relics. But let me finish about stadiums, of course I would like to see Bulgarian grounds modern and posh, but as I already said I'd still go there not to watch the ground itself, but to enjoy the game and support my beloved club.

- **Would you name the top 5 Bulgarian firms/crews/mobs?**

I'll put it straight, in response to my mate K. who in face-to-face conversations has told me a few times that nowadays Levski mob and their youth outclass CSKA… It was similar in the past, when, no matter how unpleasant I find it to admit it, CSKA were much better organised. But naturally, Levski mob is Levski mob and that's all there is to it! Botev Plovdiv were also a formidable force, but in recent years Lokomotiv Plovdiv excel them. Every dog has its day, you know. Let me finish with Pirin Blagoevgrad and Minyor Pernik, who were vicious rivals back in those days, not exactly in terms of organised firms, but more like tough and unfriendly crowds.

- **What do you think of English football hooligans and their influence on the scene now and before?**

I've always tried to stick to the Anglo-Saxon style not only in terms of fandom, but also in terms of music and traditions. I hate guys who claim to belong to a certain subculture, but dress and behave as real assholes. I like the English cause that is a kind of genuine culture for them (even not a subculture). At least in the past, they had a symbolic way of dressing and behaving across stadia. Their contribution to the world of music and football is unparalleled. The difference between them and the Germans is exactly their free style of behaviour and their willingness to defy all that is forbidden. While the English strip down to the waist and show all kinds of tattoos and banners, the Germans, as they usually do, stick to discipline and display no excessive flamboyance and showiness. So somewhere in-between those two nations lie my general attitudes to fandom as a whole. Unfortunately, I couldn't visit England during their so called 'golden era' of music and football.

- **Who are your rivals (in the general sense of the word, in life, on the ring or at the stadium), what are they like and what is your opinion of them?**

I have no definite personal enemies or rivals; it's rather a mixture of a communist, a vulgar cheeky bastard with boorish manners and huge self-confidence. We have loads of them football players in Bulgaria. I just loathe people like Hristo Stoichkov and Valeri Bozhinov and no matter how good players they are, for me they are the epitome of all of the aforesaid, fully accomplished morons. Even their recent behaviour is just additional evidence that they will never, ever change no matter where they live, who they play for and what they do. For me they are just ignorance legends.

As far as rivalry on the terraces is concerned, after all that's been said so far and despite the hatred breeding between reds and blues, I dare say we do share a lot of acknowledgement and respect (at least, we, old-school fans of both teams do. We just know each other too well! And the ring... well, there's nothing else there but aggression and respect. Actually, respect is a must on the ring if you want to succeed and every self-respecting boxer knows that. You turn into a machine, you go out on the ring, you fight and finally, no matter the outcome, you bow your head and shake your rival's hand.

- **Have you ever been engaged in fights (either football related or not) ...
  and have you ever been seriously wounded or injured while fighting?**

Wounded would be a strong word. I'd rather say it was all minor injuries like sprains, scratches and bruises... Cuts in boxing are quite common, but generally speaking, due to boxing I had learnt how to defend and parry blows when I got involved in street fighting. In fist fighting you first learn the ways of defence.

- **Have you ever been involved in civil disobedience (riots and violence)
  and, if yes, would you tell us something more about it?**

Sure! Everybody was in Sofia in 1989 to attend the million-strong protest march that saw the much-hated communist regime off, but as an example of a well organised and yet spontaneous mission I would quote what we did in 1997 when we blocked the Shipka mountain pass, but i wouldn't like to go into any further details about it.

- **What do you think of politics (in general), the current political system in
  Bulgaria and the past regime?**

I'll start from the past... There was this occasion at school when I had a dispute with my history teacher (something unheard of back in those times) regarding the date of 9th September[12], the events afterwards and whether it was all a kind of new bondage disguised in the form of liberation... Something we had been studying about the Soviet (Russian) army and the Bulgarian liberation from the Ottoman rule. So, broadly speaking, it turned out I was right then, and I still have the same opinion nowadays... The communist regime was a new kind of bondage. As far as politics and the current political system are concerned... actually communism collapsed in the natural course of events way back in 1981 with no one waging war or fighting against it... It was just that before that there was this period when the West was in crisis and Bulgaria used to re- export Soviet oil and so we probably must have had a kind of economic growth and it was good, but for a short period of time. Afterwards it all collapsed with Gorbachev coming to power in the USSR and the restrictions in the power and water supply started, along with the endless queues in front of the virtually empty food stores. Actually, when there's no opposition in politics, those in power (i.e. dictators) run out of resources and fall down and so the very system collapses in the natural course of events. The same goes for business and football, if you like, where the absence of competition means you simply stop developing. So, what actually happened after 1981, as far as commies are concerned, was their inevitable and expected demise. One could still feel this bitter taste from the past, but after 1989 one way or other things changed for all of us. For example, I, after quitting sports, had the opportunity to go abroad and so in 1990 I went to Germany. I know many guys who did the same and there each of us had the opportunity to feel the Western world hoping we could change our motherland on its way to democracy. Some managed to gain experience abroad and really changed their mentality, but the majority stayed the same, and that's the main issue if you ask me. It is in our mentality! We are somehow used to look for excuses and in particular blame the politicians, but aren't we those who elect them? Politics is necessary, OK; let's call it necessary evil in our case, but it is a reflection of the society we live in… So, in other words, to a certain extent it is us who define the political system and if we stay the same and do not change our mentality, there's no way for the system to be different from the current one.

- **What do you think of the police (the repressive machinery) in Bulgaria and in general?**

There has to be police and it has to be strong. Repressive machinery is not something bad unless it is used for political purposes as it was in our case for many decades!

There are good cops, I know cops that have treated my right and showed understanding and I know others who poked me in the ribs many a times. So generally speaking you cannot label everybody and treat them the same way. We shouldn't forget that they follow a line of subordination and they follow orders and commands in doing their duties. A totally different question is who issues such orders and commands.

- **Do you have any favourite designer labels and would you tell us something more about the clothes in the past?**

Well, the designer labels issue is something trendy and fashionable and I won't go into that. In the past I tried to follow fashion though I found it rather hard to get clothes because there was no proper supply. As I said before, I was quite big and tall and whenever I'd find a nice T-shirt it would look like a bra on my broad chest (laughing). What I'm still into is biker jackets, leather garments, camouflage and bombers, Doc Martens shoes… But if I have to play a modern and fashion-conscious guy, well my favourite brand is Everlast as I wear Everlast sweatshirts. But naturally, that's a legacy from my boxing years.

- **What do you think of younger generations and how would you describe** in general the 'scene' nowadays?

Questions like these make me feel old... I'm not into dividing people into young and old, I don't like being nostalgic, so I won't simply say "Fuck it, nowadays the young generation is worthless". Not definitely. On the contrary, we should try and encourage youngsters. Times have changed and there are no grounds for making comparisons actually. And there's absolutely no point in drawing dividing lines! There are good boys and there are worthless shits, but that's the way it is, always been and will be. That's why I find this very question kinda odd.

- **How would you define yourself nowadays?**

An honest guy, tax-payer and voter who'd like to live in a normal country. A patriot who rather criticises to pseudo-patriots.

12 9TH SEPTEMBER 1944 IS THE DATE THE BULGARIAN COMMUNISTS TOOK POWER IN THE COUNTRY AFTER IT WAS INVADED BY THE SOVIET TROOPS IN WORLD WAR II

T. T. (T.) - G. Oryahovitsa

Meet and greet

- **Where and when were you born?**

I was born in Gorna Oryahovitsa on 16th August 1974.

- **Would you tell us something more about yourself, something about your childhood like childhood hobbies and dreams?**

My times were rough... To survive and make a name for yourself in circles like ours you had to be more or less brutal. I never used to be into anything special, it was all the usual kids' street games and stuff, but sometimes things would get out of control and turn into real warfare between different neighbourhoods and the craziest blokes would meet up and go to the football. I'm talking about dangerous games, you know, like slings, etc. We'd often fight each other as we were urchins, streetwise hooligans straight from the beginning.

- **What sports did you do when you were young?**

I've done come wrestling, then sambo and amateur boxing. My uncle gave me a pair of boxing gloves and at first; they just stood there hung on the wall at home. I had this powerful punch and I'd often fight at school. My parents had a number of pretty bad meetings with my teachers and after a similar incident Mum burnt the gloves in question.

- **How would you define yourself in those times?**

Well, we were all metalheads with a few exceptions, but I was a pretty devoted follower of the heavy metal movement in its hardest form possible then.

- **When did you first get acquainted with punk rock, heavy metal and skinhead culture and the movements in general?**

I must have been in the 6th or 7th grade. We started with bands like D.R.I. (Dirty Rotten Imbeciles), S.O.D. (Stormtroopers of Death), M.O.D. (Method of Destruction) and other ones from the fashionable then 'crossover' and 'hardcore' trends. Our idol was the vocalist of the last two New York bands, Billy Milano, who skilfully managed to mix punk with thrash and thus set up a new metal style.

- **Would you tell us something about the setting up of your gang (firm/ mob), movement in your town and your experience when partying in other towns (in your region and at the seaside)?**

As I said before it came from the streets... There were 10-15 of us proper lads almost the same age from the Prolet Quarter in Gorna Oryahovitsa and then we'd meet some other urchins downtown and so at some point it all escalated into intercity meets (of all kinds) with boys from Tarnovo and Gabrovo, the so-called exchange parties and the wild summer parties at the seaside. We'd run wild around Sozopol and the Golden Fish camping site, where they still shudder at the memories of our invasions. Being penniless, we'd sleep on the beach; we'd collect empty glass bottles and deliver them for reuse so that we can buy full bottles of our beloved frothy beverage.

We'd also drown cheap cocktails on the jetty and in the evenings, we'd go to the amphitheatre where we could also sleep in our sleeping bags. The cops would get sick and tired of driving us outta there in the mornings, nicking and then releasing us just to find us at the same place again (laughing). I remember we'd sing the Old Bill a song (or rather a chant): "Here we are again, here we are again..." and they'd get even crazier. However, our best performances included tearing down the corrugated iron walls of a café and leaving its owner and his barbecue under the open sky and hijacking a horse-drawn carriage and riding it all across the town (laughing out loud). I am thankful for my close mates who I shared all those great funny times with.

- **Which is your favourite football club and how important it is in your life?**

Naturally, that's Lokomotiv, the one and only football club! I stopped going to the football long time ago, but I am still interested in the club and what is going on with it. I have the same thrill and particularly when I'm away all these feelings get so much stronger. Now I'd like to thank the authors of this book for the honour to participate in it and I'd like to tell them that I'm really proud that lads from our town started and will finish such projects... Someone had to do it and with their first book, which brought tears to my eyes while I was reading it, they took me back to all those precious moments I'm telling about now! Well, you know, we had forgotten a thing or two and in general we had not been in touch for a while, but thanks to those lads we now have the unique opportunity to tell our stories here so that they could be read by the younger generations of fans and to meet up (all old-school boys) after so many years for the book launch, once again at the seaside (winking).

- **What is your wildest favourite club related dream?**

I have no such dreams, being a fan of my club is my dream come true!

- **Which is your favourite football match of all times?**

The victory over Levski, which was then named Vitosha FC after they had been renamed by the commies. We beat them 2-1 thanks to goals scored by Valyo Ganev and Nako Doichev. I think it was in the autumn of 1988. A unique game, there were people on the floodlight posts... Priceless!

- **Favourite players (Bulgaria, Europe, worldwide)?**

The classic Lokomotiv duo Bore Iliev (RIP) and Nako Doichev. Globally it's the Milan's Dutch trio Basten, Gullit and Rijkaard.

- **Which are the best and the worst football grounds you've ever been to and why?**

The ground in Stara Zagora was not bad in terms of structure for those times. The worst one is in the town of Pernik because of the local inhabitants... I think there's no point in further explaining why... Everyone's in the know will understand (winking).

- **Would you name the top 5 Bulgarian firms/crews/mobs?**

Levski, CSKA, Lokomotiv Plovdiv, Botev and Lokomotiv G.O.

- **What do you think of English football hooligans and their influence on the scene now and before?**

I see they're still putting up English flags at stadia, so they must still have some kind of influence though not as strong as before... No matter how hard they try to deny them nowadays and literally close them down, be it for the very game or for what they did on the terraces in the past, they will remain a huge factor and symbol. Especially for us, old-school lads, they'll be our role models forever and anyone claiming the opposite simply does not belong to this old-school fandom.

- **Who are your rivals (in the general sense of the word, in life, on the ring or at the stadium), what are they like and what is your opinion of them?**

I presume I have to mention the 'Boyars', but we knew each other too well in the past and I dare say we used to have a lot of friends among them. Yeah, there was hatred, there still is and there will be, but it's ranging, I mean it's like a volcano that's either dormant or active. So, for a rival deserving our attention I'll nominate the Gabrovo folks. Not that we didn't know each other well, not that we haven't had those three-party sprees with them and the guys from Tarnovo, but they, being highlanders, are kinda different tough guys.

- **Have you ever been engaged in fights (either football related or not) ... and have you ever been seriously wounded or injured while fighting?**

I've been seriously injured only as a result of police brutality. Everybody knows how they used to beat us, but we, being the tough lads, we still are, just took those beatings for granted (winking). Anyway, we've had all the fights we'd want. On an away day in Gabrovo we fought like hell to save a flag they'd nicked from us and we managed to have it back. In the town of Shumen, we had a good ruck inside the ground. We had some good times everywhere we'd come across large numbers of people from the minorities, but I won't go into details cause the authors to have brilliantly described all those cases in their first book Beyond the Hatred.

- **Have you ever been involved in civil disobedience (riots and violence) and, if yes, would you tell us something more about it?**

Well, if we count the pursuit, relegation and beating up of cops, yes, I've been involved, and I've also been champion (laughing). Of course, I'm not proud of that anymore and I've paid my dues! If you're asking about protest marches, rallies and the like, no, I've never been involved. I like to face problems and find solutions to them myself, on my own. There was this funny incident in a park when I was chasing the local cop and he was running like hell, blowing a whistle and screaming 'Help! I need backup!' Wow! Those were the times (laughing out loud)!

- **What do you think of politics (in general), the current political system in Bulgaria and the past regime?**

I'm totally apolitical and utterly indifferent to such a disgusting topic and I'm extremely proud of being such a person when I look at everything that's been going on. I've never belonged to a political party and I've never voted for one, either. As I said before, I'm self-taught and streetwise and I've never been one of those cowards who hide behind something or someone, be it political interests, parties and leaders.

- **What do you think of the police (the repressive machinery) in Bulgaria and in general?**

They're good friends of mine (laughing).

- **Do you have any favourite designer labels and would you tell us something more about the clothes in the past?**

Ooh, at present I'm too far away from fashion trends, believe me. Speaking about the past, my favourite classics are still denim vests, stretch jeans and high-top white trainers, i.e. clobber I'd also wear nowadays, but for my age and weight (laughing).

- **What do you think of younger generations and how would you describe in general the 'scene' nowadays?**

It's so far away from me so I can't have any reliable opinion, but from what I watch on telly I can say youngsters try to do their best though in general our scene and our game are on the decline.

- **How would you define yourself nowadays?**

The same as I ever was... I haven't changed at all (winking).

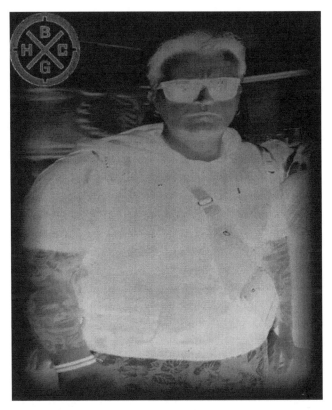

(B.) - Pleven

Meet and greet

- **Where and when were you born?**

I was born on 3rd February 1976 in the town of Pleven.

- **Would you tell us something more about yourself, something about your childhood like childhood hobbies and dreams?**

I used to read a lot (I've got two master's Degrees now), but by and large I was a bully. I don't say that fighting was my hobby or inclination. I'd rather say aggression fascinated me. I used to live with my mother only ever since I was just a small kid (for one reason or another) and though she'd try to control and punish me quite often, I had no father to control me and that fact had its influence on me in my teens. On quite a few occasions there would be people queuing in front of my front door to complain about my behaviour, 'He did this... he did that...'

- **What sports did you do when you were young?**

First, I took up rowing and for some time I was convinced that was my kind of sport. It develops all your muscles, but like all sports do, it requires strict discipline. Then it became almost impossible for me to train (due to a change in my whereabouts), I grew up very fast and I had those problems with my knees and so the doctors advised me to quit rowing. I switched to boxing as recommended by my older cousin who was an ex-champion of Bulgaria. He still believes that there was bright future for me in this sport. I had a great coach (a multiple republican champion), impressive talent, which I managed to master to a street level only, but as I said, I felt fighting was in my very nature, in my blood.

- **How would you define yourself in those times?**

If it is possible at all for anyone to define themselves at their early age, I'd rather say I was an urchin... Looking back now, I'd define myself as the ultimate, incorrigible rascal (laughing). I remember occasions from my early childhood when we used to play in the streets. There was this real war between the different residential buildings. We'd mob up and attack the kids from the neighbouring tower block with slings and bits of wood, plastic swords and shields and whet the going would get tough we'd resort to throwing stones at each other. Veritable warfare it was as I'm talking of dozens of kids involved. What most occasions like those need is an orchestrator, a leader. So, I'd take up this role with pleasure, but the problem was that there were more girls than boys living in my building. Well, somehow, I did manage to make them beat the boys from the next tower block, so I must have been a genuine urchin (laughing).

- **When did you first get acquainted with punk rock, heavy metal and skinhead culture and movements in general?**

Surely it was back in 1986 when I heard Accept's 'Balls to the wall' mega hit... I remember it crystal clear and I'll always do. I remember my first recordings on audio cassettes. Hitachi cassette recorders, quite fashionable for those times as compared to Soviet VEF or Bulgarian Resprom. I remember the big, drum-like batteries we used to hit against each other hoping to get them charged for a little more (since they'd easily run flat after long hours of listening to our favourite music), so that we could listen to at least one more Metallica song at parties or on the Black sea beaches. At an earlier stage, probably it was the Europe band that paved my path and predetermined the style of music I was about to fall in love with... Rock & Roll All Day, baby (winking).

- **Would you tell us something about the setting up of your gang (firm/mob), movement in your town and your experience when partying in other towns (in your region and at the seaside)?**

Probably in these interviews and in particular, in the answers to this question, you'd quite often come across the words 'lone wolf'! Being a fighter means you can't stand anyone beside you and if you wanna be a leader, then it is your decisions that are the right ones. It was no different for me... I had, and I still have friends all over Bulgaria, but that was the way I felt back then, and I still believe I am a lone wolf up to this day.

By the early 1990s I had already been expelled from 7 schools, the last one being a night school. They claimed there was no way to expel anyone from a night school as it was the last resort for those undisciplined. Well, they were wrong! Once you beat up the headmaster in his own office, you'll surely get expelled from a night school, too. They expelled me from all the schools in the entire Pleven district. After a gap year I graduated a vocational school in the neighbouring district!

Then I did my military service in the town of Belene! I made a lot of friends there and I still keep in touch with some of them.

However, in the town of Belene, I naturally founded a new crew of like-minded blokes and to anyone who'd easily underestimate this small town I'll tell you, you're terribly wrong! The town has its own vibe, maybe due to its dark past and the death camps built by the communists there, but the heavy metal subculture (to which I belonged) definitely had good grounds there. I already mentioned the Black Sea coast parties and the never-ending binges. Now naturally, I'll add up the 'July Morning' fest on the beach with all those camp fires and acoustic guitars on which some hippies would play all night long and we would all sing along. Oh, those were the times!!!

After I did my military service I used to travel abroad every week, so I'd spend only 2 or 3 days at home out of 7. It would mainly be Mondays to Thursdays. Each Tuesday I'd travel to Varna and Dobrich as I was into shipping passengers and goods both home and abroad. So, I met some great blokes, mates with the same attitude as mine. They belonged to one of the strongest Levski firm, i.e. Ultra Varna! They were a homogeneous group of great mates. I'll name a few, like I.T., The B., C., but there were many others from all corners of Bulgaria.

- **Which is your favourite football club and how important it is in your life?**

Levski Sofia, my beloved club, the one and only! They have always been the top of my priorities, up to this very day. I will never change. I'd even die for Levski!

I also like foreign clubs like FC Internazionale Milano and Boca Juniors, that latter because of Don Diego and the fanatical supporters and great atmosphere at La Bombonera.

I can assure you I have fulfilled all my dreams (even my wildest ones) as far as my favourite clubs are concerned. Now I live abroad, and I go to Milan more often than to Sofia, and that's something that was also a dream come true for me.

- **Which is your favourite football match of all times?**

No doubt about it, its Levski vs Glasgow Rangers and the killing shot by The Kaiser[13]. There are things that cannot be described with words, they'd rather be seen and experienced. I'll do my best to find the right words, though, and leave the rest to the readers' imagination. A young fan, a sea and waves of blue supporters...

A capacity filled ground... Unbelievable atmosphere featuring the Scottish brave hearts and Levski mighty crowd...

- **Favourite players (Bulgaria, Europe, worldwide)?**

In Bulgaria there's no doubt about it, it's Georgi Asparuhov - Gundi! No further comment is needed; he was the greatest football player and the greatest gentleman. In Europe it is the Dutch player Marco van Basten (though he played for FC Internazionale's rivals, i.e. AC Milan) – for me he was the greatest player of the past. On a worldwide scale, quite understandably in view of my club affiliations, I'd say Zanetti, Riquelme and last but not least Maradona the Great.

- **Which are the best and the worst football grounds you've ever been to and why?**

The best one is Giuseppe Meazza, while the worst are in Bulgaria and they are quite a few (most of them are real shitholes). I visited all of them several times in the past and I find it difficult to say which the worst is.

- **Would you name the top 5 Bulgarian firms/crews/mobs?**

That's fucking easy... In a non-chronological order, I would name Levski, Lokomotiv Plovdiv, CSKA, Botev Plovdiv, and Minyor.

- **What do you think of English football hooligans and their influence on the scene now and before?**

A big disappointment these days, particularly after they raised the bar so high themselves in the past. And even at their height, the Poles beat them a few times barehanded. Now the Russians did them by the book as they say, but I blame it on the banning orders the English got and, on the fact, that the Ivans seem to have a lot of unemployed military (laughing) ... We'll see, it will be an eventful summer in Russia this year, but I think they'll be ultimately dethroned as top hooligans once and for all. Come to think of it, however, it won't be easy for the Russians either, no matter the home ground, due to the Special Forces and the measures Putin is bound to take in order to save Russia World Cup's good reputation.

- **Who are your rivals (in the general sense of the word, in life, on the ring or at the stadium), what are they like and what is your opinion of them?**

I don't have a particular person, or a negative image shaped up... I can't stand a number of guys, but that's absolutely normal. I really hate CSKA fans, though I say it rather conventionally as my town is divided into blue and red halves. Through all these years we've had quite a few top lads in both firms (not to say leading figures). I had and I still have a few top CSKA lads in my friend list, and the best of them unfortunately is no longer with us (may he rest in peace), and if you allow me, I'd like to send him a message in this interview and this particular book: Gibby, I know you hear and see me from above. I dedicate these words to you, bro! And let me finish this topic by saying that … it is not only hatred and animosity on the terraces, there is also respect and shared values and friendships like mine with Gibby just come to prove my words. Let him rest in peace!

- **Have you ever been engaged in fights (either football related or not) … and have you ever been seriously wounded or injured while fighting?**

Many a times, but I won't go into details… All I can say is that I am one of the few who were stabbed in the back, both literally and figuratively.

- **Have you ever been involved in civil disobedience (riots and violence) and, if yes, would you tell us something more about it?**

I won't go into detail here either due to the nature of things I may share.

- **What do you think of politics (in general), the current political system in Bulgaria and the past regime?**

To put it briefly - an endless shitty circle!

- **What do you think of the police (the repressive machinery) in Bulgaria and in general?**

These are all short answer questions for me. But this one… I'll answer it in a slightly different way and from a point of view of a man, whose father is a cop. I did get into trouble and naturally he helped me out, but in general corruption rates with the police are rather high since that is exactly the machinery in charge of control. As far as repressions are concerned you have to spend a few years' ling in Belene to hear some stories and know what it is all about.

- **Do you have any favourite designer labels and would you tell us something more about the clothes in the past?**

Though I am a metalhead, I didn't use to dress the way metalheads usually do. I didn't even have long hair. I grew my hair long after I did my military service and I had it long for years. So maybe it's the camouflage items that come first just the way it was for most boys in those times. Now I always put on my New Balance trainers, and I also like Fred Perry but after I saw gypsies wearing that brand I started to hesitate (laughing). I also wear Pull & Bear and Lacoste.

- **What do you think of younger generations and how would you describe in general the 'scene' nowadays?**

There are decent and proper lads. The go to the gym, their tifos look fine, etc. But sometimes it takes more than pyro and tifo… it takes a heart etc. There's definitely something that modern ultras don't have, and I think this is identity. They just seem all the same to me and one way or another there's no originality, let alone the fact that chemistry (in all aspects of this word) quite seriously penetrated the fans' environment.

- **How would you define yourself nowadays?**

A Bulgarian patriot, a man who's always ready to come back and fight for his motherland. Whatever people say about immigrants living abroad, don't forget that Vasil Levski organised his entire revolutionary network from abroad during the secret conventions they had in the Romanian town of Braila as he found most of the things in his native land 'rotten'. I have almost all Bulgarian khans and tsars tattooed all over my body and, believe me, the saviour of Europe Khan Tervel and his feat in 718 AD mean a lot to me when I have to define myself as a per.

13 THE NICKNAME OF LEVSKI PLAYER NIKOLAI TODOROV WHO SCORED A 90-MINUTE SCREAMER TO KNOCK RANGERS FC OUT OF EUROPE IN 1993

Other representatives

K. I. (K.) - CSKA (Sofia)

Meet and greet

Well, I've been drawing and painting all my life cause that's a decent way to propagate your ideas (I find terraces as the perfect place for propaganda). Painting is also a good way to relax and besides, there's a lot of money in it, which in our commercialised world means ... freedom. My job also takes a lot of travelling, which allows me to go to different parties, gigs of favourite bands, meet interesting people and, unfortunately, I cannot go to football that often. The last game I attended abroad was 4 years ago, the Belgrade derby, and the best derby on the Balkans for many.

I define myself as an extreme nationalist and CSKA supporter. Quite logically I go by the nickname of "The Painter". That's not my nickname in our circles anyway, but I don't think it matters so much. Except for the records of our 'mates' 1312.

- **How old are you and when did you become a fan of your favourite club?**

I am so old that now when I look at the young fans around me I understand I might as well be their father (laughing). Unfortunately, the age limit for the majority of Bulgarian fans is rather low, which explains the big problems with our 'off-the-pitch" situation...

In my case it all happened quite surprisingly, and I cannot boast that my father, mates or anyone else took me to a football ground because none of my family was interested in football (Dad was an engineer and Mum was a teacher). Besides, the quarter I was living in (a still live there, btw) was all "blue" (inhabited by fans of our rivals Levski). So, it all happened to a great extent probably out of spite.

By the late 1980s I had entered the underground (heavy metal and after 1989 a skinhead). In those times, the rule was that metalheads, punks and later skinheads were all CSKA fans. On the contrary, the hit squads of the 'Blues' were made up of the so called 'hotshots' (geezers with country-boy haircuts wearing wide-legged trousers with sweaters tucked in and moccasins) along with dark-skinned, hairy and moustached fellas listening to Turbo-folk. By and large those two subcultures (heavy metal and Turbo-hotshots) would endlessly fight each other, so if you belonged to any of those backgrounds, then you had to support the relevant football club.

Naturally, the aforesaid type of humans ultimately put me off and that feeling predetermined my joining the ranks of the Army club fans. I believe I was 16 or 17 years old when I first went to football games and I went straight to the end behind the goal along with my mates.

- **Would you tell us how your firm (crew/mob) was established?**

Actually 'firm' is not an appropriate word for our company (nor it is for the other similar groups in Bulgaria). I'd rather call it a 'brotherhood of pirates', cause as I said in the previous answer, football affiliations in the late 1980s and the early 1990s were based on social backgrounds, i.e. the advance of the skinhead movement in Sofia in the late 1980s and early 1990s (those new blokes were actually former metalheads or punks) determined their belonging to the army club. Our gathering point was the park around the National Palace of Culture in Sofia and we made this area subject to the so-called cleansing, which meant ultimately terrorising all those who were not to our liking. In their majority those were the so-called minorities and certain swarthy foreigners. To tell the truth, football related fights became rare and they would happen on match days mainly. Our major targets were immigrants and all the scum, the minorities that democracy was already generating.

What was interesting was that by the mid-1990s Levski mob also had some small groups of skinheads who'd join our raids on the scum across Sofia streets. For those actions of theirs they were continually terrorised by their older lads on their south stand and that was the reason why many of them turned to our side eventually. By 1999 there was a kind of casting for our crew and so CSKA SS FRONT was born.

- **How would you define yourself as a fan?**

As I said before, I entered the terrace culture as a young metalhead, eventually a skinhead, and I was more anti-Levski than pro-CSKA. I loathed Levski fans cause as I already mentioned in those years they were simply disgusting with their musical preferences, appearance and ethnic origin. In the past they had people from the minorities, i.e. gypsies, but now I'm glad they don't have such creatures any more, at least not in their South stand, and their fan culture is at a pretty decent nationalistic level.

I have always had race and nationality as my top priorities, and very often I'd learn about the game result as early as the following day because I have always found the off-the-pitch events much more important and I have always paid more attention to our 'game' before and after kick-off, on the streets and in the parks. Traditionally, before a game we'd visit the parks where anti-fascists used to meet, and we'd clean the town from all kinds of scum. After kick-off we'd usually bust an Arab kebab house. In addition, when so many black players started signing for my club, I found going to games pointless as I was not able to support them and take delight in them scoring goals. Anyway, I still find stadia as an appropriate ground for propaganda and recruiting young blood for our movement.

- **Would you tell us in more details about some fights you have been involved at stadia and on the streets?**

As mentioned above, in the early 1990s, skinheads and football hooligans were connected so it was a kind of living a dual life. I mean, when there was no football we'd go on our routine skinhead missions doing the so called 'racial cleansing' of the area we used to meet up. In Sofia we found only Levski as our rivals, so football related fights were not that frequent, and they'd usually happen on derby days. In addition, there was this unwritten law saying that skinheads from other football mobs must not be attacked, but as I already mentioned in those times probably 90% of them were CSKA fans, which meant that encounters with Levski skinheads were quite rare.

Away days in the country were great fun cause we used to travel by rail in those days, which meant heavy drinking and long walks from stations to stadia and exciting encounters on our way to grounds. Imagine a street full of 200 or 300 fans, mostly skinheads who had been drinking all they long, and a group of gypsies walking the pavement across. Those were really years of great fun.

Vandalism and brawls with the police could be seen at almost every big game, one of the first massive clashes with the cops being our game against Atletico Madrid in 1998. Naturally, when the Bulgarian national squad was playing, we'd go hunting for away fans. In the late 1990s we did our famous charge against English fans ahead of the game, which was stopped by the police and many of our lads ended up in the nick. After we played Germany we captured a VfB Stuttgart flag and a few German scarves.

One of our greatest victories over our eternal enemy Levski was in 2000 when we done them two hours before kick-off at their traditional rally point, the Blue Café. Back in those years such raids were spontaneous and impulsive. We got lucky then as at the crossroads where we were supposed to be diverted to our regular route, there were only 4 or 5 cops who couldn't stop us (there were more than 200 of us) and so we rather unexpectedly turned into the street that leads to their meeting point. We stormed into them like a tornado, we smashed them and chased them away from their sacred ground (no one else has done that since then). In 2008 we tried to repeat our triumph as we raided their fan club ahead of a derby, but the coppers' timely response made our plans fail.

- **Who are your rivals (in the general sense of the word, in life or at the stadium), what are they like and what is your opinion of them?**

I used to be more of an anti-Levski fan than a CSKA supporter. In the early 1990s Levski fans were for me the lowest strata of society and football supporters as they totally lack nationalistic feelings and their mob included all sorts of low quality human beings. They called themselves 'the people's club' and we defined them as the 'peoples' club' since their stand was full of people from all ethnicities and all sorts of brainless lowlifes who were in love with cheap booze, Serbian music and Levski FC (probably 90% of them don't know the date of birth of their idol, the national revolutionary Vasil Levski).

They also hated anything that's red. We all know about one of their top boys who cut down the cherry tree in his garden and there is another one who left his hometown because of its name Cherven Bryag (Red Bank in English). For me they were the incarnation of the worst features and qualities a human can have. And it was all due to the lack of skinheads in their sector, which even resulted for some time in the appearance of anti-nationalist elements (RASH & Anti-FA) among them.

Everything changed around 2000 when their top firm Sofia West was founded. It was originally set up by nationalistic hooligans living in the western quarters of Sofia, but eventually it spread all over the capital and the country and as time went by it turned into a crime syndicate, I may say. Almost immediately they took control of Sector B or their South stand and started cleansing it from the characters I already mentioned above. Fortunately, they cleaned themselves from the enemy I hated so much.

I dare say that at this stage my enemies and rivals are any other (foreign) firms or mobs made up of Muslims or followers of anti-nationalistic ideas.

- **Have you ever been seriously wounded or injured while fighting?**

I don't believe there is a single bloke who has spent, let's say, 20-25 years in hooligan and skinhead circles, and has not been injured, hurt or arrested. As we say, 'it's a part of the game'.

]My most serious injuries were caused in police departments, but surely, they don't count here. In 2004 after a fight in Zagreb where Croatia played Bulgaria I was arrested and sentenced to two weeks in jail and banned from entering the country a second time. During a beer fest there was this fight with the aforesaid Levski top firm and a bakelite baton was thrown at me and it hit me on the head. It was rather stupid because if the one who threw it had hit me instead, he would have caused much greater damage to my head. I've also had minor traumas like a bitten finger that was caused by one of the top boys of the already mentioned Levski firm. Naturally, those were incidents that happened more than 13 or 14 years ago, and they can only make me feel nostalgic now. Nostalgia for my long past youth (laughing).

- **Where does your favourite football club stand in your life and how important is it for you?**

Now it stands on a few tattoos all over my body and at a couple of scarves nailed on my guest room walls. I'm joking, of course, my club will forever stay in my heart.

Whatever games I have attended in Europe, when asked which of the two clubs I support, I have always pulled up my trouser leg and showed the CSKA logo, saying that's the only club I love!

But as I said, the racial issue has always been my top priority. At the beginning of 2000, Bulgarian football was invaded by black players and it reached to a point when 5 or 6 of them had signed CSKA. Now I'd like to point out that we, CSKA, were the only Bulgarian side that organised a protest and set up a boycott against those black players. Naturally, I was not able to get any delight from the goals they'd score, and I dare say they killed the joy I used to get from football. I got into absurd situations when, after CSKA had scored and I hadn't seen the goal, I'd ask the lads around me whether the goal scorer was white or black, and accordingly, I cheered or not. This surely was a stupid thing to do, but it really is one of the reasons I stopped going to games.

In my youth I really used to segregate people into CSKA and Levski fans, but now a separate them into Bulgarians and minorities. I'd like to paraphrase a mate of mine who supports Spartak Moscow and who says, "A love for a football club is great, but one should know that in addition to that, one's love for one's family, friends and most of all one's motherland, should be much greater."

- **Which are your favourite designer brands?**

Surely one may say that designer clothes and shoes go along with the subcultures one belongs to. During the 1990s skinhead period popular classic were Fred Perry T-shirts, Lonsdale sweatshirts, Alpha bombers and Get a Grip boots.

Those boots were really great for kicking and breaking, but when it came to be running they were useless and besides, anyone wearing such boots was easily recognisable. Around 2000, New Balance trainers became fashionable in Bulgaria (I still prefer wearing this brand now). Anyway, what mostly matters to me is that a piece of clothing is comfortable, strong enough, and naturally, affordable. I prefer dark colours as they make you less identifiable and as people say, they don't easily get dirty (laughing). I found the English fashion of white trainers and colourful clothes rather ridiculous, because when you get into a fight and possibly get knocked down on the ground, you become easily identifiable due to the dirt and mud on you.

Naturally, after the campaign started by famous brands such as Lonsdale and Fred Perry for getting rid of the bad NS image by donating profits to anti-racist organisations I stopped buying them. For some time now, I've been keen on nationalist brands such as Thor Steinar, Ansgar Aryan and Beloyar, but still, Alpha remains my favourite jacket as it is light and yet quite strong. A black Aquascutum, Lonsdale or Fred Perry cap that covers your eyes will always be my favourite.

- **What is your wildest favourite club related dream?**

Wow, any football fan's wildest dream is of course watching their beloved club play a European final and naturally win the title, possibly after penalties so that the adrenaline could fly higher. However, we are down-to-earth pragmatists and we know that we won't witness that, not in this life anyway. It's true that my club CSKA is the most successful Bulgarian club, 31 times champions of Bulgaria, twice semi-finalists in the former European Champions Cup, once semi-finalists in the former Cup Winners Cup, but those were years of glory and pride that are long gone now. Nowadays football is way too commercialised and dominated by foreign players, which I find absolutely inappropriate cause in the majority of cases it is a matter of a medley of mercenaries and black players who have nothing to do with either the relevant club or its fans or the country they live in. What unites them is only their bank account and when it fails to be credited those "stars" come out on the pitch with their pockets turned upside down or refuse to come out at all. Most often their names are associated with scandals in local night clubs or with some sexual achievement, but never with anything to do with the football game.

I think the national team concept is also totally perverted by signing so many foreign and black players when the national stars of a given country are very few as youth academies get ruined and those academies are the foundations for developing any kind of sports.

The most appropriate thing to do, if you ask, me, would be each team to have only players from the corresponding town and so we could really see which town, which country and which nation are the best in football and who the fittest and tactically best prepared footballers are. However, this is just a utopia. To put it briefly, my dream is to see my club as it used to be in its past years of fame, made up of Bulgarian lads only defeating any opponent... Unfortunately, this is increasingly turning into nostalgia for youth and times gone by.

- **Which is your favourite game of all times?**

As I said, what matters most to me is the 'off-the-pitch' result, i.e. the number of times our rivals are given a good hiding, the acts of vandalism inside and outside grounds, the number of arrests made, if you like.

One of my sweetest memories goes back to 2001 when we played our eternal rivals Levski at their ground. In those years it had become quite popular to organise chorteos from our ground, located downtown, to Levski ground, located in the suburbs. The march involved drinking loads of booze, skirmishes with the cops, and pursuits around tower blocks in the vicinity of the ground, throwing of bottles and bombs at the blue fans they were getting more and more numerous as we neared their ground. An hour before kick-off we went on a rampage all across the away end and all through the game, which resulted in a total devastation and setting on fire of probably 80% of the seats in there (on the following day the media reported some 2500-3000 ripped off seats). Eventually our mob was driven out of the ground by the cops and what followed was another violent rampage on the streets and dozens of ruined cars and buses. I think it was not earlier than the following day that I did become aware of the score. CSKA had lost 2-1, but what mattered to me was that we had won the battle on the terraces. There is a famous video where you can see the rampage that started 3 minutes into the game.

I also keep great memories from the game we played against Cherno More in Varna in 2000, where the drunk and disorderly behaviour started in the early morning on the city beaches and then it all escalated into pursuits and fights with the locals and the Old Bill and ended up in another total destruction of the away end. I'd like to point out that summer away games in towns along the coast always feature loads of adrenaline, alcohol and a couple of days of free holiday rides to the seaside (in those times we used to travel by rail only and generally we didn't use to buy any train tickets so games at the seaside were long waited for by the entire CSKA fan communities.

A year earlier we had another memorable away day to Belasitsa FC in the town of Petrich. The fights and arrests started as early as dawn, they went on during the game and finished with a wild rampage in the train back to Sofia. We foresightedly got off at the station before our destination as we knew that cordons of cops would be waiting for us at Sofia Central Station. So by and large, the late 1990s were full of great unforgettable memories.

- **Who are your favourite players?**

My favourite player was Trifon Ivanov (RIP). My criteria are not football skills exactly (well, surely a player has to have some), but rather one's frame of mind and spirit, one's merits such as honour, duty and love for one's motherland. To put it briefly, one has to be a real man on and off the pitch. Trifon had it all. He played as a centre-back, which according to some is the most ill-favoured position on the pitch, but for me it is the most important one as it was all up to him whether we'd conceive a goal or not. People used to joke about him that he was the type of player who'd let the ball pass him, but he'd never let a player do it. They even said he'd play that kind of scary face trick when he'd turn his eyelids inside out, which, when added to his bearded face and the bags under his eyes, would surely distract a forward upon his entry into the penalty box for a brief second, which was long enough for Trifon to get hold of the ball.

During his period at SK Rapid they used to say that some mums and grandmas used Trifon's name as a threat in disciplining kids instead of the Boogeyman. He scored a screamer after an acrobatic scissor-kick against Wales back in 1994 (still considered as one of the best goals ever scored by the Bulgarian national squad). After he scored it, right there, on the spot, I promised I would have a tattoo of Trifon Ivanov, and I did keep my promise.

Once I had the opportunity of meeting him in a bar (beer in hand) and I showed him my tattoo. Naturally, he was happy to see it. Unfortunately, this whole generation of football players is long gone now only to be replaced by some worthless fuckers.

- **Would you name the top 5 Bulgarian firms/crews/mobs?**

This is a tough one... maybe we have to make clear the criteria used for assessing the so called 'firms', whether it would be the firm racketeering the football club (making money by all means imaginable) or ... would it be the firm taking over all kinds of businesses both inside and outside football stadia, varying from security companies, fan shops, fan clubs, cafes, gyms, tattoo studios, etc.

Also, I firm can be granted some 'shady business orders', even related to politics, such as orchestrating riots, election campaigns (a quite common practice in Bulgaria for the last decade or two), etc. Surely, that kind of business is possible only for top clubs as they have those huge numbers of supporters that can be used for such activities. Small clubs are not part of that 'game'.

The problem is that top club supporters' leaders are usually burdened by their criminal past as they used to do time, or they are doing time at present, which makes them kinda dependent on the police and even on the political situation in the country. This, in turn, results in their reluctance to orchestrate or participate in hooligan acts in order for them to save their top boys as they need them not for football related, but for shady business-related activities.

So, to answer your question, I'll have to go 10 or 15 years back when I used to go to football (I'm not acquainted with the current situation, so I can't comment on it. So, number one of course is the Kravai crew (CSKA SS FRONT), who were never, ever, defeated. A good number of them eventually joined Animals. 2. Levski Sofia West; 3. Lokomotiv Plovdiv Gott Mit Uns; 4. Beroe Zara Boys (a relatively young firm); 5. Botev Plovdiv Izgrev Boys (notorious for their anarchist behaviour across stadia).

- **Which are the best and the worst football grounds you've ever been to and why?**

I wonder what you mean by that, is it the most comfortable and the most uncomfortable one, or the most modern and the most rundown one? I've been to all kinds of weed-grown and brushy grounds where animals graze. I've also been to gigantic modern stadia (mostly abroad).

Talking about the most hostile stadium that would be Belasitsa ground. They didn't use to have a separate away fans entrance so travelling fans would be made to enter the ground through one of their main entrances, then escorted along the racing track and finally taken to the away end 'cage'. So all the way you'd walk up to there, you'd get spat on, insulted and pelted with stones and any other debris by the locals, who had come to watch the "junkies and skinheads from Sofia" rather than their own beloved hometown club. We felt like being animals in zoo cages. And the most ridiculous thing is that the ground is surrounded all the way by hills (it was built like that), on which the locals would stand and watch the game drinking tons of homemade booze.

During one of the fights we had against the cops in the away end, a plastic bottle full of red liquid fell down right beside me and almost hit me. I opened it to see it was a delicious homemade wine (laughing), hurled by the over agitated peasants who were watching the game on one of the steep hills right above the away fans cage. Naturally, the bottle was drunk in seconds. There used to be endless aggravation and, naturally, our drunk lads would always be up for it but would most probably end up in the backs of the police vans and down in the police cells where they'd be nicked for a week or two.

As far as the best ground is concerned I'd pick Go Ahead Eagles' Deventer Holland as there is this huge club selling alcohol and playing on hardcore music and everything looked so fine. There was also a nice stall selling beer and tasty sausages, no cops, but only friendly stewards (most of them young girls). The fans were older than us, casually dressed and absolutely friendly. So, people there really knew how to have fun and it was a real pleasure watching football in the flesh at such a ground.

- **What do you think of the Bulgarian police?**

What do you think I think of them? Nothing good for sure. They are just slaves to the system. I remember the pre-democracy times (the late 1980s) when they'd eject a whole row of guys because of a single bloke who stood up and started cheering loud or abusing the referee or the opponent team.

Some of the biggest and most tormented as kid's losers from my neighbourhood joined the police... what else is there to add?!

The way they storm in to nick a minor supporter who's lit up a flare, well, why don't they storm over gypsy ghettos with the same brutality to arrest a real criminal and so deserve a little bit of my respect? Why don't they do it? While gypsy gangs go on a rampage and literally kill elderly people in little villages, 'our' police are engaged in securing yet another football game, dressed in the latest fashion and all of them wearing sunglasses while their media teams are standing back in the background. Of course, the advance of CCTV, phone tapping and email monitoring facilitated their job a lot, though the Russian, Polish and other hooligan scenes come to prove that if lads are really up for it, they are really bound to get it and they do deserve it.

- **What do you think of the youths in your firm/crew/mob?**

Well, this is a tough one. Unfortunately, my assessment of the modern-day young generation would be rather low as I'm sad to see that each generation that follows is weaker than the previous one. I really don't know what this consistent degradation will lead to. What I know is that youth is the future of both firm and country. That's why I feel so much pity. The destructive processes in our society affected our youth to the greatest extent and had its negative effects in all spheres of life, including subcultures. Unfortunately, the fight for our kids and teens' minds was won by the liberal propaganda and its tolerance and multiculturalism bullshit managed to brainwash them and steal their hearts, minds and souls. Now words like duty, honour, respect for the elderly and motherland mean nothing to them. Right in front of our eyes there is this generation notorious for their extreme insolence, widespread illiteracy (blokes who have not read a single book in their entire lives), defiance of all authorities and rules both at home and on the streets. Those are fellas that do not respect in any way their older ones and disobey all kinds of rules whatsoever. In football fan circles (as well as in any other subcultures), what matters most is succession and heritage, which means that some day, when the time has come for the older generations to step aside and make way for the younger ones, they are to be replaced by the latter, who are supposed to continue their path and their fight. It can happen only when the elder hand down their knowledge and experience to the young. However, it will only happen if the young are willing to do so cause if they're not, passing of the torch will become impossible. Instead of growing and developing, a firm will start tearing apart due to internal conflicts between young and old, which will ultimately destroy it (such processes keep going on almost everywhere). Take for example the famous ULTRAS SUR, who as far as I know are irrevocably separated between young and old, fights between them are quite common, which is naturally facilitated to a great extent by the use of cheap synthetic drugs.

If we try to sound a little bit funny, fancy that: 50 or 60-kg, leg (and sometimes eyebrow) shaving, casually dressed (though in second-hand attire mostly), amphetamine overdosed and having a fierce look in their eyes. Upon meeting someone older, they usually greet him, but once he's passed them by they start talking bullshit behind his back, and if they are taken to task, they start swearing on their mums that they never said that bullshit. And if they are given a hiding, first thing they do is go to the police and file a complaint and then the cops make them add they've been robbed of their phones so that a case could be filed not only for affray, but also mugging. Snitching is something normal for them. There are some exceptions, though. Let me say it again, they (youngsters) are just a reflection of things going on in our society. Societies with a background of teaching their youngsters love for their motherland, respect for the elder and following Christian values and traditions are much stronger and more united. Once again, I'll give you the examples of Russia, Poland, Serbia and other countries from Eastern Europe mainly, where hooliganism level is much higher.

- **What do you think of the modern-day 'scene'?**

As I said earlier, I've not been on the active side for more than 10 years and since I have no good grounds to do it, I cannot comment on the current scene. From what I see or hear, I think that modern-day fan (hooligan) scene in Bulgaria is in a kind of standstill, kind of apathetic. While our neighbouring Balkan and some other Eastern European countries are witnessing certain processes aimed at forming an alliance of different mobs in the name of common causes such as protests against migrants, gay parades and other activities aimed at protecting their nations, in Bulgaria the situation is rather different. The hatred between the different clubs (mostly the Sofia ones) is so intense that at this stage no unity and national value protection can even be dreamed about.

Truth to tell, there were some attempts in this respect after certain ethnic riots involving gypsies and Bulgarians several years ago, as well as the ratification of a Code of Conduct, which unfortunately is not observed by any of the football mobs.

Until recently CSKA was mostly famous for its nationalist fans. The very skinhead movement was founded in Bulgaria by CSKA fans and respect was due to them both home and abroad. However, times have changed, fashion styles have changed and the rules for fighting have changed, too. The advance of drugs and the fact that criminals stood on top of the mobs also contributed to the change in the ways and methods of fighting and as a result, the carrying of knives, batons and other weapons is nowadays considered acceptable. Ambushing people in front of their homes and attacking single lads are not rare cases now.

Those in power in Bulgaria are well aware that the armies of fans are quite dangerous due to their good organisation and their experience in street wars. We've seen a squad of 50-100 cops successfully confronting a demonstration of thousands of rank and file protestors, but if among those protestors there are a few hundred hooligans, it would be quite a different story, wouldn't it. That's the reason why the authorities managed to 'buy' football mobs in the different ways that I already mentioned above.

Frankly speaking, there were those times when fights were prearranged, I believe there were 4 such fights, one against Dynamo Moscow and the others against Lokomotiv Plovdiv and Litex, CSKA fans winning two and losing the other two. However, those fair fights are now long gone...

Unfortunately, the top firms of CSKA and Levski have never prearranged such fights that could give the answer to many questions. I think it is impossible for them to prearrange a fight because neither firm would like to afford to lose such a fight as a defeat would result in losing its control over the entire stand, the respect of the rest of firms and the businesses I mentioned above.

- **What do you think of English hooligans and their influence?**

I can only pay due respect to the founders and pioneers of both football and football related hooliganism. Britain is a strange island that gave birth to numerous music trends (Punk, Ska, Oi!) and to various subcultures like skinhead, punk, football hooliganism, etc. Everybody used to watch movies and documentaries and we all watched and learned. Films like Clockwork Orange played the role of the Bible for my generation. The late 1980s and the early 1990s were the best years for English hooligans and in my opinion the decent organisation and the alliance between all firms for England games were the main reasons for their total domination. The English fans' high standard of living (as compared to Eastern European fans in those times) and their clubs' European fame allowed them to travel in large numbers all over Europe leaving behind a trial of smashed pubs and crushed local fans. Naturally, the sanctions and banning orders that followed were part of the strict measures taken against hooligans. Ringleaders and top lads had police records, and some were even jailed. They were banned from leaving the UK while the advance of CCTV marked the beginning of a thorough control over stadia, which predetermined the end of football related violence or at least its reduction to insignificant levels.

At the same time, after the fall of communism, the Eastern bloc countries wanted to prove themselves on that scene and for that purpose they had to defeat their 'masters'. That's how the hunt for Englishmen started. First it was Legia fans back in 1999 in Warsaw, where the English could no longer rely on their top lads and fell easy prey to the young, fame pursuing continental firms. The methods of fighting also changed. The good old British style of taking over pubs, excessive drinking and spreading chaos and terror all around was challenged by Polish and Russian crews mainly consisting of young athletes who do not touch any booze or drugs and who are strictly disciplined and organised in combat units that plan their action in military style. Naturally, in most cases the English did not stand a chance in such battles as clearly seen during the last Euro played in France. The right to an answer now lies in the hands of the English when they go to the 2018 World Cup in Russia.

(T.) - CSKA (Sofia)

Meet and greet

- **How old are you and when did you become a fan of your favourite club?**

My nickname is T. I was born in 1966 and so in August (when this book will be launched) I'll be 52. I've been a CSKA fan since I was a small kid. Dad used to be a die-hard red, but he passed away when I was only 9 months old. His last wish was that I should become a 'red' and so my cousins and uncles started taking me to CSKA ground when I was a small kid in the mid-1970s. So, it was then I became hooked and most of my life was spent across stadia!

- **Would you tell us how your firm (crew/mob) was established?**

I'm not a member of any organisations! I'm far right and I meet up with like-minded fellas, no matter what firm they belong to as long as they are reds! Back in the days (the 1980s), when people of my age were at the top, there were no firms. We all stood together, no matter what part of Sofia we came from. Our rally point was called Tsarevets (right at the Eagles Bridge), and in the evenings we'd go to Yalta disco club, have a few drinks, sing a few songs and have a great time. After that we'd go hunting for blue 'cattle' and every time we'd come across Levski fans we'd beat the shit out of them. We were strong because we stood together, one for all and all for one... and besides, no one used to snitch to the cops then!!!

- **How would you define yourself as a fan?**

I define myself as far right wing and an old school fan.

- **Would you tell us in more details about some fights you have been involved at stadia and on the streets?**

The fights I've been involved in are so many that we'll need a separate book to describe them all, but some of the most memorable ones are against Lokomotiv fans in Plovdiv ahead of, during and after games. Once they were waiting for us at the railway station, but we were well up for it, had good numbers and we went toe-to-toe plus the occasional home-made bombs and other missiles across the entire town. The brawl went on in the vicinity of the ground, on the terraces during the very game and after the final whistle once again it kicked off everywhere. The cops were at a complete loss what to do and the precincts and hospitals were full. A good number of our lads stayed in Plovdiv brickfields for two weeks due to community service orders (laughing).

In 1980s, CSKA played away to Botev Vratsa, who at that time were a satellite club of Levski and so were much hostile to us. We took the early train from Sofia drinking heavily and were later joined by lads who'd made the trip by cars. All day long we roamed the streets in downtown Vratsa, chanting and drinking beer and raki. The locals would hurl insults at us from a distance but didn't dare to have a go at us. There were only small-scale skirmishes, nothing worth mentioning... We took over the entire centre. About 500 CSKA (a huge number for those years) turned up and we went on having fun. The locals were in the opposite end and their numbers were 3 or four times greater than ours. CSKA opened the score, the mobs went on hurling insults at each other and the tension was rising higher and higher. There were a few cops only as they must have underestimated the game. At some point the locals decided to have a go at us and A huge mob headed towards us. They jumped over the low fencing and started running in our direction. The Old Bill looked absolutely helpless. One of our lads then screamed, 'Start ripping off benches!' (all stadia then had wooden benches, so we broke them down to lumps and armed ourselves with them). The locals were getting nearer and then another red lad roared out loud, 'Let's have it' and we steamed into their mob, the lumps of wood up front (laughing). It escalated into a massive brawl, the locals were absolutely stunned, and they simply bottled it. That was exactly what we hoped for! We ran after them and started hitting them all over with our wooden bars. Besides, we nicked a number of their scarves and flags. We chased them all the way to their home end, we took over it and we did them all. Meanwhile police backups arrived, and the coppers began beating us with their truncheons. They arrested loads of us, but we had indisputably won the battle! At the end of the game they escorted us back to the station, where the locals had been waiting for us. The moment they saw us they started throwing stones at us. We broke through the police lines and had a go at them so once again they bottled it. Finally, we boarded the train and it slowly started pulling out of the station. The local thugs went on hurling stones and bricks at us, to which we responded with bottles and bombs. The party was at full swing all the way back to Sofia. We were celebrating our (off-the-pitch) victory and the adrenaline was flying high in our blood!

CSKA was playing away to Beroe in their town of Stara Zagora (I think it was a cup game) so a few coachloads of us made the trip. As usual, it was all booze and chants and songs and a great party all the way. We arrived in Stara Zagora and roamed the streets for a couple of hours before the game. There were quite a few red fans everywhere and the locals would just hurl abuse at us but did not dare to come any closer. The game was uneventful (the usual banter only because it was full of Old Bill everywhere) and CSKA won. After the final whistle we got on our coaches and set off back to Sofia. Before leaving the town, Beroe fans ambushed us and our coaches came under a shower of stones and bottles. Some windows got shattered and the driver of our coach (also a CSKA fan) stopped the vehicle, opened the doors and out we came and steamed into the local mob. It was out of the blue for them and they were given a good hiding. They tried to take shelter in a pub, but we stormed it and we beat the shit out of everyone in there. Probably there were also some innocent victims, unfortunately. So, having nicked loads of Beroe scarves, we hurriedly boarded back our coaches as we could hear the distinct sound of police sirens approaching. The coaches set off and everybody inside (girls included) took our pants off and stuck our arses to the windows. We copycatted this trick from a film that was pretty popular then, i.e. the SlapShot movie about Canadian ice hockey fans. The rear window (quite big, you know) was all taken up by the huge ass of Fat K. (laughing). So that was the end of the story, loads of adrenaline and party at full swing.

Another memorable day in the 1980s when we played the 'cattle'. The beat us thanks to a penalty they scored, and we went fucking mad. A considerable mob of top boys set off for their usual meeting point called "The Mortuary" (Memento bar nowadays). Along the way we broke into a worker's caravan and we armed ourselves with picks, shovels and other tools and then we had a go at them. They took shelter in the boozer and locked the door, but we threw a few large benches at the big French windows and shattered them and then we stormed in and smashed the Levski mob! That kept them out of the game for quite a long time.

- **Who are your rivals (in the general sense of the word, in life or at the stadium), what are they like and what is your opinion of them?**

We have rivals all over Bulgaria, but naturally, the most loathsome ones are Levski! They've always been the dregs of society, filthy scum of subhumans, I mean the majority of Levski fans cause naturally they do have some (though only a few) decent lads, who I suppose are part of this despicable scum by sheer mistake!

- **Have you ever been seriously wounded or injured while fighting?**

Yes, a number of times (that's quite normal for guys like us), but fortunately nothing too serious.

- **Where does your favourite football club stand in your life and how important is it for you?**

CSKA has always been the most important thing for me when I was growing up (more important than school, job, birds, etc.), but it all changed in the late 1990s when they started bringing black players to sign the club. I cannot go to games and cheer for or applaud 'monkeys' (you go to a zoo to do that, not to a football ground, don't you)? So, I started attending games more and more rarely, and now I've been living abroad for quite some time. Anyway, I will forever remain faithful to the reds and I'll always be interested in what's going with CSKA.

- **Which are your favourite designer brands?**

My favourite brands are Lonsdale, Fred Perry, Ansgar Aryan, Aryan Wear, etc.

- **What is your wildest favourite club related dream?**

My dream is CSKA once again to become the 'white' club it used to be in the 1980s with no coloured players and play a European Cup final. The first part of it almost came true 2 years ago when CSKA was sent to 3rd Division and all foreigners were gone, and we started using Bulgarian boys only who won all the games! The fans also returned and travelled all across the country in large numbers despite the lower division.

- **Which is your favourite game of all times?**

I've been to many great games, but probably the most memorable was when we knocked out Liverpool 2-0 and went on to the semi-final to play Bayern Munich! The ground was so overcrowded that I still wonder why it didn't collapse and our entire country celebrated for days on end!

- **Who are your favourite players?**

All good Bulgarian players have played for CSKA, so it is extremely hard to name them all, so I'll stick to just a few names from my times and they are Lyubo Penev, Hristo Stoichkov, Spas Dzhevizov, Georgi Dimitrov, Georgi Velinov, and Tsonyo Vasilev... It's an endless list, you know!

- **Would you name the top 5 Bulgarian firms/crews/mobs?**

I'll talk about clubs, I mean fans in general, because as I said before, I've been living abroad so I'm not so familiar with the modern mobs, firms, crews, etc. So CSKA fans have naturally always been number one (no doubt about it), followed by Botev Plovdiv, Lokomotiv Plovdiv, probably Cherno, more Varna, and unfortunately, no matter how reluctant I am, I have to mention the scum from Poduyane quarter, i.e. Levski (laughing).

- **Which are the best and the worst football grounds you've ever been to and why?**

The best one for me is CSKA ground 'Narodna Armia' because I grew up there and I spent the best years of my life there (it was a 4-minute walk from where I used to live to the stadium). It's hard to tell which the worst one is because there are a number of shitholes in Bulgaria, but in my opinion, it is Levski stadium Gerena and

I need not give you any more grounds. I just loathe its filthy occupants, the mud and the stench you have to go through in order to get there!

- **What do you think of the Bulgarian police?**

Quite understandably, my opinion of the Old Bill has never been and will never be a positive one. First of all, most of them are Levski fans, and secondly, the majority of them are corrupt bastards, servants of those in powers and not of the people. Of course, I'm talking about the majority, though there are a few decent guys there… a drop of water in the sea.

- **What do you think of the youths in your firm/crew/mob?**

Though I try to follow things and I do keep in touch with a few people, I can't attend games in Bulgaria, so my opinion may not be relevant, but I can say I do not like what I see and hear! I personally don't know the youths in our mob now, but I can say they do great tifos (flares, smoke bombs, crackers, flags, etc.) What I don't like, however, is that they are divided into hundreds of firms and they quarrel and fight each other. That's what the blue scum are waiting for, so they even dare to go to our stadium (after midnight, when most of our lads are gone), put their masks on and start beating old men and innocent fellas. I wish they could put an end to their personal clashes and be united so that no one could stop them then. The Reds should be united and should not quarrel and fight each other for some stupid reasons, no matter what they really are. It is inadmissible and let me say it again, the 'cattle' simply take advantage of that and enter our territory late at night like the cowards they are and beat whoever they bump into. Otherwise, I already said, the tifos are magnificent and I love them because we didn't have such opportunities back in the days.

- **What do you think of the modern-day 'scene'?**

Here we go again… Well, I don't live in Bulgaria and since I don't witness things first hand, I cannot give you an expert opinion, but I do see that there is a hooligan scene in Bulgaria now, though it's way different than the one in the 1980s. Now you've got pre-arranged fights, smartphones, Internet forums, social networks (where they arrange those fights), you've got the dozens of separate firms, and the Jews have installed the thousands of CCTV, so it's all different now, but I am really glad that there are still crazy lads like us (30 years ago) to keep the fire burning and share the same ideas! All around the world the scene has also changed through all those years, so it is not only us.

- **What do you think of English hooligans and their influence?**

I think highly of English hooligans as they were the first to start it and spread chaos and mayhem wherever they went. All ideas, subcultures, movements, etc. originate from the English. They were our idols. I'll mention a few mobs only, but in general my respect goes to all of them except the Yids from Tottenham (laughing), so let's say Millwall, Leeds, Chelsea, Liverpool, Arsenal… Unfortunately, that old vermin

Margaret Thatcher ruined it all with her laws and cameras and spies at every corner. I wish they could regain their past fame some day!

Now I'll take some time and tell you a story related to English or rather British fans. It was November 1983. Freezing cold and snowy, Bulgaria playing a Euro qualifier against Wales (I think we won 1-0). We, CSKA fans, had met up as usual before kick-off at Tsarevets and were drinking raki, etc. As I said, it was cold and miserable and not many people were going to the game. Word had spread there were Welsh fans in Sofia, who were to be escorted by the Old Bill to the main stand. At some point, about 40 of us decided to head for the stadium through the park. We were almost there when we suddenly bumped into a mob of some 20 Welsh hooligans who had deliberately slipped out of the police escort looking for some party. We went at them right away! They were the proverbial in those times British hools, waist-naked (despite the icy weather), front teeth missing, all tattooed and pissed like us (laughing). Instead of bottling it, they roared something in English and had a go at us, though our number was twice bigger than theirs. We had a great fight, headbutts, fists, kicks, no weapons at all. The fight did not last long cause the cops quickly intervened and started beating us with their batons and nicking us (most of the arrested fans were Bulgarians). Then, much to our surprise, the Welsh interceded for us and started hugging us, persuading the cops we were mates who were only joking and having fun! So those blokes actually saved us from the Old Bill and all of us together (CSKA and the Welsh) went our way to the ground all covered in blood, lips split, and eyes bruised. And now we were drinking together... naturally it was our raki (winking). We were all happy, we'd hug each other, and we'd sing and chant in different languages one and the same song against the Old Bill (they also hated them and hurled insults at the cops all the time). So, we took them to our end and the rest just couldn't believe their eyes when they saw their own men, though few in numbers, fly their flags and scarves in our end. After the game (I couldn't tell the score) we literally became blood brothers, we drank for hours and finally we saw them off to their hotel. We parted as some good mates sharing great memories. So, this is what British fans mean to me in general... Hooligans in the truest sense of the word, bold, crazy, funny men of honour... I'll always remember them!

P.S.

Now I'd like to mention the nicknames of some lads we used to spend time together across stadia and form the core of the red mob. Most of them are my personal friends up to this day. These are guys from different generations united by a single idea, i.e. CSKA! Unfortunately, some of them are not with us any longer, but though they are gone, they shall never be forgotten!

Chenzo, The Hairdresser (RIP), The Plight, Pots, The Pomeranian, Duce, AC/DC, Denis, Zozo (RIP), Rumpo, Dachshund, The Eagle, The Felt, The Nightmare, Manov, Delov, Leo (RIP), Little and Big Jap, Cutty, Birov, Texas, The Fireman, The Jukebox, The Sock, Kaine, Forest, The Cur, The Secretary, Naso The Swine, The Muscle and hundreds of other red lions (unfortunately I cannot name them all), among them some decent younger lads who carried on with and even further developed our cause, e.g. Denny (RIP), Kacho, Zaggi, Orlin, The Monkey, etc.

I wish good luck to the authors of this unique for Bulgaria joint book and I do believe it will be successful. I didn't know about their first book, but it sounds interesting and I think it's a must for any Bulgarian hooligan, so I'll surely buy it and I do look forward to the launch of their second one!

T. -CSKA 88- Respect

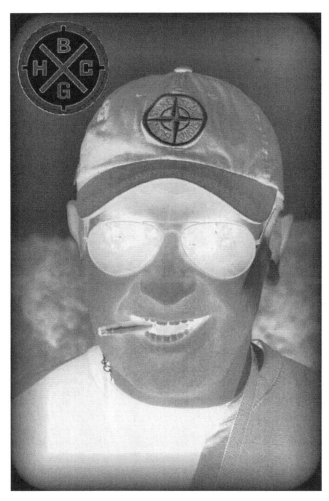

M. P. (P.) - Levski (Sofia)

Meet and greet

M. P., a.k.a. P, a Levski fan from Sofia, Mladost Quarter in particular, married, with a beautiful daughter, I work as a translator, I have two master's degrees, I speak English and in my spare time I write books about Levski or to be more exact, about Levski fans. I'm far right wing, a staunch anti-communist. I'd rather say I'm not religious because I don't believe in God, I believe in me! A fan of English football and of anything English in general, I have liked Chelsea since the late 1980s and I've been to several Chelsea games, including away games abroad.

- **How old are you and when did you become a fan of your favourite club?**

I'm 47. I became a Levski fan in the late 1970s. My first memories are Levski winning the title in 1979 and the games we played in 1980. I started going to football on my own in the mid-1980s. my childhood heroes are the incredible Levski generation then featuring Bozhidar Iskrenov (Gibby), Emil Velev (Kokala), Nikolai Iliev, Nasko Sirakov, Borislav Mihailov, etc., the glorious blue team from the 1980s.

- **Would you tell us how your firm (crew/mob) was established?**

I'm a member of Sofia West, the biggest, the strongest and the post powerful Levski firm in Bulgaria since its establishment in 1999 up to this day. I've been close friends with Sofia West founders since the late 1980s! 'A lot of water has gone under the bridge' since then, there have been a number of ups and downs, a series of new generations, but with new generation SW are becoming increasingly stronger! SW is the ones who have never lost a single battle for almost two decades now! SW are the ones who have given birth and are still giving birth to terrace legends! They were the ones who threw the police out of not only Sector B, but out of all Bulgaria stadia and paved the way for the new practice of introducing stewards and stopping the long-year continual confrontation with the coppers during games! SW are the ones who are always at the front line when it comes to protecting the honour and pride of Levski and Bulgaria! SW are the ones feared by all the other firms and crews in Bulgaria, without any exception! SW are the ones without whom Sector B will simply no longer exist! Yes, surely, we have enemies, surely a great number of people do not like us, but … we don't fucking care! We fear no foe! 'Alone against all' was SW motto way back in the year of our establishment, 1999! Better have enemies than false friends! And… you'd better look around!

- **How would you define yourself as a fan?**

Well, it's difficult for me to define myself. Some twenty years ago I'd answer this question on the spot, without a single trace of doubt, using the word 'hooligan'. Now… am I an 'ex-hooligan'? I don't know… People say there's no such thing as an ex-whore or an ex-nigger, so are there ex- hooligans?! Or am I an intellectual hooligan (laughing)?! Up to this day, there are games, quite a few in fact, when I'm more interested in what is going on in the stands and not on the pitch. The thrill of seeing what is happening on the terraces and the mobs there is still alive, and I guess it will be alive till my last breath. I don't give a fuck about the way a left back has mastered the ball or a right wing has crossed it in the penalty area. Much more interesting to me is a melee or another incident on the terraces. Mobs take part in the football game as much as players do. That's what I believe in and that's what I think about the game.

- **Would you tell us in more details about some fights you have been involved at stadia and on the streets?**

I'll never forget one particular fight that happened, I think, in 1990. Communism had just collapsed and there were those futsal games in Sofia. One of the tournaments featured the Russian side Dynamo from Moscow. Some Russians living Sofia had come to watch their team. The venue was packed and so they had brought some additional chairs and put them behind the goals. Well, our entire hatred for the Soviet kept deep inside and long forbidden by the commies was let loose and we steamed into the Russians shouting, "Sofia is not Moscow", etc. It was a brilliant fight, a really great one. In fits of uncontrolled anger, I grabbed the first chair that stood in front of me and crashed it down on the head of the nearest Ivan. I still remember the thrill and the joy I felt. It was simply wonderful!

And probably the most massive and brutal fight I've been involved in was again in 1990, after a game we played at home vs Minyor. We mobbed up about 500 of us and the away mob was at least 200 handed, but I tell you it was a tough one. It was a real battle, a fucking war. The away fans stood on one side of a halted bus and we stood on the other side when we started hurling at each other stones and bricks and bombs and other debris... Fucking hell! Respect to Minyor fans because they didn't bottle it and bravely fought until they could fight. I think the last bomb in the exchange of fire was mine. Finally, they gave in to our bigger numbers as they didn't stand a chance in the toe-to-toe and the whole street was strewn in bits of bricks, stones, marks from the bombs, blood stains, missing teeth and even ... trainers. It looked like a real war zone. The emergency units were crowded that night. Grandiose!

- **Who are your rivals (in the general sense of the word, in life or at the stadium), what are they like and what is your opinion of them?**

The 'pigs', the fans of that four-letter club, that tumour artificially created in the red corridors of power in Moscow and then fetidly shat and copycatted in Sofia following the red comrades' orders. In their majority they were born through incest, offspring of military, imbeciles who have been involved in homosexual practices since early childhood. Genetically defective individuals, Nature's Mistake with a capital 'M'. They are lowlife creatures whose presence on Mother Earth is absolutely unjustified.

- **Have you ever been seriously wounded or injured while fighting?**

Sure, back in 1996 at Gerena during the first leg of a cup tie against CSKA, minutes into the second half, we, 20-30 lads (ONLY!) Steamed into the CSKA fans end and started beating them. They bottled it right away but started throwing stones at us and one of those stones hit my head. Blood started pouring down my face and I had to seek medical help from the doctor on duty at the ground, so I missed Levski's winner scored by Marian Hristov.

- **Where does your favourite football club stand in your life and how important is it for you?**

Now I'm gonna try to skip all those clichés that it means everything to me, it is my religion, etc. However, one's beloved club is forever, I mean you may change your wives, cars, homes, everything else except your beloved football club! And you ought to support it in both good and bad times, for better or for worse as they say.

Even if it is relegation down to the lowest division possible. Even if it has 20 defeats in a row! You just ought to! And you do not comment on your favourite club, you just love it! And you must me ready to do your best, give everything you've got and make sacrifices for your club on a daily basis. Where does Levski stand in my life!? I'll give you one example only to make it clear for everyone. On one of my wife's birthdays, instead of celebrating together with my family, I went to the airport to meet Djurgardens IF official delegation because we were playing an anniversary friendly with them on the following day. My wife is still cross with me for that up to this very day, but I just had to be there, it was my sense of duty. Someone had to do it. For Levski and for all Levski fans. And in this particular case it was not a matter of a football game, but a matter of something else related to my beloved club. Actually, it was a matter of duty!

- **Which are your favourite designer brands?**

Ben Sherman, Henry Lloyd, Stone Island, Fred Perry, Lacoste.

- **What is your wildest favourite club related dream?**

Watch Levski play a European Cup final!

- **Which is your favourite game of all times?**

Well, I hesitate between two games, the one we beat Stuttgart 1-0 at home with a goal scored in 90th minute and the one we knocked out Scottish giant Rangers 2-1 with a screamer scored by The Kaiser in the dying seconds of the game. Unbelievable experiences, unforgettable moments!

- **Who are your favourite players?**

In Bulgaria I have no doubt about it, its' Gibby! Along with him came the entire generation of Dobromir Zhechev (our great coach) babes like Velev, Iliev, Sirakov … but they all stand in the shadow of His Majesty Gibby! Worldwide it is Gazza! Well, now, they may not be among the most successful players, but they were magicians, they were made of a different clay and different from all the rest! Geniuses! Let's add John Terry from my favourite English club...You won't see a player, a captain and a leader of his character for quite a long time, that's for sure!

- **Would you name the top 5 Bulgarian firms/crews/mobs?**

Beyond a shadow of a doubt, the number one Bulgarian firm since its very establishment back in 1999 has been the one and only Sofia West. Runners-up are Levski Ultra Varna as they have proven themselves for all those years. We continue the Top Five with Q.D.V.P., Lauta Hools and probably NUP (Napoletani Ultras Plovdiv). Well, of course I am biased and opinionated but that's the way it is and that's the way it should be (laughing)

- **Which are the best and the worst football grounds you've ever been to and why?**

The best one is Stamford Bridge. I've been to three of its stands. No need to explain in much detail, great location, wonderful facilities, catering, Chelsea Megastore, loads of pubs in its vicinity and so on and so forth. The worst one? Shitholes in Bulgaria are quite a few, so it is hard to tell which exactly the most abominable one is. Probably the one in the town of Montana, right amidst a gypsy ghetto you park your car in a wild muddy wasteland and the view you get comprises some unfinished or half-dilapidated houses with gypsies standing on top of their roofs. Horrible stench, lack of toilets, no water and the dumbest cops you've ever seen. And to top it all, some shabby moronic country girls are selling tickets standing by the away end gate taking them out of dirty carton boxes. Extreme surrealism at a football game. Or barbarism in its pure sense.

- **What do you think of the Bulgarian police?**

97% of the cops in Bulgaria are totally worthless, brainless and spineless scum. The lowest strata of lowlifes in the so called 'society'. Those who are not capable of mastering any other jobs in the world because they are too stupid or worthless become cops. It's a fact! The total IQ of the entire police force in Bulgaria is probably equal to the IQ of a medium-sized amoeba!

- **What do you think of the youths in your firm/crew/mob?**

I think youths should respect their elders. That's the way we were taught, that's what we did and that's how it's supposed to be in the future. They have to give respect in order to be given respect by the next generation in the years to come! Because those who are young now won't stay forever young and before they even know it they will get old. Time flies and it flies terribly fast! Respect – to ensure succession, to ensure heritage because they are essential for the very existence of football mobs. Not fear, but respect is the key word! Nobody is insured against the mistakes made in the process of growth and development. We've made mistakes, everybody's made mistakes, and we're making mistakes even now. But respect and succession should be the foundations on which a firm or any other football related organisation is built and developed.

- **What do you think of the modern-day 'scene'?**

It's much better developed than before. In terms of organisation, things are looking good. Now, probably a lot of guys my age will tell you how good the past was, the romantic away days, the train trips, bla-bla... OK, but everything is good in its season! You can't stay stuck in the mid-1980s or 1990s! Everything changes and develops! The world develops! And unless you keep abreast with the times you simply don't live a full life. It's simple. And we can't do without organised fan clubs, firms, etc. Talking about Levski in particular, if there weren't fan clubs, we wouldn't have played a centenary game against Lazio, nor the anniversary friendly against Djurgardens IF, and a few years ago we wouldn't have taken 15.000, but

149

probably 1500 to the cup final at the seaside town of Bourgas. Nowadays we take at least 300 to each away game every other Saturday. Back in those days we took much smaller numbers travelling by rail! So, the modern-day scene is well organised, a lot of efforts are made, and resources spent, and we have visible results like flags, tifos, conventions... Lads know each other, keep each other's back, help each other, and stick together... What I don't like, however, is the use of weapons by some. There are morons in every mob, we have them too. I don't understand why one has to be armed to one's teeth in order to feel safe. Some day someone will die and then we'll all be harmed! What is more, if you carry a weapon, you have to know how to use it because when you take a tool out and you don't know what to do with it, they may take it from you and someone else may get hurt. We had this case recently. Well, I could approve of a stone, a chair, a bit of wood, or whatever you may lay your hands on impulsively in a fight, but knives, iron bars, knuckledusters and any other tools specially made to kill and maim - NEVER!

- **What do you think of English hooligans and their influence?**

Top notch of all times! The inventors of the 'game'! What they did for years, even for decades, across stadia and streets, cannot be done by anyone else! And I'm talking about ordinary blokes, not some MMA fighters or anabolic workout monsters like the modern-day Russian, Polish, Hungarian and other hooligans. And it was the influence of the English hooligans that gave birth to all the other firms across Europe. With no exception! Each and every one has consciously or subconsciously followed and copycatted the English model and has been affected by the English disease as the press liked to call it. Therefore, respect, and huge respect only to the English!

B. (B.) - Botev (Plovdiv)

Meet and greet

- **How old are you and when did you become a fan of your favourite club?**

My name's B. B., I'm 48 and I support Botev from the town of Plovdiv. I used to live close to the stadium, so I've been a football fan for as long as I can remember. I was drawn into the game big time and the rest is just history…There was no other way for a kid like me. When I was 15 or 16 I got into that ultras and hardcore thing.

- **Would you tell us how your firm (crew/mob) was established?**

I dare say I was one of the founders of one of the oldest and probably the first Bulgarian firm called Izgrev Boys. It happened in 1991-92 right after I did my military service. In the beginning it was a suburban firm as in the late 1980s I moved to a suburb in Plovdiv. It was a typical poor, working-class area full of crime; you know what they call "rough areas". Maybe in a year or two we managed to shape up a good-sized crew that went together to games from our neighbourhood. Later on, we set up a more serious organisation with its prominent leaders and better preparation for games. Flags, trips, ambushes and the like. So, if you ask me (and I guess others, too) Izgrev Boys was one of the first orderly and

152

well-structured hooligan-style organisations in Bulgaria. Come to think of it after all I've seen, the 1990s were really the heyday of hooliganism. It was not only Botev, but all the rest. It was then this trend was born (in its more refined form). Maybe it was the result of all democratic changes and the social vacuum and chaos that reigned. Also, it was the clear separation between rich and poor. It all led to the formation of the so called marginal groups as cops like to call us. Going even deeper whatever, we may say about this period, we were rather nasty and mean motherfuckers (laughing). We wouldn't go to stadia for the sake of football only. Surely, we went to support our club, but our major goals were getting drunk, fighting and going on a rampage. So, all in all, we have to admit we were bad boys and that's not only my opinion, but the opinion of everyone I have talked to. In their modern-day condition, Bulgarian football mobs are not capable of doing that. I always used to live alone, so we'd meet up at my place, some 15-20 lads, 2 or 3 days before match day. There we'd go on the piss and we'd make dozens of red lead and bronze bombs. Each time we'd take at least 20 bombs and for some games we'd take up to 50-60. Chains, knuckledusters, pool cues and generally everything you can think of, with one goal only – to challenge the locals and fight them with no fear just in order to get the thrill of it. I'll not conceal it that I was always in the front rows that would start the fight without ever thinking twice. It was just that at some point, after all those fights and riots and gangster lifestyle, fear is gone, and you start to consider it as something quite normal. Me and my mates have never avoided confrontation and clashes, on the contrary, we'd always be up for it (winking). We'd often go through the Shipka mountain pass on our way to towns in Northern Bulgaria and we'd loot all the shops and pubs and cafes we'd come across. They even started to leave a box of beer outside only to prevent us from going inside boozers as sometimes we'd even steal their fridges (laughing).

- **How would you define yourself as a fan?**

Taking into account that I am pretty old but still active and I go on being involved in this stuff, I must be pretty extreme.

- **Would you tell us in more details about some fights you have been involved at stadia and on the streets?**

As I said before, life was a constant fight so there's a lot to tell. We had some great fights with Levski back in the days, then it was Neftochimic once or twice before we became allies. We'd go at Spartak Varna, Beroe, Dunav, Lokomotiv G.O., where we had two battles inside the ground, one of them being a pitch invasion. Also, there was this pitch invasion in the town of Samokov, where we fought the security guards of that arrogant feudal tyrant, who proposed live wires being installed on top of fencing because of us! In your first book Beyond the Hatred you mentioned our cup game in Tarnovo against Levski that you must have attended in the flesh. So, I won't repeat it here, but I'd just highlight it as a great example of brutal fight. There is another brawl with Levski, where we were outnumbered. We crossed paths at the seaside, on the road between Nesebar and Sunny Beach. We were playing Chernomorets (if I'm not mistaken) so we went up with some ten cars to Sunny Beach. It was summer already and there we were in the head, waist-naked and drinking beers. On our way to Burgas we made the huge mistake of splitting up. Some of us took the ring-road and the rest of us (4-5 cars) made it through the town centre. What we didn't know was that on the same day Levski were playing Cherno More at a neutral venue in Nesebar. As we were passing by the ground (long before their kick-off time), bottles, stones and debris were hurled at us. Some 15 of us got out and had a go at them. However, it turned out they were more than 30 and well up for it. We had it toe to toe. One of them went down hanging down my neck. I turned around and saw they'd nicked one of our scarves. We started fighting to get it back and there were those 5-6 minutes of brutal fighting. More Levski appeared and we had to withdraw as we also heard some police sirens. One of our cars was with a shattered back window, a metal pipe sticking out of it. The cops stopped us, and I was taken back for identification. Naturally, neither we, nor they identified each other, which must be added to both sides' credit. Some were taken away to hospitals and I think one of their top lads got a broken leg.

If I have to share with you the opponents that have been given the best hiding by us, that's definitely Lokomotiv Sofia. It happened at the 1995 cup final played in Sofia and the accident got a lot of coverage in the media. After the game we got on our coaches and were off to Plovdiv. Unfortunately for them, our coach was the last to leave. On board there were top faces only. As we were leaving, we felt the coach was being hit by stones. We told the driver to stop and out we were. The first bloke I saw was one of those who were abusing us the most during the game. A long-haired metalhead (very typical of those times). I've beaten guys and I have been beaten, but, I'll tell you what, never have I seen a man been beaten like that! In the end, I rolled up a lock of his hair around my finger and pulled it as hard as I could, peel off a part of his skin. Long time afterwards that scalp stood in the room of a mate of mine, like a real war trophy (laughing). I got tired of hitting him, so I let the others finish him. I looked around and it was a battlefield. We scattered all around the park on a punitive mission all the way down to the Eagles Bridge. There we met our doom, got into a prostrate position and nicked. Some 15 of us got arrested, three of them went to an expedited trial and the rest were ordered a 15-day community service in a brick field where the party went on... (laughing).

There was a good ruck in Croatia, where we managed to almost join forces for the Bulgarian national team game. In the beginning there were some 10-12 of us drinking in a boozer. The other Bulgarians were downtown and when we set off to join them, out of the blue came some 40-50 guys, all dressed in black and some carrying baseball bats. That was Dynamo Zagreb BBB (Bad Blue Boys) crew and they expected us to leg it just because of their reputation, but that simply didn't happen and soon they realised they were wrong. We stood back-to-back right there, in the middle of the street and they ran towards us. At some point it got rather confusing as we wouldn't give up an inch and they just stopped in front of us and even tried to start a kind of conversation. One of our lads had this glass of whiskey and it was the thing that sparked off the events to happen as they tried to take away from him the most valuable thing he had, i.e. booze. The moment someone grabbed for his glass, it all kicked off big time. For about a minute there were punches and kicks and falls and rises... again and again. All of a sudden, it ended just as abruptly as it had started. Both groups stepped back and, in the middle, between us, there was this Croatian lad lying on the ground, unconscious and choking! Immediately, without thinking twice, I shoved a cigarette lighter in between his teeth, we turned him round and got his tongue out, opening his airway. Next thing we saw were the riot police arriving on the scene. They just couldn't believe their eyes. They asked us what the matter was, but both we and the Croats kept silent. The set us apart and while I was passing by the BBB ranks one of their guys whispered, "Thank you, bro!" Finally, I'll mention our fights with the Lokomotiv Plovdiv gypsies, but I won't tell you stories about them as they are simply a daily routine for us (laughing).

- **Who are your rivals (in the general sense of the word, in life or at the stadium), what are they like and what is your opinion of them?**

If I have to name a proper rival, I did that in my stories involving Levski and our other rival is crystal clear, and it is Lokomotiv Plovdiv, but I won't spare much of my time for them, nor waste the readers' time telling what I think of them. Everybody knows my opinion of them (winking).

- **Have you ever been seriously wounded or injured while fighting?**

Of course, I have... Once you're in the front rows fighting there's no other way. I have had my head cracked at least 4 or 5 times. I've had some serious problems with my elbow joint as once it was so swollen that I couldn't move my elbow for 20 days following a ruck with the Neftochimic mob. I had my eyebrow cut in the town of Ruse and so on and so forth.

- **Where does your favourite football club stand in your life and how important is it for you?**

Family, friends, club, that's my order of priority, though friends and clap overlap in my case as most of my friends are Botev fans. Be it the mob or the football club, I've always tried to belong to a great and united family. Well, I do have friends supporting other clubs, but my closest ones are the ones I go out with, work with and go to the football. Now, my top priority is my real family and they are the most important people for me and I do put them on pedestal!

- **Which are your favourite designer brands?**

We're a wee bit old school for that stuff. Not that we have old-fashioned views and avoid wearing such brands, but they came in strong with the casual wave and we simply didn't give a fuck about such things back in the days. There was no time to waste dressing up in front of a mirror! So, following this chain of ideas, I'm no slave to brands and I still don't pay much attention to this stuff. I don't think it matters much whether it is Fred Perry or Stone Island and my opinion is that fandom should not be so dependent on fashion. My personal favourite is Adidas.

- **What is your wildest favourite club related dream?**

At present, my biggest dream is finishing the construction of our home, our own football ground. In any case, in terms of football, we've established a certain style and we are recognised by that style. We made our comeback to where we belong, i.e. the Bulgarian top flight. Naturally, as a supporter of a big club that have become champions, I'd like to see Botev once again winning the league, but currently there are other things on the agenda.

- **Which is your favourite game of all times?**

This question is like asking a kid in a candy store which his or her favourite cookie is (laughing). It's so hard to answer. How can I pick a single game when I've been to so many epic ones!? Some of them were lost, but still they remain great games! Probably our European adventures with Bayern and Barcelona were our peak, our best achievement as a football club.

- **Who are your favourite players?**

I'll tell you right now, these are the players that got me into football and made me a Botev fan, our old generation guys like Zehtinski, Pashev, Pehlivanov, etc. They were not just players, they were magicians playing the game not for money and fame, but for the sake of the game itself.

- **Would you name the top 5 Bulgarian firms/crews/mobs?**

Easy question, short answer. I don't need to focus on us or even mention Lokomotiv Plovdiv as it goes without saying (winking). Sofia West and Animals go on top! No matter how much controversy there may be regarding them being football mobs or criminal gangs, they are at the top!

- **Which are the best and the worst football grounds you've ever been to and why?**

Oooh, I've seen more than enough of poor grounds when we played in the lower divisions during one of the most disgraceful periods in our club's history that went for almost 10 years. We've seen enough of similarities of stadia in the 2nd and 3rd divisions, not to mention the fact that even some stadia in the top division look more like training grounds. The best grounds I've been to are European ones that hosted Botev's away games.

- **What do you think of the Bulgarian police?**

Parasites! I'll tell you what I mean. In Bulgaria, the problem with football hooliganism is way too exaggerated so that some people are deliberately involved, separate units are set up to prevent it and so significant resources are allocated to fight something that actually does not exist. Small clubs are having their arms twisted as they are forced to pay the police for providing security at small games that might as well be guarded by private security companies.

- **What do you think of the youths in your firm/crew/mob?**

Oh, it's hard to judge now. It was much different in the times when we used to raise hell and there's no ground for comparison. I mean, you had to do something really bad in those days in order to end up in court. I, for example, for all the silly things I've done, have been sued for football hooliganism three times only. First it was the town of Sliven where I got a 5-year ban not only for their ground but for the entire town (not that I've had to, or I've ever missed it). The second time was in my hometown Plovdiv after fighting Levski. But in the majority of cases you'd get nicked for 24 hours. You'd be given a good hiding to sober up and, in the morning, you'd be outta it. That's what I call a proper punishment for a football fan that was well up for it. Nowadays it's much more complicated for the youths. You get nicked and you get sued. A speedy trial and you're doing time before you realise it. So, it logically had its negative effects on youngsters and they had their good reasons to hide and end up making ambushes and prearranging fights while at the same time grounds are still empty. For all those reasons, Botev in particular lost one or two generations and wasted 5-10 years, but now I see there are decent lads that think in a slightly different way. I am happy to see such boys and I do hope they keep the hooligan spirit alive!

- **What do you think of the modern-day 'scene'?**

If you're asking me about the football scene, it's an absolute shit, and if football is a disgrace, then everything else also is. As far as the hooligan scene is concerned, I don't think much of this modern trend in Eastern Europe that has also affected our country. Lads going to gyms instead of stadia, drink water instead of beer so that they don't have beer bellies and therefore look better... Allegedly a healthier lifestyle, but ultimately involving chemicals and drugs. I already mentioned the pre-arranged 20 vs 20 or 30 vs 30 fights and then, ultimately, we have those ambushes and weapons ignoring the agreed Code of Conduct! I find all of this not even close to football hooliganism and after the recent events I expect it will soon be included in the Olympics (laughing).

- **What do you think of English hooligans and their influence?**

There's no way we can deny that we all learned from them. Truth to tell, they really were my role models though I've never copycatted any foreign models and I don't have a favourite English or other foreign football club apart from my native Botev! Anyway, we looked more like Italians, using long-pole flags, pyro and other similar ways of support. However, there were also the Union Jack tops, flags, etc. I think we resembled the English not so much in terms of appearance and clothes, but in terms of their famous tireless support and adamant spirit, which, especially in our punk years, made us feel free to do whatever we wanted wherever we wanted and feel proud that nothing and no one could stop us! Going back to your particular question I'll finish by saying that the English were hooligans in the 70s and 80s and then their influence was pretty strong.

P.S.

Now I'd like to mention my long-time mate Chelsea George, who recently went to play the hooligan game at some other place beyond... We miss you... Hools Never Die!

K. A. (M.) - Lokomotiv (Plovdiv)

Meet and greet

They call me K. M.; I'm a die-hard supporter of Lokomotiv Plovdiv and Manchester Utd. I was invited by the authors of this book (I've known them for years) to share some memorable experiences from my life either as a football supporter or hooligan, it's up to you to judge.

- **How old are you and when did you become a fan of your favourite club?**

I'm 43, third generation Lokomotiv fan.

- **Would you tell us how your firm (crew/mob) was established?**

Our firm was founded way back in 1992 under the name of Tequila Boys, which came from the boozer I was running then under the same name. Before that, in the 1980s, football related hooliganism did exist as there were quite a lot of fights, but it was all chaotic and disorganised. In 1990 I first went to England to watch my other favourite club Manchester Utd. Afterwards I started going to United games on a regular basis (I still do), my mates being active members of the Red Army and ICJ (Inter City Jibbers). There I saw a lot of things related to organisation, mentality, dress code and football culture in general. Eventually what I saw helped us establish the first casual crew in Bulgaria. So, in 1992 we founded a small firm of like-minded people, some of which still belong to it up to this day. We also made our first flag, i.e. Tequila Boys. To pay respect to British football culture we'd also put up the Union Jack, which is still present at football grounds and is actually the main flag of our firm. We started going together to away games, meet up before home games and soon we became recognisable on the Bulgarian scene. Years later, when the boozer closed down, we decided to change our name to Lauta Hools, the name that earned us fame and still stands for the beginning of casual culture in Bulgaria. After long years of troubles and riots we instigated, the police started giving us a hard time, so we decided to change our name to The Usual Suspects and that's the name we are known by nowadays.

- **How would you define yourself as a fan?**

Radical, loyal till death to my club.

- **Would you tell us in more details about some fights you have been involved at stadia and on the streets?**

There are many. Back in the 1980s there were fights after almost every game, especially when we played the 'parrots' (Botev) and the 'pigs' (CSKA). It was anarchy. Glorious days. Night trains, fights at railway stations, no escorts to stadia and you're free to fight anyone, arrests and after a few slaps they'd let you out. It was great fun and it was unforgettable.

In the 1990s things became slightly more organised. We'd meet up and walk in groups having clearer aims and ideas. We started making a difference between rank and file fans and radical ones and tried to lay down those unwritten laws not to harm ordinary supporters. As I already said, we had numerous fights, but some of the recent ones deserve special attention.

First, it's the Ariana pond case involving CSKA. Everything was perfectly planned. The start of the journey, the route, the arrival, the attack and all our actions. Though we had smaller numbers we had a go at them in front of their own ground. We just did them. There were no more than 60-70 of us and they came from all sides. They must have been hundreds. Mounted police were brought in to separate us. It was a vicious melee. What we did then is still unparalleled, no other firm has ever done that in Bulgaria.

I remember a friendly we played with the 'parrots'. Four of us separated and went to the ticket desks at their ground. It was full of yellow fans. We had a good ruck as no one bottled it an inch. The cops themselves told us afterwards that we must be pretty insane to do such things. Later on, that day we suspended the game as we started a fight with the Botev fans inside the ground. I used a police truncheon that I had taken from a cop during the fight. After the game there were more riots on the streets. A crazy day. We were in top shape then. At the end of the day we sat down to have a few beers, all of us having bruises and cuts. Unforgettable (laughing).

The street fights with the 'parrots' are also quite memorable. There were two brawls involving 100-150 lads each side. Our famous attack on 24th May in front of their ground turned into a vicious clash, something that could hardly ever happen again. Last year there was a brutal fight on the highway and we did them good. Shame for them that in the end their top boys just surrendered and raised their hands high so that we could stop beating them.

The pre-arranged 40 vs 40 fight with CSKA on the field, though contrary to my football hooliganism beliefs, was a quite nice encounter and our victory seemed to settle the current discussions which the toughest firm is. I still remember what monsters they brought there, but we just proved that what really matters in a fight is one's heart and not one's size.

There is also another incident when the reds lied to us and we were waiting for them in a schoolyard for a pre-arranged fight. Meanwhile they tried to get through our ground main stand entrance, but we realised what they were up to and we crossed paths with them near the ground and we crushed them badly chasing them for almost half a mile. They took a really good hiding that day.

Sandanski[14] was another incident that will forever remain in history. After CSKA refused to meet us on the road between Sandanski and the town of Blagoevgrad and told us to go to Sandanski if we wanted to have a fight, we first drove past Blagoevgrad, where Lokomotiv was playing and headed on for Sandanski. We got stopped by the cops and they asked us where we were going, and we said we were CSKA supporters, so they let us drive on (laughing). There were two coach loads of us. Only top boys. We stopped right in front of the away end and had a go at them. They escaped and took shelter inside the ground and locked the doors. Those of them who couldn't make it inside were given a vicious hiding. We also fought the cops so one of them fired his pistol in the air. We were on all evening news and even the President at that time made a statement regarding hooliganism. Then the Old Bill nicked us all, two coaches, on our return to Blagoevgrad. They ran out of handcuffs, so they only arrested 40 lads. Some were detained for a month in the local nicks and some did four months in prison in Plovdiv. The worst result of that incident was the first sentence given by a Bulgarian court for football hooliganism to our mate I. V. (B.), who spent 3 years in jail. The whole story is still unprecedented for our country up to this very day.

I'll never forget how I went into Botev's end at their ground with another mate of mine. It was years ago when they used their former stand. One of their top boys came to 'talk' to me and we were about to have it right there on the terraces, but the cops set us apart. However, years later we did settle our arguments. He knows the score (winking).

When we played Neftochimic in their town of Burgas we had a go at them in front of their home end. Baseball bats, bombs, stones, great ruck it really was. They took quite a good hiding and then they came to our end with the police in order to help the cops identify us. Loads of lads got nicked then. There is nothing more despicable and vile than a snitch.

In Europe we had a good ruck with OFK Beograd after our game in Bourgas. The two coachloads from Belgrade were really top notch, but we did well on that pitch-dark night. Unfortunately, one of our lads got stabbed and his condition was rather serious. It was also interesting in Brugge as we had a good ruck in the central square the night before kick-off. And, of course, we did Bolton. We chased them down all over Bourgas, but our mob then was brutal, top lads only. There must have been about 200 of us in 1993, when we attacked Lazio near the ground and the cops fired shotguns.

Most of the accidents mentioned above are well documented both on video and paper. There are many other stories from 1980s, the 1990s and up to this day, but I'll need a separate book to tell them all (laughing).

- **Who are your rivals (in the general sense of the word, in life or at the stadium), what are they like and what is your opinion of them?**

The 'parrots' have always been our main rivals. You know, we come from the same town. I've had dozens of fights with them through the years. They have never had any morals and dignity. After each negative incident, and believe me, there are many, they come up with the same old story, same old lies and they twist things in such a ridiculous way that they even start believing their own lies. That's how they got their nickname, i.e. 'parrots'. The other reason is that they've been copying and stealing our songs ever since the 1980s. I can't have any respect for such people. They'll always be second in our town of Plovdiv. CSKA are also our enemies, but I do have some respect for them!

- **Have you ever been seriously wounded or injured while fighting?**

Yes, I have. Broken front teeth after being hit with a stone, a broken arm, stitches in my upper lip, cracked leg and left-hand bones. I don't count the bruises and shiners (laughing).

- **Where does your favourite football club stand in your life and how important is it for you?**

Lokomotiv Plovdiv is and will be a way of life for me.

- **Which are your favourite designer brands?**

Armani Jeans, Hugo Boss, Adidas Originals and Puma trainers.

- **What is your wildest favourite club related dream?**

European games, where we could try our strength against foreign mobs. It's a pity we very rarely qualify for European games, but when we do, we have a great time as was the case with Lazio, Brugge KV, OFK Beograd, and Bolton.

- **Which is your favourite game of all times?**

Probably the game against the 'parrots' at Lauta when we won 1-0, the goal being scored by Salamanov in 86th minute.

- **Who are your favourite players?**

Lokomotiv Plovdiv's Kurbanov and Ayan Sadukov and United's Brian Robson.

- **Would you name the top 5 Bulgarian firms/crews/mobs?**

Lokomotiv Plovdiv, Levski, CSKA, the 'parrots' and Minyor Pernik from the 1980s.

- **Which are the best and the worst football grounds you've ever been to and why?**

That's maybe Brugge stadium we went to on our European away days. The bad grounds are countless (laughing). But Metalurg Pernik ground is probably the worst of all (laughing).

- **What do you think of the Bulgarian police?**

In the past it was easy dealing with them. Now they are more in the know and it's much harder for us, but if there is a will, there is a way.

- **What do you think of the youths in your firm/crew/mob?**

Young lads who are devoted to our cause. We try to get them into the habits of our trade because we won't last forever.

- **What do you think of the modern-day 'scene'?**

In general, our scene is rather poor save for a few firms. There are some rays of light, but they are not willing to follow the unwritten rules and even a Code of Conduct has been signed, things between hools are going on in the same old way. Lads are still being ambushed and heavily outnumbered, rank and file supporters are still being attacked, guns are still being used and every second boy is always carrying a knife. I hope nobody gets killed soon!

- **What do you think of English hooligans and their influence?**

Respect for them for everything they did throughout the years. They first introduced what everybody else in Europe followed 20 years later. For me they'll always be Number One!

14 SANDANSKI – A SMALL TOWN IN SOUTHWEST BULGARIA, NEAR THE BORDER WITH GREECE

A. S. (D.) - Neftochimic (Bourgas)

Meet and greet

- **How old are you and when did you become a fan of your favourite club?**

I'm 47 now, I became Neftochimic fan when I was 14 and they were still playing in the third division. It was my uncle who got me into the "greens".

- **Would you tell us how your firm (crew/mob) was established?**

A year before we got promotion to the top division, in the early 1990s, we had this promotion decisive feature against Spartak in Varna. Though still tacitly. Lukoil had already started sponsoring our club and invested loads of money so that we could reach our much-cherished goal. Spartak Varna beat us 1-0 scoring from a ridiculous penalty and so we failed. Our President Portochanov swore that we would not fail ever again so in the next campaign we finished top of the table with a huge gap between us and the runners-up and we got promoted to the top flight. I consider

166

that period as the origin of our relatively young organisation and in addition to the very football; we also had to develop as support. In the beginning there were only about 50 of us, Chernomorets being the club of Burgas at that time, so we had only some 5% of the supporters in town. However, things gradually started going our way. I cannot deny that this was due to strong propaganda and serious investments. They started manufacturing fans' items (in thousands), we had cheap coach trips on away days and that was how our numbers grew to hundreds. The very firm set up in Sarafovo Quarter, most of us being far right-wing. Our flags and banners featured bulldogs, Celtic crosses and other symbols of similar kinds.

- **How would you define yourself as a fan?**

Hardcore, far-right wing (winking).

- **Would you tell us in more details about some fights you have been involved at stadia and on the streets?**

I remember more than 30 fights and I've got a sentence for football related hooliganism, so I guess you understand there's no way I can tell include all of them in my story. The biggest fight I've been involved in was in the town of Varna, not against Spartak, but Cherno More. In general, we hate the Gagauz (quite justifiably taking into account the struggle for domination at the seaside), but we hate Spartak more than Cherno More because the former were punks and anarchists while the latter at least shared our ideas. We had a great time on that day... We brought 6-7 coach loads... Tickets for away fans cost 3 BGN and those for the home ones only 1 BGN so we rose against it because the difference of 2 BGN cost a few beers (laughing). We stormed the ground and entered ticketless. Inside they regrouped and had a go at us using stones and bombs and poles. A toe-to-toe followed, both parties standing their ground for almost 5 minutes. Finally, we got the upper hand after lots of head butts, punches and kicks, but the OB intervened in full riot gear and beat the shit out of us! After the final whistle the home mob wanted to lynch us, and they had primed themselves well with home-made bombs. Another brilliant and to some extent pre-arranged fight we had with Lokomotiv Plovdiv. I'll give you the background. We had already made alliance with Botev when we played the cup final against Levski in Plovdiv (the yellow-and-blacks lending us a hand) and then we had to play another cup tie against Lokomotiv on a Wednesday. We prearranged a 10 vs 10 fight, away from the eyes of the cops in a village called Zhitarovo, but they were late, so we left. We sat in a boozer and we saw 4 or 5 blokes wearing black-and-white jerseys, so we naturally took them off from them. They must have called their mob then and in less than half an hour they had a go at us from both sides. They were armed with pipes, baseball bats, planks of wood and in the melee that followed my blood brother M. was seriously hurt after being hit with a cobblestone in his knee. Once he was down, I tried to drag him away and then I also got injured but I'll tell you more about it later.

- **Who are your rivals (in the general sense of the word, in life or at the stadium), what are they like and what is your opinion of them?**

Maybe my words will come as a surprise for many who are not into fans' animosities and expect I'd say Chernomorets (our town rivals), but actually most of them are good friends of mine and we go on the piss together. Back in the days I used to run a heavy metal store and they'd all come to shop (winking). I already mentioned Spartak Varna as major rivals but despite our hostility, I also give credit for them for certain past occasions. Well, you find me in a good and friendly mood today (laughing out loud). The only ones who won't be given credit by anyone are Beroe cunts. I won't go into details, but we have nicked each other's flags (they did it in a rather mean way), on another occasion they snitched on us to the cops and on yet another one they hurled bombs at the train we were on. So that's where our animosity comes from. We've tried to close them down a few times, but in the meantime, they'd come to buy pyro from us (laughing). And if we're talking of rivals on the pitch I'll say Levski.

- **Have you ever been seriously wounded or injured while fighting?**

During the afore said brawl with Lokomotiv Plovdiv, while I was trying to save my mate I got my nose broken, my head cracked, and my ear torn so our club doctors had to put a few stitches in me ahead of the game.

- **Where does your favourite football club stand in your life and how important is it for you?**

We should have become wiser, but I doubt it (laughing)... Have we!? Long time ago, when I got engaged at the age of 25, I lied to my fiancée that I'm not going to a match, but somewhere else. Sadly enough, I got nicked and to make matters worse I was on the local TV with the handcuffs on. She watched me, and she asked me to choose, so she didn't become my wife, but to answer your question in a more indirect way: NO, I don't regret anything, and I'd do the same things again! My heart beats like that and my club is an inseparable part of it. To cut the long story short, I hate to choose!

- **Which are your favourite designer brands?**

First it is French Lacoste followed by the English Fred Perry and Italian Stone Island. Though I am old-school and almost 50, white trainers are still a must for me (winking).

- **What is your wildest favourite club related dream?**

Right now, it is Neftochimic going back to the top and playing at our own ground, but I doubt it will happen in the near future. At present, Burgas is full of people who are into anything else but not football. But the same goes for all other towns, too! Everywhere!

- **Which is your favourite game of all times?**

My favourite game is when we played Levski in Sofia beating them 2-3, but I don't remember many details. I think we came from behind after Milen Georgiev scored and they were a pretty strong side then.

- **Who are your favourite players?**

No doubt about it, it was Velian Parushev. He had it all, heart and soul and football skills. He was a real man. May God rest his soul in peace! Also, Mitko Trendafilov though he wasn't that successful due to the huge number of great players in his time. Being a Liverpool fan, my favourite foreign player is Stevie G.

- **Would you name the top 5 Bulgarian firms/crews/mobs?**

I'll name cities: Sofia, Plovdiv and Bourgas and I'm not talking about Slavia, Lokomotiv Sofia, Maritsa or Chernomorets of course (winking).

- **Which are the best and the worst football grounds you've ever been to and why?**

Undoubtedly, the worst one is in Pernik (Minyor's ground) and the best one is our ground in Lazur Quarter. The best foreign ground I've been to is Mercedes-Benz Arena in Stuttgart.

- **What do you think of the Bulgarian police?**

I'll go to the fight against Lokomotiv Plovdiv again and I'll tell you what happened afterwards. While both sides were in the nick, we together turned against our common enemy, i.e. the cops. So, we were sitting there wondering who was gonna get in and who would be let go and then we heard them talking about me, 'This guy has done more than enough, it's high time he went to prison...'. So, as I was standing there with all my head injuries, my stitches and freshly torn ear, I banged my head against the sink, blacked out and was directly taken to hospital. That how I got away then. Years later, however, after a fight we had with Chernomorets, the inevitable happened and I did time for football related hooliganism, playing cards in the cell with a Chernomorets lad who is no longer with us... may he rest in peace! Then they started keeping us on a short leash. You couldn't even fart without getting nicked. No way can I have a good opinion of the Old Bill. At one point I loathed them so much that even now, when I think of that, I start feeling really sick.

- **What do you think of the youths in your firm/crew/mob?**

We had some decent generations. They set up a fight club. They go training, but more or less, when the club went into decline and there is no interest, their support is gradually dying out.

- **What do you think of the modern-day 'scene'?**

We have to go back to the topic involving the police, who adopted laws and measures for prevention and fight against people like us and so there was no way for our 'scene' not to get affected. I think football hooliganism is generally dead and soon the time will come for all those Russians and Poles and all that will be left will be books like yours. In fact, that's why I agreed to give this interview and I'd like to congratulate you for what you're doing. Good job, lads!

- **What do you think of English hooligans and their influence?**

I have always believed this issue is related more or less to a country's economic situation and the fans' financial status. Yes, they were class, but as we know it comes from numbers and the English have always been able to bring huge numbers, which resulted in quality. Look now, we also went here and there a few times and we did show the cloven hoof doing a good deal of harm. Suppose we had their resources, forget about paying the bills and other daily stuff and imagine we could afford it. Don't you think we'd also mob up and do the trips!? Anyway, they do deserve a huge respect for what they really did for football and fandom. Truth to tell, they have always been beer monsters (laughing) and I really can't imagine them in a toe-to-toe with some of those sporty lads, but let's wait and see what the future really holds for us (winking).

Y. B. - Beroe (Stara Zagora)

Meet and greet

My name's Y. B. and I was born in 1967. I was invited by the authors of this book and I thank them for that, it's a privilege for me to participate in such a project.

- **How old are you and when did you become a fan of your favourite club?**

I don't remember. I've been going to football since a very early age. First, I went with my Dad and after 1988 on my own.

- **Would you tell us how your firm (crew/mob) was established?**

Beroe fans had no organised firms before 2009. There was just some kind of attraction to the Ultras culture. In 1996 the flag ZARA BOYS appeared and up till now this is the general name of our mob in our sector. In 1999 a few lads made the ULTRAS BEROE flag, but until 2009 they didn't think of themselves as a separate group. My crew (I consider a 'firm' as the next stage of development) CP12 was established in the autumn of 2008, but the official date in view of going to football games in an organised manner and getting involved in any other football related activities (incl. hooliganism) is 14.01.2009.

- **How would you define yourself as a fan?**

As the years go by, I become calmer and more level-headed in terms of football, but blood is thicker than water, you know.

- **Would you tell us in more details about some fights you have been involved at stadia and on the streets?**

There are loads of them, both small and big ones, but I'd rather not talk about it.

- **Who are your rivals (in the general sense of the word, in life or at the stadium), what are they like and what is your opinion of them?**

The ones I hate most are Levski fans, i.e. the 'cattle' and then our enemies from Neftochimic. Levski are one of the two biggest mobs in our country, but I have hated their club since I was a kid and so I also despise Levski fans. As far as Neftochimic is concerned, let there be death! They are nothing else but bitter subhumans and we will beat the shit out of them with no mercy whatsoever every time we meet them, anywhere!

- **Have you ever been seriously wounded or injured while fighting?**

Cracked head, smashed nose, trivial things, you know.

- **Where does your favourite football club stand in your life and how important is it for you?**

Beroe, my family, my homeland, my job…this is the order of my priorities.

- **Which are your favourite designer brands?**

Ben Sherman, Fred Perry, the usual ones. Also, CP and Stone Island, but what matters for me most is the cut and quality. A garment has to be convenient for your hobby.

- **What is your wildest favourite club related dream?**

A European breakthrough, a semi-final in either of the tournaments. I've already been through anything else.

- **Which is your favourite game of all times?**

Beroe vs Levski in 2004. We drew 4-4.

- **Who are your favourite players?**

Players who have proven their love for our club like Vanya Dzhaferovic, Stoycho Dragov, Petar Vinkov. From the current squad I like Ivo Ivanov.

- **Would you name the top 5 Bulgarian firms/crews/mobs?**

CSKA ANIMALS; Levski SOFIA WEST; CSKA TP; Beroe CP 12; Levski South Division

- **Which are the best and the worst football grounds you've ever been to and why?**

The worst one is in the town of Targovishte and the best I've been to is Rapid Wien ground.

- **What do you think of the Bulgarian police?**

Incompetent and illiterate morons. But naturally, there's an exception to every rule.

- **What do you think of the youths in your firm/crew/mob?**

There are no youngsters in our crew, but currently the youth prevails in our club. We don't have the time and it seems we no longer have the same enthusiasm to orchestrate things on match days. We feel somewhat exhausted, drained...We have done time, we have trials pending, cops all over Bulgaria know us by our names. We are a small mob and generally easy to deal with. However, whenever they need us, we're there to help.

- **What do you think of the modern-day 'scene'?**

Chaos, organised chaos...Everyone is a member of something, but there's not a trace of unity either at a club or at a national level. I think that 20 years ago, when fans used to stay away from the club's policy, things were much more transparent and honest. Nowadays everyone's trying to take advantage of the club for their own personal benefit.

- **What do you think of English hooligans and their influence?**

Pure classics, though they look like dinosaurs in the modern environment. The well-built workings out boys have replaced the proverbial pissheads in our modern

Ultras culture. I and my boys are the classic example of OLD SCHOOL HOOLIGANS. We don't need excessive make-believe and too much storytelling and we don't need any flamboyant tifos and pyro works. We are the rough and tough chanting boys.

D. H. (D.) - Lokomotiv (G. O)

Meet and greet

My name's D. and some call me D. I was asked by my mates, authors of this book, to tell in brief about my experience as a Lokomotiv G.O. fan.

- **How old are you and when did you become a fan of your favourite club?**

I'm 42 now, a dedicated football fan since 1989. I was 15-year-old then, but I remember a lot of games from the 1986/87 season when my beloved Lokomotiv got promoted to the top division and stayed there until 1995. It was a real pleasure for me to follow my club everywhere and witness this most successful period in its history.

- **Would you tell us how your firm (crew/mob) was established?**

I'm not much into the modern fan terminology so what kind of firm are you talking about (sounds sarcastic)!? In my times there were no firms, crews and the like. We all stood together and that's why it was way better than nowadays. We'd meet up in old pubs (taprooms), hunter chalets, wine cellars, taverns, garages and basements, where we'd learn and rehearse songs about our beloved club. There were those huge tankards full of cheap beer and our flags were plain sheets, which after getting soaked would get mouldy and heavy and would stinks like a polecat (laughing). There were no organised fan clubs to sponsor away days and tifos, so we'd cup up newspapers until we get blisters on our fingers, roll them up, dip the rolls in Ammonium nitrate and dry them up in the sun just in order to get some choking smoke at games. We'd find cash register rolls and we'd toss them to unwind and fall down the stands. We'd steal curtains from school gyms to make flags and we'd make bombs from red lead and bronze and we'd stick them down our tight elastic jeans crotches... What else is there to say!? You (the authors of this book) are well in the know, but let them younger readers read and know all about it... Wasn't the Jolly Roger firm founded in a basement to the sound of Running Wild way back in 1994 (winking)?

- **How would you define yourself as a fan?**

Now I'd rather say I'm a moderate fan, one who'd hardly lose his temper and do the things he used to do decades ago. But you never know... It's all up to the circumstances and the irritating factor... There are things and people that could definitely awake the beast in me (laughing).

- **Would you tell us in more details about some fights you have been involved at stadia and on the streets?**

Oh, they're so many, and you already wrote a book about us that tells most of those fights and so everybody can buy this book and read all about them (it's worth reading, believe me), so I'll just outline some of them. So starting with the regular brawls with the 'violet shits', I remember at least 5 or 6 of them, 2 or 3 being over the hill as we call the area between Gorna Oryahovitsa and Veliko Tarnovo), deep into enemy lines. Once we tried to take over their home ground main stand and we got involved in a fierce fight in their stand with people rolling all over down the seats. Also, we did this glorious raid (went through them like a hot knife through butter) right in front of the same stand outside the ground before another derby. And then there was the melee in front of the Law Courts in Tarnovo, where they used knives and the next game in our town when we took sweet revenge at the steps that wind all the way from the train station to downtown. Ahead of another derby played in our town we steamed into them as they were strolling round our stadium as if they owned it. We jammed the crossroads, and, in the end, they had to pick up their casualties from the pavement and roads as they simply couldn't walk on their own! But speaking of fights on real away days (because we don't consider Tarnovo as an away game since we spend every weekend there chatting up birds and last time we played there we took 2000 black-and-whites), I remember a brawl in the town of Stara Zagora in front of a rock club when we got defeated (laughing). Now I find it funny, but come to think of it, our youth firm then did not have much fun on that day. But when one gets occasionally defeated there's nothing wrong with admitting to it. And I believe everyone has been defeated at least once, some time, some place, ain't this the truth (winking)?! It wasn't funny in the town of Pernik, when in the second half they chased us down the racetrack after a continuous exchange of punches, but I still think we did relatively well as there were only 6 of us feeling like 'Hobbits in the land of the Orcs'.... Super thrill (laughing). Going back to Stara Zagora, we had great away days there. They weren't a match for us (except for the club incident I already mentioned), so we'd go on a rampage on the streets fighting gypsies at gypsy weddings, playing street rugby with a rag ballin the so-called Faggots Park near the train station, overturning waste bins in bus lanes and even overturning cars. And if it was quite easy to overturn a Trabant, well, try and do it with a Moskvich (laughing)... We did it only because it was green (laughing again).

Now let's turn to bigger and more important events like those in the town of Gabrovo. Every time we'd go there, there would be serious trouble all the way from the railway station to the stadium, inside the ground and on the way back. Each minute and at every corner you'd see more and more blokes joining the fights. Once they nicked a British flag of ours, but then we took it back in a fair fight. It was not fair play, though, when it was us who used knives on another occasion. Pleven was another great destination as early as 1987, when 2000 black and white lunatics went on a rampage there. We'd have good rows with the locals every time we'd play there, both inside the ground when we stormed their main stand and at the railway station. We also had some great time in the town of Shumen going on another rampage and fighting gypsies. There was a hail of stones, smashed ticket booths, fights on the terraces, lads handcuffed to the fencing inside the ground and in the end emergency brake on our train back. So, there were really many occasions and Lokomotiv G.O. have a lot to tell and we are doing it (winking). I'll finish with probably the greatest hooligan classic not only for us, but maybe for the entire Bulgarian hoolie scene. That's the old school classic pitch invasion in Gorna and the fight on the pitch with the 'parrots' from Plovdiv! Well, no one can really deny that it was Botev who started it (they've always been tough and aggressive lot). I think we stood our ground more than well and the fight itself had a little bit of everything: great energy, hatred, cops injured and broken parrots' beaks (laughing). Of course, I have to make it clear that most of those events are documented in pictures and on video, but who cares anyway!? In any case, few are willing to recognise the others in our circles! However, we shouldn't take it too seriously as we were just having fun the way we thought it was best, so full respect to all those involved!

- **Who are your rivals (in the general sense of the word, in life or at the stadium), what are they like and what is your opinion of them?**

Rival in the general sense?! I don't think I have one or at least I hope so. Our stadium rivals are crystal clear, and they wear violet, so I'll spare any more abuse for them. However, as the years went by, we learned that we have to respect our rivals, so I have a couple of friends that wear violet!

- **Have you ever been seriously wounded or injured while fighting?**

The most serious injuries I've had are, quite understandably, the result of exchange of stones, bottles and any other debris, mostly at places with great concentration of minorities like Sliven, for example. It was a real street war and a hail of debris that one could hardly survive unscathed! Otherwise, in a toe-to-toe (full contact), I didn't have much trouble and I've never had a scarf or anything else nicked. By and large, I wouldn't let anybody take liberties close to me (winking).

- **Where does your favourite football club stand in your life and how important is it for you?**

It has a definite place in my life and there's no substitute for it. As far as importance is concerned, currently I have some other priorities, but I definitely put my club on a pedestal and I believe that, though it may be hard, if you really love it, it can go hand in hand with family life. The rest is just excuses.

- **Which are your favourite designer brands?**

I'm not a slave to brands for the simple reason that I take a bigger size and we all know that designer clobber is meant for models, not for beer monsters like us (laughing). Besides, they're rather expensive and I really can't see the point of wearing designer clothes, especially when I go to the football. I find it ridiculous when they wear their best clothes to games and start pouring down beer, climbing up rusty fences, lighting up flares and fighting all over after games. Who needs designer clobber to do that and why they are doing it is a complete mystery for me. I remember the times in the early 1990s when we'd go to football wearing dungarees and when it would get rough we'd go waist-naked, which I still consider as the most suitable and comfortable clobber for us, hardcore fans, for wearing at games! I like to dress nice and tidy. Jackets, jeans, shirts and shoes no matter the brand. And of course, it depends on the particular case because there are formal occasions, you know, but let's say that some Armani sunglasses are more than enough for me (winking).

- **What is your wildest favourite club related dream?**

The wildest? I wish Lokomotiv G.O. had stayed in the top flight, but from what I see is going on there I now have mixed feelings and I think we'd better stay in the lower echelons and turn our attention to youngsters. Yes, probably this is my wildest football related dream, to see my club play with native boys only who are ready to die on the pitch for their fans! Well, is it too wild ... almost chimerical?! Well, it's as good as it gets…the power and the glory are temporary, while honour and dignity are forever!

- **Which is your favourite game of all times?**

It's hard for me to tell, but probably it's CSKA away back in the autumn of 1993, if

I'm not mistaken, when Valyo Ignatov scored a long-distance screamer and we won 1-0.

- **Who are your favourite players?**

Globally, it's Alessandro Del Piero. Some would say we support a club for the club itself and not for the players as they are always temporary, but everybody has their idols. In Bulgaria and in particular in my hometown Gorna Oryahovitsa my favourite is Lyubo Rusev. I just like that type of tireless players. Those who do the hard job on the pitch but are often underestimated and stay in the shadow of all those stars. Even up to this very day, such people continue to have great contribution to my native club and in particular Rusev's sons Vlado and Lucho are exceptionally talented coaches in our youth academy and they simply revived it to a great extent. Hopefully, with their help, my wildest dream will come true someday (winking).

- **Would you name the top 5 Bulgarian firms/crews/mobs?**

Good question, but I guess you get the same answers because the options are not that many. I won't be able to escape from predictability and though I'll try to give a most impartial answer, at the top I'll put Lauta Hools and all of its current subdivisions. Well, when it comes to the past (and modern times also), they were probably the first who dared to set up an organisation that followed a, shall I call it, European (western) model. CSKA also had a notorious skinhead firm called SS Front or the so called Kravai boys. Though they were (and still are) anarchists, Botev Plovdiv had a decent core named Izgrev Boys. Back in the days Levski were rather blokes of all kinds, which presumably meant no organised groups, but nowadays Sofia West are a proper firm and last but not least, without being much biased, (Jolly Roger Firm). Although some may not realise and recognise it, our firm was founded much earlier than some of the above-mentioned firms (no matter how stronger and more numerous they may be), back in the mid-1990s, and I'll make yet another comparison. The leading CSKA firm now, Animals, was established not earlier than the 21st century!

- **Which are the best and the worst football grounds you've ever been to and why?**

When I was a regular at football the worst one was probably the ground in Lovech (when their club was still named Osam). Afterwards it became one of the most modern ones. As far as the best ones are concerned, the grounds in Stara Zagora and Sliven were pretty decent in those times, except for the gypsy crowds that used to gather in the latter (laughing). At present I wouldn't highlight any ground, but for the Lazur Stadium in Buorgas.

- **What do you think of the Bulgarian police?**

Despite the problems we faced in the past (the totalitarian regime and its repressions), it was much easier for us, hools. Nowadays it's much harder and stricter for young hardcore fans. I remember the cops used to beat the shit out of us. A mate of mine was kicked all the way down under a police car and he got a couple of teeth missing. I hated them then and I hate them now, of course. Now they won't kick you in the face but punish you with all the power and all the laws they've got, which makes people hate them even more!

- **What do you think of the youths in your firm/crew/mob?**

I don't have many observations on the 'young wave' so I won't give any judgment or opinion whatsoever. It's a matter of different times and manners and ways. My friendly advice would be that youngsters should respect their elders! I wish them good luck and no surrender.

- **What do you think of the modern-day 'scene'?**

Once again, without being in the know, I find the modern scene as pretty bold, innovative, advanced, progressive and well developed. It relies on much more potential, resources and opportunities. Unfortunately, the most important thing it lacks is … sheer numbers!

- **What do you think of English hooligans and their influence?**

You know my answer to this question. I've never been keen on English football, so I can't answer this. I love Italian football and I follow Juventus (winking).

Y. G. (G.) - Etar (V. Tarnovo)

Meet and greet

My name's Y. G., but they call me G. not only in my hometown of Veliko Tarnovo. I've been living abroad for 15 years... Until recently in Italy (Rome and Naples) and now it is the Czech Republic. Dad was a military and Mum was an accountant.

- **How old are you and when did you become a fan of your favourite club?**

I'm 44, an Etar fan since about 1981-2... I started going to the football when I was only 10, first with my Dad and then with my classmates and friends. Week in, week out, home and away and we got too much carried away (laughing). I grew up in had a relatively decent environment and I had an ordinary childhood. As a military man, my father insisted on discipline and training and he encouraged me to take up sports, so I did wrestling for 10 years. They had great hopes and expectations about me... The sports school wanted me (coaches used to come home), but in the end, a man chooses his own destiny, and no one can predetermine and control it.

The rising movements and trends dragged me into them. As we used to joke then, we became prominent rascals who were into merry-making, parties, beer and football... Our vocation was fandom (laughing).

- **Would you tell us how your firm (crew/mob) was established?**

As I said before and I presume most of the old school lads have also said here... things got shaped up rather spontaneously and soon there was this separate circle, a core of boys of about the same age plus all the younger ones who were attracted to it, willing to copycat and also become somebody in the mob. There were such things and no matter how bad an example they may have seemed back then, nowadays we seem to realise and understand that it wasn't exactly like that. I was also got carried away trying to copycat the elder, but I'm not ashamed of that and now I can boldly state that I'm really proud of it and to some extent it helped us grow up and become men! I remember an away day (I still get the goosebumps when I think about it) with all of its clashes against the locals so typical of those days. A few bombs went off and there was this curtain of smoke and all through that chaos one of our older lads emerged with the Union Jack around his shoulders looking like the Trooper from the Iron Maiden album covers. Well, how could you not get hooked on, having seen all that in the flesh, and how would you not want to feel all those thrills, adrenaline and emotions again and again. It's absolutely priceless and beyond words. You have to experience it.

It all started with heavy metal, loud parties, the feeling of rebellion, the desire to be free and do whatever you want and quite reasonably it was all passed on and reflected on the terraces where we'd express our true selves. In those years of communism, it was progressive and fashionable, and everyone was attracted and wanted to be involved in it. When you see all those people around you are wearing long hair, jeans and sneakers, the Western style in general, well, you can't help being drawn to the modern ways. Some of those people are no longer with us (may God have mercy on their souls), but I can't do without mentioning Ventsi the Pedagogue, who was one of the founders of the movement in Tarnovo and respectively the top boy, the leader of the Etar mob.

Then followed the years of going to pubs, and my home town had plenty of boozers, so I started meeting the older lads there and listened to their stories of their experiences at stadia all over Bulgaria. Stories of buses smashed, fights with rival fans, lads taken off from trains and nicked by the Old Bill. So, I really couldn't help getting involved in it and I started regularly going with them to away games. I skipped school, got fake medical certificates and all kinds of problems with discipline in general. I'd get into more and more quarrels and fights and at some point, it escalated into a much wider scale. Then the intercity parties began. G.O.-Gabrovo-Tarnovo-Lovech-Pleven, for me that region in north central Bulgaria was and still is the Heavy Metal capital of our country.

Even nowadays, when I get to think about it, I'd say we were born and raised for that kind of stuff. It was started suddenly, and it also finished this way for us, but we did experience it, we were really there. Somehow, the very scene and the terraces demanded it and things started and developed easily and in the natural course of events. One thing led to another and quite naturally we grew up and became what we became. It had nothing to do with modern times, where some plastic fans and pampered kids come and go, constantly grumble about something and are always discontented, but I think it's a different topic. And probably the answer to a different question in this interview (winking).

- **How would you define yourself as a fan?**

Well, we, old school boys, were not really hooligans. Anyway, there were no modern and complicated terms back then. We were rascals, urchins (laughing). In modern times I had the opportunity to dip into the ultras culture; I mean the very heart of it, since I lived in Italy, both in Naples and Rome in particular, though I won't be comparing things. I'm not into classifying things and putting them within frames and dogmas. At the end of the day, a man is what he wants to be, an expression of his own feelings and of what he has in his mind and soul.

There's an occasion I'd like to quote as an example and I'd have to confess something. We were playing Botev Plovdiv at home, we won the game and they left the ground prior to the final whistle. I used to live near the ground and I also had to leave it earlier (I don't recall the reason, however), anyway. So, I bumped into them outside, they were just wandering about. I knew what wild mob was about to come out and I felt kinda awkward. It was pretty ridiculous as there were only some 20 of them, 4-5 of which were girls. Not that I betrayed my lot, but I showed the away fans a shortcut to the train station and I even guided them along part of their way. Afterwards we became good mates with one of their lot and when I was doing my military service in their town of Plovdiv, he'd often come and visit me in my unit. That's what we, old school hools, actually were. A punch where a punch is due, respect where respect is due!

- **Would you tell us in more details about some fights you have been involved at stadia and on the streets?**

They are numerous so if I tell you about some of them I'll recall some others also, but among the most vicious ones that come right to my mind now is a game against Cherno More in their town of Varna. It must have been 1989, the campaign we finished third, if I'm not mistaken. It was the final game of the season, crucial for the bronze medals. There were some 120 of us, the core of about 70 went on Friday and the rest (me including) on Saturday, match day. Allegedly, some of our lads knew their top boys at the time, but our core must have started it big time with their mob the previous night as they met us with volleys of bombs and flares and it kicked off all over the seaside park. The cops arrived almost immediately with their truncheons and a mate of mine, who's no longer on this Earth, got injured then. Lots of our lads couldn't watch the game as they got nicked and after the game we were escorted back to the railway station, 8 of us missing in the local nicks. But that was surely not the end of it as at each station on our way back more and more lads were arrested for being involved in fights and only 8 of us made it back home safe and sound.

On another occasion, about 200 of us went on an away game against Slavia and no matter how strange and funny it may seem now (not that they had big numbers or a strong mob back then, either) they were well up for it and it kicked off everywhere, on the streets and between tower blocks, where car windows got shattered and balcony windows were smashed with panes falling down right on our heads. Sheer terror and madness for the residents as some of us went inside their buildings to seek shelter or go on fighting.

Naturally, the majority of accidents would happen during local derbies against Lokomotiv G.O., of which we are about to speak later (laughing)

- **Who are your rivals (in the general sense of the word, in life or at the stadium), what are they like and what is your opinion of them?**

Oh, here's the question right away. I won't think twice, and I won't play up to the authors for a single second, but it's Lokomotiv G.O. My opinion of them is pretty varied (laughing and winking). Truth to tell, for all of us Lokomotiv were a great stimulant and no matter how we'd deny each other's merit, the Bulgarian scene badly misses this derby nowadays.

What is interesting in our case (many would find it surprising) was that ahead of games, no matter whether they were to be played in G.O. or Tarnovo (it would most often be in our town), where nightlife was much better, fellas from G.O. would come almost on a weekly basis, though they did have a few cute Heavy Metal joints that we also liked visiting. However, on match days, all those friendly terms were gone, and we'd confront each other throwing stones over the police lines. It's really pretty weird to see someone who you'd had a few drinks with the other night being hit by a stone that you'd just hurled at the opposite lines. We got involved in some funny incidents where we'd bump into each other in an underground bar in Tarnovo and instead of demolishing the boozer, we'd fling at each other folded up notes with threats written and beers would go from our table to theirs and vice versa but in the form of treats and not missiles (laughing).

Our animosity is really bizarre, but still it exists, and I dare say it is pretty genuine unlike the one claimed to exist between other clubs. Here's my personal explanation: the two towns are so close to each other that they might as well be a bigger city rivalling some of the biggest in our countries (as far as I know, there used to be such an idea in the past), but at the same time they are so far apart and so different in terms of infrastructure and social status of their populations. The working class railway town against the former and eternal cultural capital. A family from Plovdiv, for example, would more often feature both fans of the local Botev and Lokomotiv, but a family from either of our towns would hardly have any fans supporting the two different rival clubs!

Following this chain of ideas, I think we and Lokomotiv G.O. are real professionals and when the two teams come onto the pitch we put all our friendships aside. Generally speaking, in our case, the word 'friendship' is rather conventional as the two towns are so near and yet so far away.

- **Have you ever been seriously wounded or injured while fighting?**

Taking into account that we, the boys from the former Bulgarian capital, were notorious for our bomb squad' skills and resourcefulness, I can assure you I didn't get many injuries. The exceptions are, of course, my stays at police departments where they'd regularly beat me black and blue with their batons and two occasions on which I got my head cracked, once with a police truncheon and the other time it was a stone hurled during a game against CSKA in Sofia. Truth to tell, I really shudder at the thought what dangerous situations we used to get involved in back in those days.

As time went by, our home-made bombs evolved into a dangerous game for advanced. They were no longer those small ones containing two pebbles and a little red lead and bronze wrapped up in sellotape. We started filling up beer cans with Berthollet's salt, Sulphur crystals and Potassium permanganate and then we'd add s few bolds and nuts. Yes, brutal we were, and I have seen it with my own eyes how a solid three-plank bench turned into splinters after such can was blown beneath it, but brutal we were to ourselves, too.

Nowadays I hear fans singing out loud they're ready to die for their club. OK then, try to hide a home-made bomb under your balls and carry it across the entire country on an endless train journey in a compartment where the temperature is as high as 30°C. Well, we'd do this kind of sacrifice to support our club; this was our choreography as we did not have the money to do anything else, but when we'd sing songs swearing allegiance to our club we meant it and we were really ready to prove our words with actions. Probably that's what is actually meant by the phrase 'have balls' cause our balls faced the danger of being blown up at any time (laughing).

- **Where does your favourite football club stand in your life and how important is it for you?**

It stands on the top of my priorities. Even far away from home, I am still interested in what is going on with my club and I try to help the youths. That's how it should be as this is the club I grew up with and the town I still have a number of good mates in. This is the club I'll always keep in my heart, no matter what!

- **Which are your favourite designer brands?**

I've been fond of Armani for many years and I've been wearing its clobber and use its perfumes. I also like Adidas trainers.

- **What is your wildest favourite club related dream?**

My dream is Etar coming back to the top flight (it came true this season), staying there and building a strong team of local lads (to hell with those foreign players purchased by the pound). Also, finishing in the upper part of the table, probably playing in Europe and why not see them becoming champions once again in my life!

- **Which is your favourite game of all times?**

The biggest game I failed to attend in my life was our CL game against FC Kaiserslautern in 1991. However, I watched it on telly and it was the experience of a lifetime. Every time we beat Lokomotiv G.O. I feel almost the same way. As far as games abroad are concerned, I once went to watch Napoli vs Avelino (small town some 40 miles away from Naples) and I remember at the same time Juventus were playing a CL game in front of some 30 00 fans. Well, Napoli hosted Avelino at Stadio San Paolo in front of 70 000! The biggest football crowd I've seen in the flesh was at the fantastic Ciro Ferrara's final game featuring stars like Maradona - 80 000 fans!

- **Who are your favourite players?**

I can't help mentioning here the golden team of Etar who went on to become the backbone of our national squad: Krasi Balakov, Tsanko Tsvetanov, Boncho Genchev, Iliyan Kiryakov and all the rest. Globally, the Manchester Utd.. and the English national team stars then, and if we speak of personalities, geniuses like Gundi, Cantona and naturally Maradona, and of underestimated, but highly talented players, I'd say Emil Spasov from Levski and United's Lee Sharpe.

- **Would you name the top 5 Bulgarian firms/crews/mobs?**

That's easy: Sofia clubs, Plovdiv clubs and in the past we, Etar, and Lokomotiv G.O. were top of the notch. Probably also Varna mobs, way above the mobs of Bourgas clubs. We had this alliance with Beroe, but I personally would not rate them among the top hardcore mobs.

- **Which are the best and the worst football grounds you've ever been to and why?**

The best is San Paolo, understandably, San Paolo because of its atmosphere. The worst must be somewhere on the Balkans and the first that comes to my mind is in the town of Sliven, but I won't go into particular details and explanations why. It's just an abominable place… infested by gypsies and I think that's more than enough.

- **What do you think of the Bulgarian police?**

At football grounds, in particular, they are the ones who start all the provocations and all the aggro. It's been like that ever since the communist era. I already told you about the black and blue beatings I've received by them so there's no way for me to have any positive thoughts about them (laughing).

- **What do you think of the youths in your firm/crew/mob?**

We have some decent lads, I know them, but they somehow lack that zeal, if I can use this word. Tifos and … that's it. They don't focus on friendship, comradeship, unanimous clapping and chanting if you like. On the contrary, it's all splits and divisions and arguments who's to take the megaphone, who's gonna to listen to him and who's not... Firms and crews and all those countless complications. Truth to tell, smaller clubs like ours are much better. Though fewer in numbers, genuineness and quality are much better. The way the grand clubs' organised supporters are doing simply makes me sick.

- **What do you think of the modern-day 'scene'?**

What I already said is to a great extent true for the Bulgarian scene in general. I dislike fans' mentality. Big clubs drain up the resources of smaller ones and so they 'kill' a good few local derbies. I tend to merge the last two questions (as I find them similar), but I'll say here that in my hometown we have a great example of that and I do have certain affinity for Levski FC, but I'll never put them before my native club as a lot of other Etar fans actually did!

- **What do you think of English hooligans and their influence?**

They are all-time Number One, and no one can take that away from them, no matter what efforts some have been putting recently. It's just that we all have learnt from them and we still keep on learning. I find all those efforts as futile and temporary. The English have always been and will always be unrivalled and out of reach as far as football related hooliganism is concerned. My English flag still stays put on my wall!

(V.) - Spartak (Pleven)

Meet and greet

- **How old are you and when did you become a fan of your favourite club?**

My name's I. and I'm 34 years old. I've been going to Spartak since 1993. Blame it on my Dad, who was also a Spartak supporter. Most fans know me also as V.

- **Would you tell us how your firm (crew/mob) was established?**

In the late 1990s Spartak fans united and set up Spartak Pleven fan club. We started making flags and fan items, organising away trips, raising money for tifos, etc. As a result of poor organisation and folks unsuitable for the job, things started going wrong and in a few years the fan club was closed down. Fans split into smaller groups called Ultra Spartak, Pleven Boys, SPUY, and Semper Fidelis and Storgo Firm.

- **How would you define yourself as a fan?**

I'd define myself as die-hard ultras and I've been following my team wherever

192

they've played through all those years. I've been taking an active part in everything our mob has been into.

- **Would you tell us in more details about some fights you have been involved at stadia and on the streets?**

My first fight was with away fans of Antibiotic Razgrad (that was the name of Razgrad club back then). We ambushed them in the car park by the ground where their coaches were, and we had a go at them. To my surprise a lot of lads joined. The cops soon came and so the travelling fans got off lightly with just a few injured and windows smashed. At an away game in Montana, some of our lads beat 3 gypsies outside the stadium. Little did we know the ground was next to the gypsy ghetto. Soon afterwards a dozen of gypos came, and we had a good ruck. We've had loads of brawls, most of them on our ground. On away days we regularly had fights with CSKA and Levski supporters. I've also had clashes with Minyor, Lokomotiv Plovdiv, Botev, Beroe, Etar, Litex, etc. Recently I have nothing worth mentioning. Spartak has been through quite a lot, from the top flight down to the regional amateur division, bankruptcies and the like and supporters are now fewer and less dedicated.

- **Who are your rivals (in the general sense of the word, in life or at the stadium), what are they like and what is your opinion of them?**

In the 1980s and the early 1990s there were rather bitter feelings against Botev Vratsa and the clubs from Sofia. Huge crowds of thugs would wait for fans arriving at the train station. Away days were also interesting as we used to take good numbers. Nowadays we do not seem to have any definite rival. Recently, hatred has been building up for clubs like Etar, Lokomotiv Sofia, Lokomotiv Mezdra, and Bdin Vidin. All lads who support their local clubs get my full respect.

- **Have you ever been seriously wounded or injured while fighting?**

I've received punches as it is inevitable in mass brawls. However, I haven't had any serious injuries, just a broken finger on an away day at Academic Svishtov.

- **Where does your favourite football club stand in your life and how important is it for you?**

Spartak has been a part of my life since I was a kid. Most of my mate's support Sofia big clubs, but my real love and passion have always been meant for my local team. I always tend to find free time in spite of all the problems, duties and the like, all in the name of my beloved Spartak. I'd quite often give my own money for making club calendars, scarves, T-shirts, etc. My love for Spartak will never die.

- **Which are your favourite designer brands?**

Probably Adidas and Fred Perry. I go to games wearing our own Spartak T-shirts and stuff.

- **What is your wildest favourite club related dream?**

To hell with silverware! I want Spartak back in the top league and I want it to stay there. I want to see people go back to the terraces. I'd like to see someone who really cares about sports in my town of Pleven and I'd like to see our rundown stadium renovated. I always leave the ground happy when there is a good atmosphere on the terraces, I personally don't care much about the score.

- **Which is your favourite game of all times?**

There are several games that I'll never forget. In 1997 Spartak beat Dobrudzha 5-1 and our club legend Plamen Getov scored three goals from free kicks. The crowd went mental. My other favourite was a few years later, a cup tie between Spartak and Slavia. It was played at the now demolished White Eagles Stadium, which did not have a racetrack. 12 000 turned up for the game and the atmosphere was terrific. Spartak won 3-1, but the most impressive thing that day was the crowd. All Pleven fans supporting Levski and CSKA joined forces with Spartak supporters.

- **Who are your favourite players?**

The most players from the Bulgarian golden team. My favourite Spartak legend is Plamen Getov, though he was a complete disaster as a manager later.

- **Would you name the top 5 Bulgarian firms/crews/mobs?**

Sofia West, Animals, South Division, Offensive (do they still exist?), Lauta Hools and Bultras. Smaller clubs also have decent crews and lads, but numbers really matter.

- **Which are the best and the worst football grounds you've ever been to and why?**

I think the best one is in the town of Lovech and it was not by chance that all away mobs had their greatest days there. The away end in the town of Razgrad definitely makes that ground the worst for away fans.

- **What do you think of the Bulgarian police?**

Personally, I dislike them, and I don't have any friends who are cops. Absolutely worthless and dumb scum in most cases. At a lot of games, they have instigated tensions instead of suppressing them.

- **What do you think of the youths in your firm/crew/mob?**

In particular, we have some 20 lads now. We've had more, and we've had less through the years, taking into account several factors. In Pleven there are significant numbers of CSKA and Levski fans so many of the ultras beginners join them. We find it hard to attract them as we can't give them what a big mob can. It's one thing being with 20 to 30 mates at the empty Pleven Stadium and another being among thousands. It's also our own fault as our internal organisation is kinda poor, but this is another story. Those who really love Spartak support it unconditionally and no matter what.

- **What do you think of the modern-day 'scene'?**

All mobs have their ups and downs. We know well what the problems are and what puts off people from going to football. Bulgarian football is pathetic; there are fixed games, etc. The scene would be much more interesting if the upper divisions featured clubs like Spartak Varna, Lokomotiv G.O., Dobrudzha, Spartak Pleven, Etar, Botev Vratsa, and others with strong fan support, instead of small clubs like Verea, Montana, Bansko, etc.

- **What do you think of English hooligans and their influence ?**

Everyone used to copycat them, and each mob would fly the Union Jack. I'd follow their feats by reading books and watching films about them. They definitely had great influence in the past. Nowadays English stadia look like theatres and the punishments for anyone breaking the rules are severe. It's another story when they go abroad, and they always have good away days.

(T.) - Spartak (Varna)

Meet and greet

My nickname is T. and I am a die-hard Spartak Varna supporter. I was invited by the authors of this book to share some memorable events in my life as a football fan though such events are numerous, and I won't have the time to tell everything I've experienced.

- **How old are you and when did you become a fan of your favourite club?**

I was born in 1975, and I became a Spartak Varna fan in 1986 when I was still 11. It was winter, in the month of March, if I'm not mistaken. I was on my way to the cinema when I saw crowds of people heading somewhere. I decided to abandon the movies and follow the fans flying white and blue flags and scarves. Mesmerised by the flow of people I reached the stadium. It was a Spartak Varna vs Beroe game. It was Beroe's champions' campaign. I remember the game ended in a 1-1 draw and our players were in no way inferior to the visiting team.

- **Would you tell us how your firm (crew/mob) was established?**

Back in the days (the late 1980s and the early 1990s) there were no firms in Bulgaria; it was all just groups of young and old fans, mixtures of metalheads, punks and skinheads. Gradually, in the mid-1990s, firms started to appear copycatting the UK style. In the beginning, our firm was simply called Mladost Boys 95 as most of us used to live in Mladost Quarter, but little by little, younger firms like Flower Hood, Brigade Hools, and Spartak Youths (founded in 2008) began to emerge, and now our youths (ultras) have a crew called Syndicate 12, whose aim is to kick out all those people who recently led our beloved club into bankruptcy and so the team went down to the amateur divisions.

- **How would you define yourself as a fan?**

I'd now define myself as ultras, though in all those years I've always been into old school hooliganism when we used to fight bare handed only. We used to support our teams only by singing, chanting and blowing off hand-made bombs. There was no pyro, neither tifo.

- **Would you tell us in more details about some fights you have been involved at stadia and on the streets?**

There are numerous incidents, but I'll only mention several that I'll never forget. One was in Stara Zagora in April 1992. There were just a few games left of the campaign. It was a crucial game for us in our fight to avoid relegation from the top division. Seven of us took a train to Stara Zagora and though few in numbers we had no fear. We stocked ourselves with booze and sang our songs throughout the journey. We walked to the ground undisturbed with no cops to escort us. Probably the locals did not expect any away fans. The game ended 1-0 for the home side. Come the end of the match, the coppers escorted us back to the railway station because a lot of local fans had gathered. It was a late afternoon game, so the Old Bill escorted us to the train station at about 8:00 pm so that we could catch our train back to Varna. Nobody suspected something would happen anymore as there were a few knackered passengers only. It must have been around 11:00 pm when, out of the blue, 40 Beroe fans had a go at us. Some of us ran to seek shelter in the nearby restaurant, the majority of the locals hot on their heels. A few of us were left to face a dozen so we steamed into them throwing punches and kicks. We were giving them a good hiding and one could hear the distinct sounds of jaws and heads being hit hard. Blood was spurting out of our mouths and heads, it was a small-scale massacre. The bystanders were looking at us, their mouths opened wide as they couldn't believe their eyes. We crushed those bastards down to the ground. Blood boiling hot, we could feel no pain after all the booze we'd drunk, and we beat the shit out of them right there, on their territory. Those who managed to escape were lucky as the rest were writhing on the pavement in pools of blood. As you'd expect, the Gendarmerie arrived on the scene armed with machine guns. They must have been afraid we'd go on beating the locals to death.

Another great fight I remember was against our eternal enemies Cherno More.

We were both playing in the top division, but I can't remember the year. I remember they were coming back from Buorgas, having played Chernomorets there while we hosted Neftochimic. The games were played on the Bulgarian national holiday, 3rd March, so it was freezing cold. They were travelling on coaches in the evening and as always, they passed through the centre of the town. There were some 12 of us, already on the piss in the bar we used to meet up after games and waiting for their coaches to pass by. First, we saw their team's coach and then came the coach with their fans. We could hear them from a distance chanting out loud in the dark. We regrouped and when they approached us we started throwing bottles (some of us were still drinking), stones and dust bins at their coach. We could hear the sounds of windows being shattered, brakes screeching and angry shouts from both sides. Their coach was full, there must have been about 40 of them. Some got off and we went toe to toe with them. Some had cuts on their hands from the pieces of glass flying from the smashed windows. One of our lads, bottle in hand, just landed it on one of the Cherno More fan's head and the latter collapsed on the ground. Our mate took the half-broken bottle with the intention to cut his face. Blood was gushing out of his head and there was already a pool of blood beneath his body. We shouted at him to stop because if he had gone on he could have ended up killing him. The fight went on for a few minutes and though they outnumbered us, they couldn't get the upper hand. On the contrary! Fortunately, later on, we were told that the victim got off lightly with only a number of cuts. Similar things happened a few years later (around 2010), during a friendly played by Spartak Varna and Neftochimic on the artificial pitch in Varna, where a toe-to-toe started after the away fans threw a bottle and it hit a mate of ours. The scuffle went on for several minutes before the cops arrived. Despite the Old Bill's intervention, 8 fans from Bourgas sought medical help in Varna emergency rooms as a result of various injuries.

I recall another incident, but this time it does not involve warring Bulgarian firms, but an international game Bulgaria vs Sweden played at Vasil Levski National Stadium in September 1993. When Bulgaria plays, most groups of supporters unite for their common cause, but sometimes there are fights between old rivals. We knew Swedish fans were coming for the game, but they are not notorious for any significant hooligan acts. Some 4 or 5 coach loads of Scandinavians arrived from the direction of the stadium main stand. There were not many cops as there were several hours before kick-off. Most of us had hidden in the bushes or had climbed up the trees in the park where the stadium is located, and we were waiting for our opponents like predators would lie in wait for their prey. The moment they stepped off their coaches we had a go at them and a mass brawl started. We could only hear the sounds of punches and fists hitting heads and jaws. We did them good! They received so many blows that I think they'll always remember that day. I was punching a Swede lying on the ground when the cops and the riot police arrived. I got nicked with a dozen of others, but most of us managed to escape. All the time I was guarded by a copper with a German shepherd, which would start barking every time I dared to move. I was pushed inside an armoured police truck and kept there till the end of the game, the dog looking at me all the time. After the game finished we were taken to the local police department where we had to choose between a fine and community service. Naturally, I went for the first option, i.e. the fine, probably thanks to the young and sexy female judge in court.

- **Who are your rivals (in the general sense of the word, in life or at the stadium), what are they like and what is your opinion of them?**

It may come as a surprise for some of you, but it's not our blood enemies from Varna, they are Etar from Veliko Tarnovo. In 1991, the year they were crowned champions of Bulgaria and had a decent support and a good mob, I was on a trip to Tarnovo with some other boys from Varna, when we accidentally learned there was a cup fixture to be played between Etar and CSKA. While we were standing at a bus stop downtown, a trolleybus stopped and out of it came more than 50 lads who surrounded us. One of them asked me where I came from and what I was doing there. I told him we were from Varna and had come sightseeing in Tarnovo, but they didn't believe us as they thought we were CSKA fans coming from Sofia. The wanker approached me and tried to take off my denim vest with all those traditional badges on it. I hit him hard in the teeth with my elbow and he let out a groan as blood started spurting out of his mouth. Then his mates went at us with kicks and punches and simply beat the shit out of us. A few against 50 did not earn them much credit, did it!?

- **Have you ever been seriously wounded or injured while fighting?**

Yeah, a few times, but after the game between Spartak Varna and Lokomotiv Plovdiv in 1992/93, I was seriously hurt after a fight on the terraces and I couldn't walk for more than a month...

- **Where does your favourite football club stand in your life and how important is it for you?**

One life, one destiny, one love and one religion!

- **Which are your favourite designer brands?**

Since I've been an English football fan for many years, I like the Umbro brand their national squad used to play in.

- **What is your wildest favourite club related dream?**

Winning the lottery and making Spartak champions of Bulgaria!

- **Which is your favourite game of all times?**

The 1999 CL final between Manchester United and Bayern.

- **Who are your favourite players?**

Zhivko Gospodinov, Ivailo Petev, Zlatin Mihailov, Trayan Dyankov, Stefan

Naidenov, Martin Zafirov, Ivailo Bogdanov, Diyan Donchev, Lyubo Penev, Ebbe Sand, Jorg Bohme, Toni Schumacher, Carrick, Beckham, Cantona...

- **Would you name the top 5 Bulgarian firms/crews/mobs?**

SVUD, Brigade Hools, D16, Spartak Youths, Izgrev Boys.

- **Which are the best and the worst football grounds you've ever been to and why?**

The worst ground I've been to is Slavia stadium, a neglected, dirty ground with an away end that's smaller than any other away ends I've seen. The best ground for travelling fans is the one in Stara Zagora, where the away end is quite comfortable.

- **What do you think of the Bulgarian police?**

ACAB.

- **What do you think of the youths in your firm/crew/mob?**

We have some 50-60 youths who follow the club everywhere, though Spartak Varna are now in crisis and play in the amateur league. To cut the long story short, they are doing their job. On the other hand, we still hope, and we believe that one day we will once again play against the big clubs in the top flight, the place that we've always belonged to! Varna is blue!

- **What do you think of the modern-day 'scene'?**

They are too much into watching films and videos. I don't approve of fighting with baseball bats, knives or knuckledusters because it's not fair play. I've always relied on, and I still keep on believing that the best tools one could use in a fight are one's own hands and feet!

- **What do you think of English hooligans and their influence?**

They've had a huge influence on European mobs as they are the originators of this trend. Although we could now often see the advance of some MMA fighters in mobs across Russia, Poland and Hungary, the English style of support and street fighting is still unmatched! Lots of people respect the English, but they wouldn't admit it. For me personally, English hoolies will always remain a unique paragon, eternal role models!

K. D. - Cherno More (Varna)

Meet and greet

My name's K. I am from Varna and I support Cherno More FC, my passion and my way of life. I met one of the authors of this book through a mate of mine, who supports our sworn enemy Spartak Varna.

- **How old are you and when did you become a fan of your favourite club?**

I'm 42 and I've been following my club for 34 years (I was an 8-year-old kid when

Dad first took me to a football ground). I still support Cherno More in any way I can.

- **Would you tell us how your firm (crew/mob) was established?**

In my time there were no firms yet. A group of 50-60 lads were the core that always supported the club, and on derby days and for big games against clubs from Sofia and Plovdiv we would bring decent numbers.

- **How would you define yourself as a fan?**

I was a dedicated one; I used to go to every Cherno More game.

- **Would you tell us in more details about some fights you have been involved at stadia and on the streets?**

The biggest fight I've been involved in was in the early 1990s in the town of Pleven when we played the local Spartak Pleven. We arrived in Pleven early in the morning, only 10 of us. Anyway, we did raise hell on that day. The rest of our mob arrived in the afternoon and our number grew to let's say 50-60 fellas. After the game about 30 Spartak fans were waiting for us at the train station. It kicked off big time, fists and kicks flying for some 5-6 minutes. We got the upper hand and they bottled it. We nicked an impressive number of their scarves and flags. On our way back to Varna they laid an ambush at a bridge. Our train was going by that bridge when they started throwing stones and other debris and as a result, several carriages were damaged.

- **Who are your rivals (in the general sense of the word, in life or at the stadium), what are they like and what is your opinion of them?**

Each Cherno More rival was also my personal rival. Naturally, our biggest rival is our deadly enemy Spartak Varna and I have to admit their fans are one of the most loyal to their club!

- **Have you ever been seriously wounded or injured while fighting?**

Yes, in the town of Ruse, in the early 1990s, ahead of a game against Lokomotiv Ruse. I had numerous grazes and bruises from the batons and boots of 5-6 coppers.

- **Where does your favourite football club stand in your life and how important is it for you?**

It comes second now, right after my family.

- **Which are your favourite designer brands?**

My favourite label is Adidas.

- **What is your wildest favourite club related dream?**

Winning the title.

- **Which is your favourite game of all times?**

My favourite game is the Levski vs. Cherno More Cup Final that we won.

- **Who are your favourite players?**

Iliyan Iliev and Georgi Iliev.

- **Would you name the top 5 Bulgarian firms/crews/mobs?**

Cherno More is first, followed by Levski, CSKA, Botev Plovdiv and Minyor Pernik.

- **Which are the best and the worst football grounds you've ever been to and why?**

The best one is Lazur Stadium in the town of Bourgas and the worst one is in Plovdiv, Maritsa FC ground.

- **What do you think of the Bulgarian police?**

Nowadays cops don't beat you the way they did in the past. It's completely different now.

- **What do you think of the youths in your firm/crew/mob?**

Youngsters are much more organised nowadays than we used to be.

- **What do you think of the modern-day 'scene'?**

It's very different, greatly influenced by the ultra movement, but in general stadia used to be crowded back in the 1980s and 1990s and now they're not.

- **What do you think of English hooligans and their influence?**

English hools are the best and loads of people try to be their copycats.

206

R. (B. V.) - Chernomorets (Bourgas)

Meet and greet

- **How old are you and when did you become a fan of your favourite club?**

Let me first point out that this is a summary of memories, both mine and of my mates, because in those times we used to go to games highly intoxicated and a good few events are not so clear in my mind after all those years. I'm 57 now and I first went to a football game when I was 12. I did it with some older boys from my neighbourhood. We were playing for a certain period at the ground located in the Lazur quarter. I remember well the cigarettes, the wine, the hustle and bustle and the long walk to the ground, which was filled to its capacity. We beat Slavia 2-0.

- **Would you tell us how your firm(crew/mob) was established?**

We started gathering as a mob back in 1976 or 1977… it just happened. We used to call them mobs and they united everybody. As time went by, the modern day crews and firms appeared. By forming a 'mob' we wanted to separate from the rank-and-file supporters. We'd mob up in the so called 'English end' (a truly legendary place for Burgas up to this day), people aged between 15 and 30. On big games we'd fill the end from its middle up to the corner-kick curve. We were the unruly youths of

207

the town, i.e. gangsters, scammers, smugglers, lazybones and regular customers of juvenile delinquency commissions and reformatories. We also had longshoremen, porters or workers who'd enjoy the commotion and the usual confrontations with the police. Times were hard and if you wanted to break the chains for a while, you could only do it at football grounds, especially when you're in the company of like-minded people. There were crowds dispersed with water jets, games abandoned, Sieg Heil shouts and appeals, away fans pursuits, though rather rare in those times. Through the years the mob changed drastically as in the early 1990s a decision was made for not allowing young kids followed by the flares wave and respectively the first split as not everyone approved of the pyro. In 1998 B.S. CREW was formed and the Blue Sharks official fan club was founded. Just like their predecessors, B.S. Crew were the proverbial crooks, so we set up a good hooligan brotherhood that was to rule over the entire town. Streets were dominated by a single master and that master was us. Bars and nightclubs were either guarded by our bouncers or closed for the public when we'd decide to get in. Then the graffiti culture emerged, and our domination was to be seen on the town walls, too. We had all sorts of people in our family and everybody got all the help they could possibly need from the other members of that big family. That was actually the Blue Sharks' golden era. At present, there is a deadlock, a complete standstill, but hopefully one day we'll rise from the ashes like a Phoenix and once again Burgas will become a rather hostile and intimidating place for all away fans.

- **How would you define yourself as a fan?**

At my age now, I'm a moderate fan, but still I try to set the pace and encourage youths. It's simply in my blood and there's no cure for it.

- **Would you tell us in more details about some fights you have been involved at stadia and on the streets?**

In the 1980s there were fights at almost every single game. We've had some exemplary brawls with Levski in Bourgas at various places. They'd always use their bombs, but we'd make up for it with sheer numbers and better knowledge of the town. At the cup semi-final we played against them in the town of Haskovo we were so many that we actually threw them out of every single pub in the town and at the very ground we went at them straight in front of their end, but yes, we did outnumber them more than heavily. We also regularly clashed Beroe and if they have been given a better hiding anywhere else than the hiding they've been given in Burgas, then they are the mob that has been most brutally beaten in Bulgarian history. Once we even took their flags without a single resistance effort by them. In more recent times we have had a go at them in different small pubs where they'd try to hide, but someone would always uncover them somewhere. We have also crushed them in their own town of Stara Zagora when we played the local Lokomotiv. We arrived the night before, we went on a piss in the bars and we offered them a prearranged fight, but they refused and never turned up, even on the next day (laughing). As far as the case involving the stolen flags and the nicking of our mates is concerned, everyone must have seen on TV what kind of pussies they really are.

Our biggest scuffles are against Lokomotiv Plovdiv and Botev Plovdiv. Unlike the big Sofia clubs, they'd always bring huge numbers. We also confronted them each in Plovdiv, where we had quite decent performance taking into account they we were heavily outnumbered on both occasions. One of the biggest brawls to have happened in Bourgas was us against Botev Plovdiv. A horrendous melee! Even the gypsies living in the nearby ghetto joined the fight; not that we are very proud of that (laughing). It was just that in their panicky retreat, Botev legged in all directions, but the ground neighbours the sea and the Roma ghetto and they were simply trapped. Oh, what a sweet victory that was! I guess some of them 'parrots' still have nightmares from that day!

The 1983 relegation play-offs with Lokomotiv Plovdiv also witnessed large-scale riots. We clashed on a bridge and both sides used stones, pipes, poles (flags were then flown on wooden poles) in addition to the punches and kicks. Both sides had casualties. More recently, we had it again with Lokomotiv, this time at the train station when their mob went at a small crew of ours. However, much to their surprise, our lads were well up for it and ultimately it all resulted in a kind of friendship with some of our youths.

We don't have much history with the Mazuts (that's how we call Neftochimic fans) as their club is newly founded, but still there was this decent row at their ground, where they had even brought an operator to videotape it. They were given such a bad hiding that the video was never shown (laughing). We've slapped them all around the town boozers, but generally speaking they are not a match for us. It was us who actually set up their mob and the big fight in Varna can be attributed to us because we were the stormtroopers who went to that game to defend the honour of our town Burgas and not them. Through all these years we've also had good rucks with Lokomotiv G.O., Sliven and the Gagauz, but I'll need another book to tell it all.

- **Who are your rivals (in the general sense of the word, in life or at the stadium), what are they like and what is your opinion of them?**

'The Gagauz'[15] as it's in our genes; we are born to hate Varna. Absolute morons, we have taken over their ground a good number of times. And they didn't dare come to Bourgas, or when they did we'd have a go at them right there, inside the stadium.

Beroe as they are primitive peasants and absolute cunts... They've never had a decent mob and the only thing we did not do to them in Burgas is shag them because we're not faggots (laughing).

The Mazuts because they are our town rivals, even up to this day. They have a short-term memory and they tend to distort history. Attacking school kids or members of youth academies are absolutely shameful and violate any kind of fans' Code of Conduct.

- **Have you ever been seriously wounded or injured while fighting?**

I haven't had any serious injuries, nor have any of my mates, as far as I know.

Grazes, bruises, shiners are normal stuff, you know, but I've never been hospitalised, etc. Once I got punched hard in the back by a Beroe fan at a quarter-final we played in the town of Sliven and I had a backache for a few days and then Yuri Galev[16] did a good cross in my face on an away game in the town of Samokov (laughing). During a fight we had with Levski in the Seaside Garden, in 1992 I think, we had some lads injured, but after the game we take a good revenge on them at the railway station.

In recent years, I suffered injuries because of the cops. They got me after the attack of the fucking Jehova's sect and held me in a cold and damp cell with bare nothing. Since then, my back has been totally fucked up.

- **Where does your favourite football club stand in your life and how important is it for you?**

Chernomorets is deep in my heart, no doubt about it. It's not only a major part of my life, it is my entire life. If my youth had not gone the way it did to make me a die-hard football fan, I would have hardly had such great and varied life experience (far away from material happiness, but who cares). I'm divorced, I have a grown-up daughter and when I think about it, I guess I don't have much in my life apart from the memories I share with the lads of events all over the country.

- **Which are your favourite designer brands?**

Back in our days there were no designer brands. The only fashion was jeans, military boots and sailor striped shirts. Years later it was bomber jackets and chequers followed by white trainers. There was not much point in wearing expensive clobber and stuff in order to be different cause we were different anyway. Besides, the cops knew us too well. It didn't matter whether we wore white trainers and shirts when we'd approach the away end entrance as the cops were ready for us with their electroshock batons and riot shields. We've had some good rows with Bourgas cops.

- **What is your wildest favourite club related dream?**

It's not easy to answer this as things have changed a lot. Once upon a time we dreamt of the title or the cup. Now I dream of a packed ground with crowds roaring no matter which division we're playing in. I dream of young lads familiar with history and traditions and defending the honour of our town, of an inseparable crew of mates, a big family who stand strong all together. And once again to rule the streets of the city and show of who's the real team of Bourgas. 'The wheel is spinning' and our time will come again, I believe.

- **Which is your favourite game of all times?**

My favourite game is the Cup semi-final against Levski in Haskovo. For a small club like ours, experiencing that is something that will forever stay in our memories. Seeing the cavalcade of coaches and cars (the first one arriving in

Haskovo while the last one departing from Burgas), the crowds of people sweeping over the town and stadium plus our unique play and victory, what more is there to say! Good clashes, hide-and-seek with the cops, we had a little bit of everything that day. I also remember a very comical situation when, instead of biting me, a police dog was bitten by me, and the hatters caught their heads in astonishment (laughing).

- **Who are your favourite players?**

They are many, but I'll mention S. Traikov. He is a 'shark' and though he was not born in Bourgas, he'll stay forever in our hearts. A true legend, who has even fought Mazuts in the streets without showing any mercy. On the pitch he hardly missed a chance to score against them, no matter if he had been on the piss till 4:00 or 5:00 in the morning.

- **Would you name the top 5 Bulgarian firms/crews/mobs?**

Botev Plovdiv, Lokomotiv Plovdiv, CSKA, Levski and Minyor Pernik. In our strong years we were also in Top 5.

- **Which are the best and the worst football grounds you've ever been to and why?**

The best in terms of atmosphere and acoustics is probably the one in Lovech. Even a small mob there can raise hell, not to speak of a huge one. There are innumerable poor and outdated grounds in Bulgaria, but Blagoevgrad was pretty hostile. Gorna Oryahovitsa too. Samokov was a horrible away experience as we took small numbers and entered the ground with no tickets. 30 minutes into the game it kicked off with Yuri Galev's thugs. We didn't know who and what they were, but they outnumbered us and were well up for it. It was our own mistake trying to go on a rampage, just 10-12 of us in an absolutely unknown territory. We didn't have the foggiest idea where we were going.

- **What do you think of the Bulgarian police?**

One word only – mercenaries!

- **What do you think of the youths in your firm/crew/mob?**

There are none at present. We are the ones to blame as we chased them away and made them feel unwelcome and worthless. We didn't trust them, and we wouldn't accept others among us. Probably it was the result of all those years of rallying around a core that used to be in a constant state of warfare, not only against rival fans, but also against the normal part of town as every one of them considered us as the unwanted citizens of Bourgas. Perhaps this triggered a protective mechanism of distrust for anyone and suddenly we decided that youngsters are not worthy of notice and the like. So currently we are just a bunch of old dogs getting fewer and fewer due as time goes by. 1983-87 were our last generations who controlled the town as our proud successors. I mean the B.S. CREW. However, it's a different story now. We just lost control of the nightlife. For years on end we owned the bars and all the bouncers and other blokes who could do any kind of dirty job were 'sharks'. We took whatever we needed, and we ran the show. Our numerous guests and friendships through the years are the best evidence of that; they all had the time of their lives. Now it' all about glamour and fashion, playing the hotshots for a year or two and there are even girls posing on the terraces trying to look like ultras. Strike a pose, make a selfie or a video and then they go studying abroad and that's it. Everything has changed, i.e. traditions, the way the terraces look, the mobs, respectively the lads. Every era has its own heroes. Maybe at last here's the time to mention our friend Toshko, a tough boy, a fighter and a real leader. It was in our hopes for him to lead the new army of 'Sharks', but unfortunately, he will not ... God rest his soul and he will remain in our hearts. He was taken from us ridiculously, after yet another stupidity (as they could not handle with fists, they took out the knives), but the retribution always exists!

- **What do you think of the modern-day 'scene'?**

Not too much of a singing, in 20 to 30 minutes it all fades away. In terms of organisation, I don't know in detail how things stand with the different clubs, but although they seem well organised and more than patriotic, I find our country is rotten from within. Everyone's dressed alike, they do their best to make fan clothes and stuff, they set up fight clubs and every firm has some kind of business, either football related or not. It all seems fine on the surface, but obviously something's missing. National squad games are a tragedy and for me this is the stage where we should prove what we are capable of doing together in the name of our Motherland. The atmosphere on the national team away games is a disaster, all those menacing looks, separate chants and prospects of fighting each other. Probably it is all because of all those traitors and business interests around us. Probably each mob has its downfalls and the stabs in the back. But it is a matter of fact, it is undeniable, we are a world apart from each other and the young generation is totally devoid of notions like morals, tradition, honour, unity, etc. Hopefully we go through this Hell and see some better days in the future.

- **What do you think of English hooligans and their influence?**

Years ago, they had the reputation of being the greatest hooligans in Europe. They had a huge impact on us as we were hotheaded and would cause havoc following their example. Carrying British flags was our way to challenge the authorities. It just came from within; those were the times we lived in. Four of us went to Varna to watch Spartak Varna vs. Manchester United in1983 so that we could get the feel of them. We entered their end but found them absolutely meek. They must have been warned to behave like that, so we witnessed no riots.

---

15 Turkic ethnic group living in Northeast Bulgaria, a derogatory term used for the residents of Varna and its area

16 Rilski Sportist FC former President, assassinated in 2010

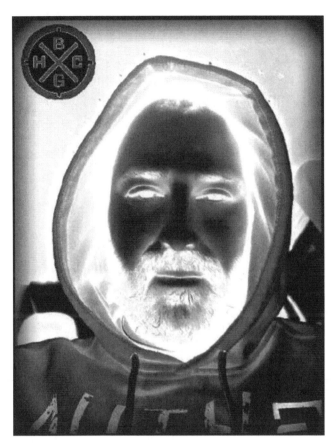

T.P. (T.) - Neftochimic (Bourgas)

Meet and greet

- **How old are you and when did you become a fan of your favourite club?**

Hello, I'm 38 years old, a Neftochimic Burgas fan since times immemorial, but a dedicated one since we knocked Levski out of the cup in 1991, when we were playing in the third division while they were the reigning champions.

- **Would you tell us how your firm(crew/mob) was established?**

I've taken part in the establishment of most firms whose aim has been to support the club and develop ultras ideas in Bourgas. One of them is Green Fighters founded in 1997. We also have some other firms like HGU, MR Hools, The Light Brigade, Bourgas Berserks, etc.

- **How would you define yourself as a fan?**

I've always put my club first and supported them unselfishly on almost all home games and many a time away from home in all divisions. I wouldn't say I'm a die-hard, though sometimes one needs to go to extremes.

- **Would you tell us in more details about some fights you have been involved at stadia and on the streets?**

Well, they come to my mind right away. For example, in Varna we did some good stuff. We were playing Cherno More away and at half time we went out to have some beers in a local shop situated right next to a building site. However, a few gulps later I felt the need to shit and I decided that the most suitable place for emptying my bowels was the second floor of the unfinished building. I jumped over a moderately high fence, I shat in what looked to me as a WC, and with a lighter body and in higher spirits I decided I would finish my beer with the lads. I went downstairs and half way through the fencing I saw faces that were unfamiliar to me. There were 7 or 8 of them and the moment they saw me they knew I did not belong to them, so they instantly had a go at me. The fence and the bricks lying there were my saviours. Three of them went down while they were climbing up. At that point I decided to get away from my trap and quickly jumped over the fencing. However, on my return to the away end the rest of the 'Cherno More' firm stood in my way. I knocked down two of them first and then my third punch hit another one, so the rest just bottled it. I made it to my mates unscathed, but unfortunately, I had forgotten my beer outside and it was almost full (laughing).

- **Who are your rivals (in the general sense of the word, in life or at the stadium), what are they like and what is your opinion of them?**

Interesting question. I try to avoid having enemies, but I quite dislike Beroe 'ladies' because they always come to pre-arranged fights in three times bigger numbers or carrying tools. Cowardly cunts. Spartak Varna are the other ones I dislike.

- **Have you ever been seriously wounded or injured while fighting?**

When in a fight, I've always tried to be on the alert and save myself from being injured with either a knife or a firearm. Well, when you often tend to end up in such situations you can't get away without a single graze, bruise or shiner.

- **Where does your favourite football club stand in your life and how important is it for you?**

I love my club and it was the reason for me to meet a lot of people that I could have never met otherwise.

- **Which are your favourite designer brands?**

I'm not so fashion-conscious, but the Stone Island clobber is definitely the best quality.

- **What is your wildest favourite club related dream?**

We, Neftochimic supporters, have never demanded any trophies from our players. What we have always wanted them to do is play their hearts out and give their best for the club and for us. Anyway, right now my biggest wish is that Neftochimic could once again have its own stadium.

- **Which is your favourite game of all times?**

Wow, they're so many... We have loads of unforgettable glorious victories over much more famous teams and players that used to be much more favoured by national squad managers and the press. Recently our game against Chernomorets remains as a pure classic. Unique atmosphere before, during and after the match.

- **Who are your favourite players?**

Krasimir Denev, Mitko Trendafilov, Velian Parushev (may he rest in peace), Dian Lefterov, Ilia Gruev and all the others who gave their hearts and souls and lives for us fans.

- **Would you name the top 5 Bulgarian firms/crews/mobs?**

I'm not into 'firms' these days, but I think that all top clubs (except for Ludogorets) keep up a decent level.

- **Which are the best and the worst football grounds you've ever been to and why?**

I've been to almost all Bulgarian and several foreign grounds and, apart from our own of course, I think Old Trafford is the best one I've ever visited. It has a unique atmosphere. And as far as the worst one is concerned I hope none of you ever go to watch a home game of Byala Reka Zaichar FC (laughing).

- **What do you think of the Bulgarian police?**

No comment!

- **What do you think of the youths in your firm/crew/mob?**

In a few words, they have nothing to do with the youths from the past. However, there must be some decent lads...

- **What do you think of the modern-day 'scene'?**

The scene changed a lot with the advance of high tech and CCTV. Now it's a bit more complicated to get away with some mischief and so, naturally, you get more self-controlled and cool-headed and you think twice before doing anything stupid. Anyway, my dream is that all we like-minded people (regardless of the petty squabbles we may have) could come together and realise that there's no sense in making our families and friends wait for us anxiously to come home safe and sound after we've been to a game just for the sake of some sports rivalry.

- **What do you think of English hooligans and their influence?**

I'm not familiar in details so I can't give you a proper answer.

A. - Hebur (Pazardzhik)

Meet and greet

- **How old are you and when did you become a fan of your favourite club?**

I'm 33 years old and I've been following Hebur since I was when my classmate's older brother first took me to the Georgi Benkovski ground. It was a game against Olympic Galata and the crowd was as big as the crowds that later on would gather to watch Hebur play Levski and CSKA, though it was a third division game, if I'm not mistaken. Unfortunately, the years of economic recession made many people leave our town and truth to tell I doubt if we'll ever see such huge crowds at our stadium. The atmosphere, the banter, and the first military smoke grenade I saw, they all made an awesome impression on me and I couldn't wait for my next game. Afterwards, I started meeting up mates from school and going to every home game, just the way it would happen to most of us who grew up in the 1990s. We became football supporters by going to the stadium, not by sticking to computers and smartphones.

- **Would you tell us how your firm(crew/mob) was established?**

219

The beginning of organised support for Hebur, as far as I know, can be traced back to the mid-1980s. In the early 1990s when the club played twice in the top division, a group of fans started calling themselves the 'gravediggers'. Nobody can tell for sure whether it was copied from Partizan Belgrade fans or was due to the location of the football ground right next to a prison and the old cemetery. Anyway, there are still lots of old writings on walls all across the country that say 'Gravediggers Pazardzhik'. Recently, this name has hardly been used as it is mostly associated with Partizan supporters. I have been going to Hebur games since 1998 and I've seen loads of lads come and go in this period. The 2000/2001 campaign, our last stay in the top flight, was our peak as since then we haven't had the opportunity to meet and clash rival fans, with a few exceptions because teams playing in the lower divisions do not attract big crowds. It was then that we last had big numbers of old-school fans who had taken part in riots and accidents plus a younger generation of fans aged between 14 and 18. Unfortunately, nowadays old-school fans no longer come to games or they do it on rare occasions, the main reason being that most of them do not live in Pazardzhik and Bulgaria. I guess the same goes for all mobs and towns of our size. Those of us who were young then are now not only the older generation at football, but unfortunately, we are the only ones who are still interested in football in our town.

- **How would you define yourself as a fan?**

I think that one of the biggest problems for football fans nowadays is their excessive tendency to define themselves as and claim they are what they actually aren't, unfortunately. In other words, we are talking of great expectations that cannot be really met. I consider myself as just a fan who tries to support his club anywhere and by any means possible.

- **Would you tell us in more details about some fights you have been involved at stadia and on the streets?**

The first one that comes to my mind was in 2001, when we hosted Botev. We mobbed up downtown, including some older lads, when the word went out that the 'parrots' were in the park by the stadium. Only the younger lads headed for the park. Upon our arrival we saw that this time it was not just a rumour as there were Botev fans there. It kicked off for the first time that day and they started hurling stones and bombs at us. Fortunately, they were small and not skilfully made as one exploded almost in the face of one of our lads and the only thing he got away with was fright and a burnt eyebrow. So, the first round was definitely won by Botev as their bombs made us retreat back to the crossroads. However, there we saw one of our lads in the back being attacked by the yellow-and-blacks, so we immediately raided the 'parrots' and they, in turn, bottled it, leaving of few of their lot behind to suffer the anger of our crowd. Well, in moments like those we can hardly speak of reason when adrenaline is flying high and when seconds earlier you witnessed what happened to a mate of yours. In addition to having their scarves nicked, those Botev fans who couldn't leg it were also given a really bad hiding. That was also the result of their own imprudence as on their way to the ground they terrorised the ordinary locals, who, in turn, not being interested in football in any way, had decided to punish the aliens and had a go at them from the other side of the park using all kinds of improvised weapons, including shovels! In the mayhem that followed, one of our lot also got hit by a shovel or two before he got the chance to explain to the angry mob that he was also from our town. Before the game there were some more minor scuffles with Botev groups where the away fans had to seek shelter with the police at the ground entrances. Amidst this chaos one of our green-and-white flags got nicked and Botev hung it down the fence in their end, which made one of our older top lads run all the way down the racetrack, take it off the fencing and run back to our end under a shower of abuse and flying debris hurled by the Botev fans. After the game, at the old bus station, there was another brief but brutal fight with another Botev crew, who were much older than us and stood their ground well but were ultimately chased down all across the centre of the town and I seriously don't envy them for what they experienced on that day.

The next more serious riot was in 2005 at a Cup quarter-final against CSKA, when we had several brawls with the reds during the day', once they were beaten and chased at the train station and then a second time, only God knows why, they tried to have a go at us downtown but what they got was another good hiding. What was funny that day was that both sides generally knew each other and though they were rivals on that occasion, a few weeks later they had beer together on another occasion, this time in Sofia. Sadly enough, such incidents involving clashes, but not extreme hatred, are rare now and we can learn a lot from, let's say, the Russians, where lads are rivals on match days, but still find it easy to unite for certain national causes and ideas.

Since in all its history Hebur FC has mainly played in the 2nd and 3rd division, we actually have not had much chance to have good rucks with top division clubs, which naturally have more numerous fans. It's crystal clear that we are a small club and do not have massive support, but events like the above-mentioned come to show that no matter how small you are, you can always stand a good chance in equal numbers and fair play fights. Otherwise it would be ridiculous for us to claim that we could really challenge the bigger mobs in our country.

In recent years, our main rivals have been the fans of Minyor Pernik. The main reason for that is probably not that they play in those horrible colours, nor that Hebur's ex-owner took over their club, but that they are the only club in our division that has a kind of mob. For our first game after Hebur's resurrection, 2 years ago, Minyor came about 15-handed and we had a go at them in their away end and most of them just left the ground. Only a couple of them remained to watch the game from the central stand. However, when we played them for a second time in August 2017, things escalated. Even prior to the game, we had info that the Orcs, as we call Minyor fans, would be coming in much greater numbers looking for revenge. However, 2 weeks before the game, they decided to ask for assistance the police in their home town, who, in turn, got in touch with their colleagues in Pazardzhik and asked them to warn Hebar fans to avoid getting into any trouble. Upon hearing this, we send an invitation to Minyor to come to a location far from the stadium, but they turned it down. On match day, there was a lot of police all around the stadium, but anyway they couldn't protect the travelling fans as they were attacked by our relatively smaller mob. There's a video uploaded on the Internet, but it shows the end of the incident, not the beginning when the Orcs legged it for the exit, though one could watch the funny moment when they all bottled it after a single boy steamed into them wielding a piece of iron bar taken off from the fencing. Unfortunately, this event had grave consequences for loads of lads, who, in the days that followed the accident got nicked and were taken to court and issued banning orders as a result of the video shown by the media and the journalists' appeals for arrests. A total of some 10 lads fell victim to those repressions, but anyway they showed the real way to do things and they proved that whenever there is a will, there is a way, even at the cost of being taken to court. Sadly, the accident in question is still being investigated and so I won't be going into any further details. Another funny thing that day was that the alleged fearless Orcs had conveniently forgotten to take their flags for the game in Pazardzhik. A complete contrast to their other away games, especially the one against CSKA 1948 in Sofia, where dozens of yellow-and-black rags were put up across the fencing. Just a few days ago we played away in Pernik. We took a small firm there with the clear intention not to enter their ground at all as we had been told that they were going to arrest us all on some false pretences in their attempt to take revenge on us for what happened in the summer. Considering our numbers, we decided not to risk having another straight-forward fight inside the ground in front of all the cameras and coppers and eventually getting banning orders. To make up for it, we decided to walk about Pernik quarters and centre, leaving the relevant messages to our rivals, sending them pictures in the hope to come across some of their lads on their own territory. However, we didn't see anyone but the dozens of cops, which, at some point, made us leave their town. The Orcs' response was asking us why we were not at the ground, which just confirmed my guess that as they were not up for it, they simply relied on us going to their ground and being repressed by the Old Bill. Once they were sure we had left their town, some 15-year-olds started bombarding us with text messages proposing a pre-arranged fight. You see how easy it can get in the virtual world when your enemies are already out of town...

- **Who are your rivals rivals (in the general sense of the word, in life or at the stadium), what are they like and what is your opinion of them?**

Since we only have 3 seasons in the top flight and just a few successful cup campaigns, it would be rather far-fetched to talk about rivals as a vowed enemy, but still, traditionally and in view of location, we may say that Hebur's major rivals are the clubs from the town of Plovdiv. In the lower echelons we've been playing in we can hardly talk about rivals because most clubs are even in a worse situation in terms of fans' support, though they didn't stop existing like Hebur did for a certain period. The only other club that gets good support in the lower divisions is Minyor. The several games we've played against them for the last 15 years have always involved a lot of tension and the incidents I already described.

- **Have you ever been seriously wounded or injured while fighting?**

I've been hurt, but fortunately it was nothing serious, just the usual stuff for the hobby we share. I'm pretty sure that each of us going to football in Bulgaria has been beaten up at least once, if not by rival fans, then surely by the bastard cops. In addition to the mandatory police truncheons and the cops' vile punches in the back, I've also been hit with a knuckleduster, stones, bottles and ripped-off seats, all the common Balkan style stuff, but as I said before, thanks God, all I got away with was just a few stitches.

- **Where does your favourite football club stand in your life and how important is it for you?**

My club is of extreme importance for me and I guess it's the same with all football fans. In the end, it is the idea that unites us and makes us meet up every time there is a match. I've heard some people say that we might as well unite behind another hobby or craze, but truth to tell, I don't see how this could ever happen. How many hobbies can you think of in which a man would have to defend at all costs the ideas he believes in against other people, who also defend their ideas whatever the cost? In the modern world that has not values and no ideas, this is something really unique and to a large extent reserved for our world only, i.e. the world of football fans.

- **Which are your favourite designer brands?**

Due to the economic situation in Bulgaria, designer clobber is something we could hardly copycat from foreign countries and … after all, do we really need to copycat everything and everyone? I think it's a matter of personal choice and preference. My favourite one's Lacoste.

- **What is your wildest favourite club related dream?**

My dream is simple and humble, and it is Hebur FC to continue its existence. I don't dream of cups and even of promotions because I know how I and many others felt between 2009 and 2016, when Hebur FC did not exist at all. Without exaggeration, a part of us was missing and it made me devoid of any megalomania and wild dreams. I just want a team to watch, a team that goes for fair play, no matter how hard it is in Bulgarian football, a team that is not related to money laundry or illegal betting, a team that is not a satellite to any big club and a team that would eventually make people return to the stands so that we could once again be strong in every game we play, all year round.

- **Which is your favourite game of all times?**

The top division promotion play-off in 2000. The sea of hand-made green scarves and flags, the dozens of coaches and cars full of fans travelling to Sofia to watch Hebur wins for the third and last time promotion to the top flight. The winner scored in the last minute, the return journey to Pazardzhik, where thousands took to the streets to celebrate, sing and cry with joy… those are memories and emotions that will hardly ever be experienced again.

- **Who are your favourite players?**

Dobri Ragin for all the goals he scored between 2000 and 2003. Despite his short stay with us, another forward will be long remembered due to his stamina and bodybuilder's physique. His name's Georgi 'Animal' Bogdanov and he was a player that would send the ball into the back of the net together with the entire defence and the goalkeeper.

- **Would you name the top 5 Bulgarian firms/crews/mobs?**

I wouldn't rank them because I think everything is temporary and a matter of current shape. Also, I'll talk about clubs as a whole and not about particular firms. For example, let's take Plovdiv clubs, where Lokomotiv dominated Botev for some long years, but recently there has been a shift of power and now Botev seem to prevail. Sofia giants Levski and CSKA get the biggest support, including fans from all over the country. Understandably, they have the biggest numbers of hardcore fans, but on the other hand, the lack of cohesion due to the great distances and sometimes the not so good coordination and the fans' interests not related to football, often lead to internal conflicts within mobs. Unfortunately, in recent years accidents involving those two giants' fans are rare as their own internal quarrels prevail. Generally speaking, this has a negative effect on our entire scene. When you add all the fellas that called it quits and all the folks who emigrated, things don't look good at all. To complete the puzzle, I'll mention all the fans supporting clubs in smaller Bulgarian towns like Beroe, Dunav, Lokomotiv G.O., Minyor, as well as the small but still managing to survive mobs of Lokomotiv Sofia and Slavia. The more people start supporting their local clubs, the better it is for the scene and the sooner we'll be able to rank them on grounds of actual events.

- **Which are the best and the worst football grounds you've ever been to and why?**

Unfortunately, I find it rather hard to pick out the worst ground I've been to in Bulgaria. Most of our grounds are in a pretty bad condition and then, I could hardly tell the best one. Don't misunderstand me. I find all those Bulgarian stadia in ruins kinda charming and I'd like to visit as many of them as possible before time finishes them off. Not always modern and luxurious grounds are a good thing really. Imagine the construction of 5-6 modern grounds and the huge increase in ticket prices that would follow. The result would be beautiful but empty grounds cause a scenario like this will surely put off the last fans standing. Of course, all those journalists and wannabe experts claim that if we had modern grounds they would immediately be filled to their capacities, but that's total bullshit and anyone who's really into football knows it is. But in order not to sound so pessimistic, I'll give you an exotic example and say a few good words about the ground they built in the town of Etropole. It is an all football one and the two posh stands make you feel as if you are in some small English town. Unfortunately, all you can hear under the roofs of both stands is dead silence.

- **What do you think of the Bulgarian police?**

Fortunately, Bulgarian police is still totally unprepared and pretty unaware of fan culture. Unfortunately, fans, or at least those who claim to be hardcore and look for rival fans, do not take advantage of that. And the day will come when we'll all be sorry that we haven't taken advantage of the cops' ignorance and stupidity. Here's some tips to all fans: whatever you do, whatever happens, don't look for the police support or assistance. You won't get anything, and you'll only end up being used by the Old Bill.

- **What do you think of the youths in your firm/crew/mob?**

Youths, particularly in our club, are something that, unfortunately, we all look forward to turning up in big numbers. Our club did not exist for some 10 years, during which period a whole new generation grew up entirely under the influence of new trends and technologies. The generation that does not care about being real men in real life but being cute in the virtual world of the Internet. Of course, there are some exceptions, but the vacuum that resulted from the absence of a local club was unfortunately filled by a much stronger influx to local Levski and CSKA fan clubs. Those are boys who have never actually seen Hebur in their lives and, though highly annoying, we shouldn't be angry with them for choosing to support a club outside their native town of Pazardzhik. And when I think of new recruits, I guess it will get even more difficult as time goes by. The temptations of modern-day life are much more numerous than before, youths tend to play fast and loose and so the fluctuation of manpower in mobs is huge.

- **What do you think of the modern-day 'scene'?**

Unfortunately, nowadays it seems not enough to go to the stadium or defeat your enemy in a street battle. What matters more for the Bulgarian hooligan or rather pseudo-hooligan modern scene is what they are going to write about it on the Internet afterwards. So even if you have won the real battle, later you may read on the computer screen that you've lost, you've been badly beaten and what not. This is a phenomenon, which along with the ever-increasing fear of real physical fights will sooner or later result in a fatality or in a total collapse of the so called 'scene'. Unfortunately, most old-school fans are now gone and there seems to be no one left to teach the youth what wrong or right is. There's a huge difference between a surprise attack on match day and a bare-hand fight and an ambush in front of people's homes and the use of sprays, batons, bats and knives. This has nothing to do with football anymore and I would like to ask anyone who's into this shit a simple question: Isn't there any Roma scum left so that Bulgarians have to hurt and cripple each other? The attempted Code of Conduct that was intended to deal with such problems unfortunately failed. It seems we are not mature yet or we have much less courage than we are willing to admit. If there is another attempt to sign such a Code, I suggest everyone goes to the venue of signing unarmed in the first place without being suspicious as to what surprise the others may have planned for them. Otherwise, sooner or later, we'll mourn the loss of someone who's no longer with us because of someone else's fear and then we'll give a handle to our enemies to have us all down and finish us once and for all.

- **What do you think of English hooligans and their influence?**

The influence of English hools is well-known for everybody, even for those beyond our countries. Due to the specific features of our country, however, I think there would be no point in us blindly copying something that happened in other times and places. But what we could definitely learn, is to enjoy the relative freedom we still have, support our clubs everywhere and try to be more fans and less online hooligans. I'd be glad if someday we could all embrace the ideas of one of the most notorious English hooligans Tony O'Neill whose attitude was 'we're going and whatever happens, happens'.

Y. (G.) - Pirin (Blagoevgrad)

Meet and greet

My name's N., put people know me by my nickname, G. I wouldn't like to describe myself as all I could say might sound like self-praise. So, anyone interested in me may ask around or Google me and then draw their own conclusion, be it positive or negative. When I don't go to football I do my best to promote healthy lifestyle among white nationalists. That includes not only football fans, but all the rest of Bulgarians, regardless of their interests and subcultures. Until recently, I and some mates of mine ran a gym in Blagoevgrad where one could train for free. At present I'm trying to attract fans' attention to the real enemies of Bulgaria and those who sit in our Parliament. I would like all those football related divisions to end and all football fans to unite against the enemies of our nation.

- **How old are you and when did you become a fan of your favourite club?**

I'm 27. I became a Pirin fan when I was 16 or 17.

- **Would you tell us how your firm (crew/mob) was established?**

Pirin SS was founded in 2000. Our original idea was to act like opposition of the club management as we were at war with them at the time. Unfortunately, Pirin SS failed to develop as a serious hooligan firm. On the whole, the firm did take part in some football related clashes, but it surely is much weaker than other similar firms in Bulgaria, though it still has some pretty decent blokes.

- **How would you define yourself as a fan?**

I'd rather define myself as a Skinhead. Skinheads are kinda different type of football fans.

- **Would you tell us in more details about some fights you have been involved at stadia and on the streets?**

Oh, they're quite a few, but in view of the lawsuits filed against me, I won't go into details cause my words can be used against me in the court room, though I do know that the readers will definitely find them interesting. For the most part, those fights have had a multi-cultural basis. It would often be the case when we would beat some folks who had darker colour of skin and chase them away from stadia. I personally once beat two such individuals and made them leave our home ground because I saw them sitting next to our end. In 2007 or 2008 we went to Greece for a friendly between Pirin and Apollon Kalamaria. Ahead of kick-off we did a local Albanian right in front of some journalists. Some of them wrote an article about it afterwards. Serious accidents have often happened ahead of or after football games, but I will refrain from saying anything further. I know most top faces from the other mobs in person and we have never been into serious fights.

- **Who are your rivals and what do you think of them?**

I've never had any football rivals. I've always been against football related separation. All my rivals are my political opponents and I define them as enemies of our nation. I hope you get the picture and see what I mean.

- **Have you ever been seriously wounded or injured while fighting?**

I wouldn't use a word like 'seriously'. Once I've had my nose broken, but the fight wasn't football related.

- **Where does your favourite football club stand in your life and how important is it for you?**

I can't say for sure how important it is. It's a part of my personal story and therefore it has its definite place in my life.

- **Which are your favourite designer brands?**

Generally, I stick to all-time classics like Lonsdale, but I do have some Fred Perry garments. Now there are a lot of new brands that are nationalistic, and I try to mainly wear such clobber. The National Resistance organisation, which I belong to, also manufactures clothes and most of my Tees and polo shirts have their logo on.

- **What is your wildest favourite club related dream?**

My club becoming many time champions featuring white players only.

- **Which is your favourite game of all times?**

The Bulgarian Cup final played between Pirin and Litex in Sofia. The euphoria we experienced then will hardly be repeated again.

- **Who are your favourite players?**

I don't have many favourites, but at the top I'll place Paolo Di Canio.

- **Would you name the top 5 Bulgarian firms/crews/mobs?**

I'll mention 4 currently active as there aren't many decent firms now: Sofia West, Animals, Gott Mit Uns, and Zara Boys.

- **Which are the best and the worst football grounds you've ever been to and why?**

I can't tell any good ones, but we haven't had any good welcome at Plovdiv stadia.

- **What do you think of the Bulgarian police?**

The police in Bulgaria is the same as everywhere else in the world, i.e. wankers protecting the system and suppressing their people's freedom.

- **What do you think of the youths in your firm/crew/mob?**

It's the same all situation like the one in the country in general. Younger generations are becoming increasingly weak and cowardly.

- **What do you think of the modern-day 'scene'?**

Worse than before. I have the impression that with each year gone by, people's devotion and commitment are getting weaker and weaker. One could see evidence of that when looking at the numbers of fans going to football. They are extremely small.

- **What do you think of English hooligans and their influence?**

I wouldn't define them as a leading factor. At present, strong firms are to be found not in England, but in the rest of Europe. It is them that have the biggest influence.

P.S.

Respect to all football fans who remained loyal through all these years and kept the Bulgarian scene the way we know it now: nationalistic and racist. I'd also like to thank the authors of this book because I'm sure that a read like this would be helpful for both us and the next generations, who will now know the history of their firms and the influence they've had.

M. (M.) - Minyor (Pernik)

Meet and greet

- **How old are you and when did you become a fan of your favourite club?**

V. Minyor Pernik, 39 years of age. I remember well my times in primary school when football was religion and Minyor FC was made a cult of by the working class. You had to be really lucky to find a vacant seat at the Stadium of Peace. In 1987-88 I started going to the football on my own, before that I don't remember much as I was too young.

- **Would you tell us how your firm (crew/mob) was established?**

Long time ago there were no fan clubs! The entire ground was a huge mob as they say now. In the 1990s we established Minyor fan club and then came the different firms like Hard Boys, Moshino, UA-13, Krakra Boys.

- **How would you define yourself as a fan?**

Personally, I don't define myself as a die-hard fan because I think such a category should not even exist. My opinion is that any proper fan should be a die-hard.

- **Would you tell us in more details about some fights you have been involved at stadia and on the streets?**

We've had millions of fights through the years, but I think our generation inherited great memories of huge riots and so wherever we went we'd feel the respect paid to our predecessors and if anyone dared to challenge us, they'd end up beaten up and humiliated. In 1997 we had a good ruck with CSKA and in 1999 the Levski cattle was given a good hiding. As a matter of fact, we beat them pretty bad any time we meet them, so...

- **Who are your rivals and what do you think of them?**

Our best and only reward is when there is no mercy for Levski. That's what I think of our enemy! Otherwise, a destination such as Lokomotiv Stolipinovo[17] can also generate hatred only.

- **Have you ever been seriously wounded or injured while fighting?**

I've never been injured, beaten, or nicked a scarf... we are Minyor for fuck's sake (laughing).

- **Where does your favourite football club stand in your life and how important is it for you?**

My favourite club stands right beside my family and country!

- **Which are your favourite designer brands?**

I don't have any!

- **What is your wildest favourite club related dream?**

My biggest dream is my club to have no money worries. I don't want any silverware, all I want is the clubs from Sofia to suffer when they play against Pernik.

- **Which is your favourite game of all times?**

All our games against Levski are my favourite cause if we didn't do them on the pitch, we surely did them in trains and at stations.

- **Who are your favourite players?**

Tony Evtimov is my favourite player and the hat-trick he scored against that Poduene scum made everybody in Bulgaria respect him.

- **Would you name the top 5 Bulgarian firms/crews/mobs?**

Top 5 of Bulgarian mobs are Minyor, Botev, CSKA, and the scum from Levski and Lokomotiv Plovdiv.

- **Which are the best and the worst football grounds you've ever been to and why?**

The best ground outside Pernik for me is Hristo Botev Stadium in Plovdiv because we've got friends over there and the worst one is in the town of Stara Zagora...

- **What do you think of the Bulgarian police?**

I don't give a shit about police! Once I invaded the pitch and some fat wankers started chasing me, but I managed to get away and the crowd cheered me in delight (laughing).

- **What do you think of the youths in your firm/crew/mob?**

Youths in Pernik...Well, they are the same as the older fans.

- **What do you think of the modern-day 'scene'?**

Modern-day on- and off the pitch scene is real and absolute shit!

- **What do you think of English hooligans and their influence?**

English hooligans? 200 Russians beat the shit out of them! What the fuck could I think of them? Thank you.

---

17 Stolipinovo is the Roma ghetto in the town of Plovdiv

M. (C.) - Lokomotiv (Plovdiv)

Meet and greet

My name's P.M. I met Gilly (one of the authors of this book and a friend of mine) in Varna one morning in March before the Lokomotiv vs Cherno More game and after a huge amount of beer we drank, things got settled(laughing).

- **How old are you and when did you become a fan of your favourite club?**

I'm 42, a Lokomotiv fan since the early 1980s. When I was 5, my dad first took me to a game to watch Lokomotiv play Maritsa, though, naturally I don't remember much of it.

- **Would you tell us how your firm(crew/mob) was established?**

I don't belong to any firm or crew. I'm just a part of the black-and-white mob and I have respect for everyone, including other mobs. But my biggest respect has always been due to the mobs of Lokomotiv G.O., Etar (to Gulisha, in particular) and Botev Vratsa.

- **How would you define yourself as a fan?**

I define myself as a die-hard fan, I love my club and I do not betray my mates! I've always been ready to give my heart and soul for Lokomotiv and for my real friends who I feel as close as brothers. We're getting older now, but I keep on following my club, come rain or sunshine.

- **Would you tell us in more details about some fights you have been involved at stadia and on the streets?**

My first fights were against Botev Plovdiv and CSKA. The ones I hate most after the yellow parrots are Slavia. I remember an occasion in Sofia that gave birth to my hatred for them. It was either 1991 or 1992 when we played away to them. There were probably 7 of us roaming around the stadium before kick-off. As we were having our beers undisturbed, out of the blue came some 40 Slavia and had a go at us. One of our lads (The Ox) legged and we followed him, but they caught us at the bus stop by the stadium and we were given a really good hiding. Well, 7 against 40, what else could you expect?

There was this away day in Varna, we were playing Cherno More in 1992/93 and only 3 of us remained after the game as the rest had got on the coach. They had a go at us and we took some kicks and punches, but I nicked the scarf of one of their top lads. Now I remember another funny story when we played away from home in the town of Dobrich and though we lost 2-4, things got better than we'd expected. There were just a few of us and we thought the locals would come looking for a fight after the game, but we were wrong. One of their lads saw us off to the railway station, bought us tickets and booze, would you believe it?! So, we went on a binge in the buffet car and we started chatting some birds up and at some point, we were considering having sex with them in the toilets (laughing).

I got badly hurt on another occasion after a game against Botev Plovdiv. As I said before the yellows or I'd rather call them the scum are one of my most hateful rivals. It happened at Plovdiv freight station, the evening after the Plovdiv derby. Some 10 of us decided to complete the night drinking in the local pub celebrating our victory against our eternal rivals. There were some other folks in the boozer, too, but we were raising hell singing songs about our beloved club and so after we had consumed huge amounts of alcohol we decided to go outside for a bit of fresh air. Then they came out of the blue. I don't know whether they traced us, or someone told them where we were but there appeared some 30 Botev hools. Being pretty drunk, we started throwing bottles and stones at them. They answered back and then went at us. We were trapped and there was nowhere to run. Being so drunk that we could hardly stand on our feet, it seemed impossible for us to cross all those railway lines. We stormed into them, but they got the upper hand. They beat us black and blue; we suffered numerous blows, kicks and punches. They got me down to the ground and a good few of them started kicking me around. Soon I was covered in blood. Thanks God the older folks from the pub came out to see what all that noise and rattle was and then they chased away the yellow cunts with a shower of bottles and glasses. Nobody knows what would have happened if they hadn't come to our rescue. I was in a real mess, so they called an ambulance that took me to hospital. I won't go into details regarding my condition, but I stayed in hospital for some 20 days. In principle I had to stay for some more days to complete my recovery, but some mates came to get me out and took me to an away game in

Shumen, passing through Gorna Oryahovitsa to pay a visit to our black and white brothers.

On an away day in Varna for a game against Spartak in the late 1990s we literally blew up their ground with loads of home-made bombs. There were only about 30-40 of us, but Spartak lads didn't stand a chance. I'll never forget how Vasko Metallica (RIP, bro!) blew off the first bomb throwing it all the way down the pitch during the very game. We had some top faces with us and we had more troubles with the cops rather than with the locals.

I remember an away day in Bourgas, when, once again pretty pissed, we had a ruck with the Sharks and then we got chased down by some gangsters downtown. It must have been 1992, a game against Chernomorets. After yet another long binge on the train and in Bourgas boozers, we headed for the ground. We were so drunk that we ended up right in the home end, amidst the Chernomorets Sharks. It kicked off big time and we had a really close shave. All we got away with was some scratches and bruises and, naturally, torn up clothes. The cops escorted us out of the ground and we caught a bus downtown. We went on the piss again, sang some more songs and then we got pursued by a bunch of local gangsters. Thanks Goodness, we weren't given another good hiding by them... (laughing).

You know we're good mates with Lokomotiv G.O. fans, but before we got on friendly terms, we used to be enemies. In 1988 when we played in Gorna Oryahovitsa we set a bus on fire with our bombs on our way from the train station to the stadium.

There are countless fights inside and outside grounds and I won't have enough time to speak about all of them.

- **Who are your rivals (in the general sense of the word, in life or at the stadium), what are they like and what is your opinion of them?**

Botev Plovdiv are our major rivals (and Slavia for me personally). I used to live in a Plovdiv quarter inhabited by yellow bastards only. My hatred for them is eternal. I also dislike Spartak Varna.

- **Have you ever been seriously wounded or injured while fighting?**

I mentioned the clashes with Slavia in Sofia and the fight at the freight station after which I was taken to hospital.

- **Where does your favourite football club stand in your life and how important is it for you?**

Where does my favourite club stand? It is my world, my soul, my love! It's the second most important thing after family. I live for Lokomotiv Plovdiv. They got me married and they got me divorced...I'm sorry that things happened this way and I and my wife separated, but I find my club important. Nothing lasts forever but the black-and-white love!

- **Which are your favourite designer brands?**

I don't have many favourite designer labels, but I've always been fond of Adidas, as well as of the black-and-white Lokomotiv Plovdiv jerseys. The club's crest is my brand.

- **What is your wildest favourite club related dream?**

I dream of Lokomotiv beating Botev every time they play and of me being proud of it. Wins against Botev are the only games that make me really happy. I want to see a capacity crowd ground and an overcrowded train full of black and white fans. What else a football fan could possibly need? Unfortunately, things now are not what they used to be... (his eyes brimming with tears)!

- **Which is your favourite game of all times?**

Botev – Lokomotiv 0-1 in 1991/1992, Yankovich scoring the winner in the 78th minute, as well as another victory over them in 1988/1989, when the winner was once again scored in the last minutes. Those are the most memorable games for me!

- **Who are your favourite players?**

Lazar Vuchkov, Eranosyan, Misho Vulchev and the entire Lokomotiv Plovdiv squad of the 1990s.

- **Would you name the top 5 Bulgarian firms/crews/mobs?**

1. Lauta Hools & Lauta Army;
2. Sofia West;
3. CSKA Animals;
4. Cherno More in the past and last, but not least
5. Lokomotiv G.O. For a small town like Gorna Oryahovitsa, always having a core of 30- 40 united and dedicated lads is a remarkable achievement!

- **Which are the best and the worst football grounds you've ever been to and why?**

The worst I've been to is the one in the town of Shumen. The best one is our home ground. There's no place like home, you know!

- **What do you think of the Bulgarian police?**

ACAB. There's no way one can deal with those pathetic bastards. A number of good lads did time for nothing. Football fans in Bulgaria and elsewhere are considered worse than criminals and paedophiles.

- **What do you think of the youths in your firm/crew/mob?**

They'll never be like us, the old-school boys; they'll never reach our level, we, old-school lads were for real!

- **What do you think of the modern-day 'scene'?**

Things ain't what they used to be, and you don't meet proper fans any more. In the past we used to be born proper fans. You must have it in your heart and you have to stand behind your club and love it even when they lose. A good example of loyal fans one could find with Lokomotiv G.O. For so many years they played in the lower divisions; they even played in the amateur leagues for a decade, but nevertheless they had always had at least 20-30 proper lads on away days playing in small villages. Such are the old-school fans. Things are much different nowadays, there's no doubt about it.

- **What do you think of English hooligans and their influence?**

They are the pioneers, and they had influenced the entire world. The English were strong in the 60s, 70s, 80s until the early 1990s, but the cruel measures taken by the Iron Lady Margaret Thatcher changed a lot of things. Prison sentences, long-term banning orders, fines, etc. The result was the decline of English hooligans. At present, the Russians and the Poles are on top of it... but they'll always remain in the shadow of the high and mighty English!

P.S.

I'd like to thank the authors (Tosh and Gilly) cause it's a great honour for me to take part in this book, and also I'd like to thank Kuncho (GMU), Plamen, Lisko, Kolyo - The Bomb, The Two Axes, Napolito, Bankov - The Taxi, Chapkuna, Danny from Cherno More and last but not least those lads who are no longer with us – Doncho, Dundie and Vasko Metallica (RIP).

M. (V.) - Lokomotiv (Sofia)

Meet and greet

- **How old are you and when did you become a fan of your favourite club?**

Hi there! Let me introduce myself, my name's M. and football fans know me by the nickname V. I've been following my club since I was a small kid, probably around 11. I'll never forget the day I first went to watch Lokomotiv Sofia in the flesh. It was a late Sunday afternoon. I was sitting with a mate of mine in front of our block of flats with nothing to do when he told me Lokomotiv Sofia (I live near Lokomotiv Stadium) were playing that day, so we decided to go and kill 2 hours. When we entered the ground, we saw the supporters in the opposite end singing, clapping and cheering on their team and we felt a kind of special thrill so in the second half we moved to their end in order to share their joy and emotions when watching their beloved club play. So that's how I got hooked on football.

- **Would you tell us how your firm (crew/mob) was established?**

I cannot tell much of the firm because I was not there when it was founded, but I know that my Drinking Boys Sofia Hooligans crew was established with the

241

purpose of separating those fans who are far right-wing and fonder of violence (the hooligans) from the other large firm called Iron Brigades, which also consists of die-hard ultras.

- **How would you define yourself as a fan?**

In the beginning, when I started going to football, I defined myself as an ultra, but then I realised that I'm actually more of a troublemaker because I take delight in fighting rival fans or the police.

- **Would you tell us in more details about some fights you have been involved at stadia and on the streets?**

I've been through a lot of riots and accidents across stadia and on the streets, but I'll tell you about our most recent one involving our biggest rivals Slavia. There was this Slavia vs Lokomotiv Sofia game, and as always, we, Lokomotiv fans took a tram to Slavia ground. When we stepped off the vehicle and headed for the ground we had only 2 or 3 cops escorting us. All of a sudden, group of 15/20 masked blokes appeared from behind and went at us shouting 'Slavia'. We were some 20/25 people, including kids and older fellas (actually not more than 10 of us took part in the fight). We steamed into them, which is recorded in a video, taped by some random guy living in the block of flats opposite and on this video, you can see how 10 Lokomotiv lads storm into and utterly defeat 15/20 Slavia lads and how the latter legged it. They just came across the wrong people (laughing). This is simply one of the many experiences I've had.

- **Who are your rivals (in the general sense of the word, in life or at the stadium), what are they like and what is your opinion of them?**

As I said, our biggest rivals are Slavia! We don't just hate them, we loathe them, we despise them, and no matter what people say about the Levski vs CSKA hatred, I'll tell you what, they don't have a fucking clue what hatred really means and how much we hate Slavia. Anyway, I think they should exist as a club because they are an old club and have good traditions, and also because we need someone to beat the shit out of from time to time (laughing).

- **Have you ever been seriously wounded or injured while fighting?**

I've had some minor injuries, but nothing too serious. Once I got hit with a baton, but maybe due to the adrenaline rush I felt nothing. On the next day I woke up with a huge lump on my head (laughing).

- **Where does your favourite football club stand in your life and how important is it for you?**

Lokomotiv Sofia is my top priority in life. I've skipped school, I've missed birthday parties of relatives and friends and I've even been absent from work in order to watch my beloved Lokomotiv and every game they play is like my first game ever, full of the same emotions and thrills.

- **Which are your favourite designer brands?**

Well, I've got quite a few favourite brands, but now we have this new BH Wear (Balkan Hooligans Wear), which is a great brand and it's taking over the market, but traditionally I'd go for Fred Perry, Lacoste, Hugo Boss, Armani, Burberry, Adidas and some stuff made by Nike.

- **What is your wildest favourite club related dream?**

My wildest dream is seeing Lokomotiv Sofia lift the Cup. I've been dreaming about it ever since I became a football fan.

- **Which is your favourite game of all times?**

My favourite game is one against Slavia. It was at their ground and in the dying seconds of the game Lokomotiv scored and we qualified for European tournaments. It was a joy that no words can describe, probably one of the happiest moments in my life, beating our bitter enemy in the very last minute and qualifying to play in Europe.

- **Who are your favourite players?**

I don't have any favourites, there are good players now and there are all those legends from the past, players that should never be forgotten, players like Nikola Kotkov, Atanas Mihailov, Georgi Asparuhov - Gundi, Trifon Ivanov, Hristo Stoichkov and many others.

- **Would you name the top 5 Bulgarian firms/crews/mobs?**

In my opinion the top Bulgarian firms are as follows: Levski Sofia West, CSKA Animals, Lokomotiv Plovdiv Lauta Hools and Beroe Zara Boys.

- **Which are the best and the worst football grounds you've ever been to and why?**

Well, the worst one is definitely Minyor Pernik ground called 'Stadium of Peace'. What the hell has it got to do with peace? (laughing). The best one, of course, is Lokomotiv Sofia ground!

- **What do you think of the Bulgarian police?**

Bulgarian cops carry a chip on their shoulders and they think they are above the law because actually they stand for the law. In their private lives cops are very often sad cunts who are able to defend only when wearing a uniform and a badge. Very few are those who are real men of honour.

- **What do you think of the youths in your firm/crew/mob?**

We don't have many youths in DBSH, I am one of the few as entry to our firm is not easy and you have to prove who you are for quite a long time in order to be allowed to join the firm. In general, our mob has a good number of youngsters, some are ordinary supporters, others are future ultras and still others are old school hooligans.

- **What do you think of the modern-day 'scene'?**

Well... it's an interesting issue, describing the scene in Bulgaria... Each year it's getting worse, ultras are getting fewer and the same goes for tifos, flags, songs, pyro, etc. Besides, hooligans do not fight with their bare hands like real men, but use tools like batons, knives, pipes, and knuckledusters and almost on every occasion not in equal numbers. The proper supporters are getting fewer at Bulgarian stadia at the expense of plastic fans, glory hunters and supporters of clubs that do not have any history and traditions. Unfortunately, Bulgarian fandom is getting worse each and every year!

- **What do you think of English hooligans and their influence?**

English hooligans marked the beginning of hooliganism on a global scale, but nowadays they are simply worthless. Countries like Bulgaria, Serbia, Greece, Turkey, Romania, Russia and Ukraine have much stronger and better hooligans than England. England does not have the hooligans it used to have in the 1980s.

G. D. (P.) - Botev (Vratsa)

Meet and greet

G.D. (P.), born on 26.11.1974, married, with one kid. Currently travelling as a sailor. I've been supporting Botev Vratsa for 35 years, and for 20 years I was the top face, the leader of their mob.

- **How old are you and when did you become a fan of your favourite club?**

I've been a Botev fan since I was just a small kid. I must have been 6 when I first went to a football game.

- **Would you tell us how your firm(crew/mob) was established?**

Walter Kalupov is the man who first organised Botev supporters in the 1970s. A great fella who's always stood beside me. Our group first started gathering in the late 1980s, but formally we were first organised in 1999.

- **How would you define yourself as a fan?**

Just an ordinary fan now, the years of hooliganism are long gone for me.

- **Would you tell us in more details about some fights you have been involved at stadia and on the streets?**

I'll tell you about the fight that will forever remain in my memories. We were playing our regional rivals Septemvriyska Slava from the town of Mihailovgrad (modern-day Montana). Nowadays they call it a derby, but it surely was not a derby before because we played for a quarter of a century in the top flight while their derbies were in the third division against Kom FC from the town of Berkovitsa and besides, Kom FC would usually win. Having been relegated from Division 1, we hosted the team from Mihailovgrad in the first rounds of the new campaign. The ground was a sellout. The away fans arrived by train, probably 100-handed. Botev Vratsa won 2-0. After the game we headed for the bus station. There we caught some of the away supporters. They pretended they were waiting for a bus to Berkovitsa, but it was 7:00 pm and we knew that buses for Berkovitsa left only at 8:00am and 11:30 am. What followed was a nasty beating they received. All hell broke loose as women started screaming and bystanders ran for cover. Next, we went to the train station, but found nobody. Two of our lads searched through the station to find two shopping bags full of our enemies' red-and-white scarves and flags. I told the lads to put on that stuff and in such a disguise to approach the platforms as I was sure the wankers had hidden somewhere. That's what we did, we took off our green-and-white scarves and put on the red and white ones. We went out at the platform and started chanting Slava, Slava... That was their usual chant and soon, one by one they started coming out of the bushes in the further end of the platform, waving at us. They must have mistaken us for their mates we beat at the bus station. Well, they recognised us eventually, but it was too late. Another vicious scuffle followed. We did them good and left them lying on the platform. Then suddenly the Old Bill appeared, and we legged. The cops naturally started chasing us. We started jumping from one train to another and I was the last man running. At some point they closed the gap and I was sure I was going to be nicked. Then I remembered I had this huge home-made bomb on me. I turned around and sent it blowing off right in front of the legs of the nearest cop. They stopped right there and then I heard one of our lads in the distance shouting that the coppers had fired a gun. They ran as hell (laughing) and when I caught up with them I shouted at them, 'For Christ sake, stop it, nobody's firing any guns' and I started rolling with laughter. Then we hung all their nicked scarves and flags on a tree by the stadium, making it all red and white. Unforgettable and unique experience.

- **Who are your rivals (in the general sense of the word, in life or at the stadium), what are they like and what is your opinion of them?**

Septemvriyska Slava from the town of Mihailovgrad, but their club is now called Montana FC and they have no support, pathetic scum.

- **Have you ever been seriously wounded or injured while fighting?**

I've never been badly hurt in a football related fight, a bleeding nose or a shiner, but nothing serious.

- **Where does your favourite football club stand in your life and how important is it for you?**

When I was a regular at Botev Vratsa games, Botev was my home and my family. Unfortunately, one day they appointed a complete moron for a club director and that was the last straw that broke my back. Now I follow things from a distance and just watch the wrong path Bulgarian football has long taken in general. On a global level, the Bosman rule and the wholesale buying of Africans ruined it all. Bulgarian football is literally a hostage to politics, which I find absolutely disgusting!

- **Which are your favourite designer brands?**

Fred Perry, Ralph Lauren.

- **What is your wildest favourite club related dream?**

I've never had much of a dream about Botev Vratsa. What I've always wanted is players doing their best on the pitch. That has always made me happy. But still; I wouldn't mind Botev winning a trophy someday…

- **Which is your favourite game of all times?**

It's very hard for me to point out a single game, but probably I'll say the Septemvri Simitli vs Botev Vratsa game that we won 2-1. In 2011, after winning this game Botev returned to the top flight after long years of exile in the lower divisions. The game was played on the same day the CL final between Barcelona and Manchester United was played. I remember that all those who saw we were going to Simitli thought we were crazy choosing not to watch such a great final. I told them that our final was to be played in Simitli because it was our Botev playing there. We brought a tough bunch of lunatics there and when Simeon Raikov scored the winner we went fucking mental.

There's another game I'll never forget. In 2009 we played away in the town of Pleven against a team called Belite Orli FC. On 15th August, the night before the game, my son was born. On the next day the game finished in a 2-2 draw. The home side opened the score and then Rumen Rangelov made it 1-1. After the equaliser the entire Botev team ran to our end, lined up in front of us, put their arms together and started doing the 'the cradle' celebration dedicating this goal to me, my wife and our newborn son. Some other memorable games for me are Levski vs Botev Vratsa 3-6, Botev vs CSKA 3-0 and an unforgettable 3-1 away victory to Trakia Plovdiv.

- **Who are your favourite players?**

Boiko Kraev, Valentin Stanchev, Hristo Mitov, Simeon Raikov and several others I find worth mentioning. But there are also those who, as time went by, bitterly disappointed me in terms of characters and personalities. That's why I say that a football player has to be a man both on and off the pitch.

- **Would you name the top 5 Bulgarian firms/crews/mobs?**

Lauta Army, Sofia West, Animals, they are the top three. Then follow several other firms, which I think are at the same lower level, though different in numbers. If I have to name them, well, here they are: Brigada Vratza, Pirin SS, Lokomotiv GO, Beroe, Neftochimic, Minyor and finally Izgrev Boys, but in their past.

- **Which are the best and the worst football grounds you've ever been to and why?**

Oooh, this is a really tough one. Almost any ground in Bulgaria could be described as the worst. In the town of Razgrad, for instance, away fans are locked up in something resembling a birdcage. I just don't wanna talk about it anymore. Here's another example, in our own ground in Vratsa, right behind the goals there are numerous rebars sticking out of the terraces. There was this young lad that once fell over and was literally impaled on one of those bars. We ran for an ambulance and first aid. Fucking hell! Once I also hurt my leg on one of those steel bars and then the club's doctor washed my wound and vaccinated me against tetanus. The worst thing is that only a few months after the accident with the young kid, one of the political parties shot a video of our main stand to show how much they did for the town and the local football. It's all a deception; it's all fake and ridiculous football in Bulgaria becoming hostage to politicians, especially municipal clubs.

The best ground I've been to is Philips Arena in Eindhoven.

- **What do you think of the Bulgarian police?**

A.C.A.B. What can I say about them? They're always on the wrong side.

- **What do you think of the youths in your firm/crew/mob?**

There are some decent lads, game as fuck. But I've got some advice for all youngsters – just leave your knives and bombs behind!

- **What do you think of the modern-day 'scene'?**

Taking into account the shitty football played in Bulgaria and the clubs' wrong policies, as well as the constant pressure from UEFA and FIFA and the police brutality, we still manage to have some decent firms. What I have always dreamt of is setting up a strong Bulgarian national firm. At one point we had almost made it, taking into consideration the games Bulgaria played in Zagreb, Budapest and Constanta... Man, it was cool! Somehow, we stood all together and then things got fucked up again, which is so typical of Bulgarians.

- **What do you think of English hooligans and their influence?**

The truth is that all that culture involving hooligans, ultras, etc. originated in England. They've stepped back a little, giving way to the Polish and the Russians, but mind you, the cops also had their contribution for such a retreat. The last thing I'll say about English hooligans is what goes around comes around, or … once a hooligan, always a hooligan.

M. - Levski (Sofia)

Meet and greet

My name's V., they call me U., and I'm a Levski Sofia fan! I first met two of the authors at their first book (Beyond the Hatred) launch. I was asked for a brief interview for their second project and I thank them for including me.

- **How old are you and when did you become a fan of your favourite club?**

I'm 32 and I've been a Levski fan ever since I was born. My first game was in 1991 against Beroe in Stara Zagora. I've been going to football since 1997.

- **Would you tell us how your firm(crew/mob) was established?**

I used to be a member of OCB (Old Capital Boys) from the town of Veliko Tarnovo for a number of years. In 2010 I moved to the town of Ruse and there with the local lads we founded Blue Terror Ruse. We're a small but solid group and though we've been through a lot of changes in all those years, as a whole I think we're moving forward in the right direction.

- **How would you define yourself as a fan?**

I'm a hooligan. Or I'd rather say I was. In 2013 I fought a long battle with cancer that had some serious consequences for me so now I try to avoid physical confrontation. However, I don't think there is such a term like 'ex-hooligan'. It's a disease that just lives inside you!

- **Would you tell us in more details about some fights you have been involved at stadia and on the streets?**

My first major fight was in 1999 in Plovdiv with Botev. There were some 30 of us and they were twice as many. They gave us some hard time in a pub. All sorts of debris came flying at us and then they went at us toe-to-toe. One of their top boys punched me so hard that I didn't recover until the end of the game. We and them 'parrots' hate each other so much. In 2013 we had another great melee with them in Plovdiv. Inside the ground we started throwing stones at them because one of their stewards stole a flag from us and we went mad. After the game we smashed them near the stadium. We nearly got nicked and one of my mates had a suspended sentence. The biggest fight I've been involved in was against the cops in 2005 during a Sofia derby game. They invaded our stand, but we brutally drove them away big time and for good! A lot of vicious brawls have happened on the streets and roads on such derby days. We used to give them hell, damn red pigs. So, in all those years the only battle I've lost was the one against Botev back in 1999. Not that I'm some kind of a Terminator, it just happened (winking).

- **Who are your rivals (in the general sense of the word, in life or at the stadium), what are they like and what is your opinion of them?**

Our biggest rivals are the CSKA pigs. They are despicable scum that has no morals and honour. They don't keep their word and they do not follow the Code of Conduct that they came up with themselves. Back in the days they had some true gentlemen among the old school Kravai boys. Now they're gone. Probably the boys from Offensive deserve some respect for not recognising their merger with Litex, something that the rest of them reds willingly did. But I've talked enough about them (laughing).

- **Have you ever been seriously wounded or injured while fighting?**

I've been injured a lot of times while fighting the police. After a game in Lovech my back stayed black and blue for a whole month. During a bar fight in Tarnovo some Albanians stabbed me in the leg. Then we beat the shit out of them. Once again in the town of Tarnovo, a Lokomotiv G.O. lad smashed a bottle in my head and cut my eyebrow open. If he is reading this, I hope he will take my apologies for the events that followed. Cheers dude!

- **Where does your favourite football club stand in your life and how important is it for you?**

After my family and the people, I love, Levski comes third in terms of importance.

It's more important than me. I've sacrificed a thousand times for Levski and I'll do it another thousand times!

- **Which are your favourite designer brands?**

I've never been a slave to designer brands, but I like wearing Adidas and Fred Perry. I've always dressed in such a way as to avoid the cops' attention. I'm not worried about the other supporters.

- **What is your wildest favourite club related dream?**

My biggest dream is to see Sector B united. I have dedicated 20 years of my life to that Sector and what is happening there right now is just killing me.

- **Which is your favourite game of all times?**

I'll never forget Levski playing Udinese! We made a fantastic comeback from 0-1 to 2-1 to qualify for the Europa League quarterfinals. I cried tears of joy on that day.

- **Who are your favourite players?**

Sasho Alexandrov, Ivankov and Georgi Ivanov (Gonzo).

- **Would you name the top 5 Bulgarian firms/crews/mobs?**

Levski Sofia West; Lokomotiv Plovdiv Lauta Army; Litex Animals; Levski South Division; Levski Ultra Varna.

- **Which are the best and the worst football grounds you've ever been to and why?**

I'll nominate two as the worst places, one is in the town of Razgrad (I'm speaking of its away end conditions) and the other in Blagoevgrad. The best one is Ljudski in Maribor.

- **What do you think of the Bulgarian police?**

Old Bill is gay. 99% are halfwits carrying a chip on their shoulders.

- **What do you think of the youths in your firm/crew/mob?**

I try to teach everyone to have respect for their elders and to love and protect their motherland. To work and behave like reasonable young people who will later become good men! I hope they learn from my off-the-pitch knowledge and experience.

- **What do you think of the modern-day 'scene'?**

Modern-day scene is pathetic. It's mainly young wannabes who have no respect for anyone or anything. They use tools and are up for it only when they outnumber their rivals. Those who are my age or older than me just quit for a number of reasons.

- **What do you think of English hooligans and their influence?**

They were the pioneers and will always deserve respect. Their big firms actually do not exist anymore, but in the lower divisions their hooligan scene is still alive, though it's a poor copy of what it used to be in the 1980s and 1990s. On a wider European scale, they considerably give way to Eastern Europe and we fully witnessed that during the last Euro held in France.

P. - Neftochimic (Burgas)

Meet and greet

- **How old are you and when did you become a fan of your favourite club?**

Hi there, I'm 29 years old and I've been following Neftochimic for 11 years.

- **Would you tell us how your firm (crew/mob) was established?**

I belong to Green Fighters, which was founded long before I became a member.

- **How would you define yourself as a fan?**

I define myself as a die-hard fan. I don't care about results and I hardly ever watch the game itself.

- **Would you tell us in more details about some fights you have been involved at stadia and on the streets?**

Some five years ago I and another GF lad were seeing off a mate at the station without knowing that Slavia were playing away to Chernomorets on the same day. I think it was a cup game. Slavia fans stepped off the train and there was this bloke pissed as hell who recognised us thanks to our tattoos and went at us. However, nothing happened as the cops appeared. Then 9 of us GF boys met up and followed them to the beach where they started taking pictures and drinking beer. We had a good row for about 5 minutes, no police around, and Slavia fans took a really good hiding.

- **Who are your rivals (in the general sense of the word, in life or at the stadium), what are they like and what is your opinion of them?**

We've had this animosity with Beroe for years. They have some decent lads, but I don't think much of them. They do those cowardly acts like ambushing rank-and-file supporters after games and beating them with tools, heavily outnumbering them, of course. We recently offered them an equal number fight, but they refused. I guess you don't wonder why.

- **Have you ever been seriously wounded or injured while fighting?**

I've never had any serious injuries while fighting.

- **Where does your favourite football club stand in your life and how important is it for you?**

It stands right below my son… as my son is my life now.

- **Which are your favourite designer brands?**

I don't have any.

- **What is your wildest favourite club related dream?**

I dream of us having a home (ground) once again cause there's no future for us without that.

- **Which is your favourite game of all times?**

I'll never forget an away game against Chernomorets (NB: at our own ground!!!), ahead of which everyone predicted our loss with a 5 or 6 goals difference...I still remember as it was yesterday how Pepi Dimitrov scored in the 90th minute to make it 2-3. I'll never forget their coach's downcast expression.

- **Who are your favourite players?**

As I said before, I don't have any and I don't care much about what's going on, on the pitch.

- **Would you name the top 5 Bulgarian firms/crews/mobs?**

Taking into account the current situation with our 'scene', I find it very hard to name five top firms. Maybe only Animals keep up the good job. The rest have made a huge step back.

- **Which are the best and the worst football grounds you've ever been to and why?**

The ground in Razgrad looks like a prison. It's a terrible cage and surely is the worst one. The best one used to be Neftochimic Stadium before Chernomorets FC started using it.

- **What do you think of the Bulgarian police?**

Morons!

- **What do you think of the youths in your firm/crew/mob?**

We surely have a lot more to give (I consider myself as one of those youths), but when I recall what we actually did when we were teens... modern-day teens are a fucking disgrace!

- **What do you think of the modern-day 'scene'?**

Our 'scene' is a tragedy...

- **What do you think of English hooligans and their influence?**

I don't give a shit about them, but I think they have not had any influence for a few good years.

(M.) - Shumen (Volov)

Meet and greet

- **How old are you and when did you become a fan of your favourite club?**

My name's I. E., but everybody knows me by my nickname M. I'm 53, born in the town of Shumen. I used to live right by the stadium and I wouldn't miss a game as a kid. I was lucky as right after I graduated high school, the local Volov FC was promoted to the top flight.

- **Would you tell us how your firm (crew/mob) was established?**

Our mob would then gather behind the goal on the North stand. We used to call it the English sector. In that campaign Volov got relegated though finishing 11th in the table (there were 16 clubs in the 1st Division then). Water cannon crowd dispersal, riot police; it's a long story... What followed were 10 years of decline until the club was taken over by a guy known as 'The Shogun'. Naturally, the mob was still there, fresh blood in it. We didn't have a name; we were just the English sector boys. The older generation, the metalheads, and a number of young nutters.

The Shogun started paying for our coaches, so we'd bring large numbers on away days.

- **How would you define yourself as a fan?**

Rather mixed (laughing).

- **Would you tell us in more details about some fights you have been involved at stadia and on the streets?**

Surely those away days did have stories to tell. For instance, when we got promoted to the top division we played our last game away in the town of Vratsa. There were 20 coach loads of us. Mind you; it's a great distance between Shumen and Vratsa! Some of us arrived for the second half. Vratsa was all yellow-and-blue[18] that day. We were drinking in a pub when the locals turned up. It ended way too fast. One of our lads, we called him Piff, asked them who their ringleader was and then directly went at him headbutting and down he was so the rest bottled it. During the game Piff broke his leg and I got nicked after the final whistle. 5-6 cops chased me down the pitch and finally one of them tripped me up. I ended up with two other Shumen lads in a police van. The Shogun, however, said our coaches would not leave the town until we got released.

- **Who are your rivals (in the general sense of the word, in life or at the stadium), what are they like and what is your opinion of them?**

We disliked Varna and Ruse fans most. In the neighbouring town of Targovishte we did them well back in my student years. All game long they wouldn't stop their banter, though they were 10-15 handed only. After the game we had a go at them before the cops could even realise it.

- **Have you ever been seriously wounded or injured while fighting?**

I rarely fought at games. Once it kicked off with you, Lokomotiv G.O. fans, and we exchanged a good couple of punches. On quite a few other occasions we did see off our 'guests' with a good slapping, but the cops were usually hard on our heels. My last serious fight was in Vienna before Rapid vs CSKA game. They had a go at us, Bulgarians, right by the away fans gate. I was a bit further talking on my mobile when two hooded guys approached me. One of them was a head taller than me and mind you, I'm 1.86 m. tall. I turned around to see none of our lads apart from the Count, who had already lost his scarf and was being chased. I said to myself, 'To hell with all! I'm up for it!', and I went straight at the tall cunt kicking and punching him in the face. They legged it, but the cops grabbed me and the Count and started questioning us. Then we took out our English passports as we already had this dual citizenship then, and they gave us that dumb look of theirs as if they had just shat in their pants (laughing).

- **Where does your favourite football club stand in your life and how important is it for you?**

I follow my club whenever I can, no matter the distances. I watch lots of football in general. I call my friends regularly to discuss football. I've been a family man and I've had my own business for years, so I can't go everywhere and meet everyone for sure. I started missing a game or two long ago, but when I was younger I went to all away games. There are a few other lads of ours who could also tell you decent stories.

- **Which are your favourite designer brands?**

I don't have any specific favourite brands, but when I think twice, maybe I wear a couple of Jack & Jones.

- **What is your wildest favourite club related dream?**

My biggest dream is to watch Shumen play in ECT, though it actually happened in 1994. We qualified for Europe (any club and town's dream), but we got done by some Cyprus team as early as the very first round.

- **Which is your favourite game of all times?**

My all time favourites are the Bulgaria vs Germany games at the 1994 World Cup and the 1995 Euro qualifier played on 7th June 1995, which I attended, and we made a fabulous comeback from 0-2 to 3-2 in the second half.

- **Who are your favourite players?**

Hristo Stoichkov, Francesco Totti and Paul Gascoigne, who I was most amazed by and would keep on watching in a kinda rapture the way he was playing his magic.

- **Would you name the top 5 Bulgarian firms/crews/mobs?**

I don't know much about modern-day firms and crews. We, Shumen, have never had any serious separate firm. As I said, we were just the English sector guys.

- **Which are the best and the worst football grounds you've ever been to and why?**

The best ground I've been to is probably Estadio Do Dragao in Porto. An incredible stadium, you get on the tube and you're straight inside without even going overground. One of the nasty ones I've been to is Fulham's ground.

- **What do you think of the Bulgarian police?**

A cop is a cop, wherever they may be. You should watch out for them (winking). I've been nicked on 5 or 6 occasions, always outside grounds. Once we got busted by the riot police after a play-off against the team from Lovech (called LEX then). We decided to have a go at the away fans at the parking lot in front of the stadium. I remember the cops arrived and went down the stairs by the main stand in their jeep without even getting off. They nicked me and a couple of other top faces, but I won't go into any further details. They are lousy bastards in general.

- **What do you think of the youths in your firm/crew/mob?**

I have no personal observations, so I'll make no comment here. Besides, it's not quite right to express any opinion when you live a thousand miles away and after all those years (winking).

- **What do you think of the modern-day 'scene'?**

Modern firms and the fresh blood on the stands are much better organised now. They spent huge funds on tifos and away trips. Back in the days we'd do our best to evade ticket collectors to travel ticketless on trains and then would do all sorts of tricks to get inside grounds for free. I remember I had this 5-seat Barkas van. Once seven of us went on an away day to Stara Zagora and on the way back there were maybe 13-14 lads on board (how could I have possibly left our lads there). We kept the fifth door open using Piff's crutch so that we could breathe inside (laughing). Absolutely no place for comparisons!

- **What do you think of English hooligans and their influence?**

Generally speaking, I was extremely impressed by them during the Italy World Cup back in 1990. The bad part is that they get aggressive when they are drunk, otherwise, when sober, they're nice guys. I wonder what would happen in Russia now as Russians are ultra aggressive even when they are sober!

Interviews

Meet our special guests from England , Scotland , Italy and France

(Millwall , Leeds, Rangers, Lazio and Strasbourg)

S. D. - Millwall (England) and Glasgow Rangers (Scotland)

Meet and greet

I was a bit hesitant to do this interview due to the fact that I am a Millwall fan and we normally do not do any interviews as every time we do one the media will twist our words and make us look like cunts. But after speaking with Tosh and his team from this book I put my trust in a fellow old school football lad who understands our way. Since opening the Facebook group Football Firms Piss-Up back in 2009 and meeting up with many firms over the years I have become a well-known face and name in our culture famous for all the wrong reasons you could say but fuck it

I'm Millwall and I don't care. This interview tells it all as it is. So, get yourself a beer and enjoy.

- **How old are you and when did you become a fan of the team?**

Age 46, getting old (laughing). But what a life, and what an experience since going to Millwall, and since moving to London in 1998. I became a football fan from the age of 12. Being from Glasgow I got took to Glasgow Rangers as a kid and followed them all my life, but when I moved to London in 1998 it was all about Millwall. I used to live near their old ground on the isle of dogs in the Docklands which funny enough was full of West Ham and Millwall pubs. All good banter though and old school south and East London piss heads you could say. However, on a Millwall vs West Ham derby it would all kick off big style OB would be on us like a hawk.

- **How did you get going with a football firm, did it have a name and how was the name established?**

When I was a kid I used to be part of the Union Bears at Rangers, but since this interview is about my time with Millwall I ended up going to Millwall with the T28, used to drink with them and go to Wall to watch the games also with the famous Millwall Bushwhackers. Nowadays all Millwall seems to be one big family. When I started going to Wall from 98 being a Scot that was the connection for me I thought I wouldn't have been welcomed by the Londoners but I was very wrong as it was the Scottish club Dundee that founded Millwall Rovers, our old name, that were workers of J.T Morton in Millwall in the East End of London on the Isle of Dogs in 1885.

J.T. Morton was first founded in Aberdeen, Scotland in 1849 to supply sailing ships with food. They opened their first English cannery and food processing plant on the Isle of Dogs at the Millwall dock in 1870, and attracted a workforce from across the whole of the country, including the East Coast of Scotland who were predominantly Dundee Dockers. Let's just say the 90s era was the time and place to be in, there were more meet ups than they are these days. The biggest firm really is the OB. It's all about the football now the beer and the banter for all of us.

- **How do you define yourself – hooligan or ultras?**

Football fan mate, as if I would say on here (laughing).

- **Who are your biggest rivals fan-wise and what do you think about them?**

Our biggest rival fans the question is .... Let me think... Probably no cunts as Millwall do not fear any other club. We have always done our own thing and are known to hate many cunts. We do hate West Ham, and Leeds to name a few. No one likes us we don't care.

- **Have you ever incurred any serious injuries or been badly beaten up at a match?**

Back in the season 2000 when Leeds came to us after the match I did get caught up in London Bridge with 5 Leeds lads who recognised me from my Facebook group Football Firms Piss Up (laughing). There was me and my mate Steve against 5 of them. We stood our ground but did get knocked fuck out of then got thrown out the pub where it all happened. No real harm done though just a bloody nose. "Always remember you are braver than you believe, stronger than you seem and smarter than you think."

- **Where does stand your favourite club in your life and how important is it for you?**

I know this is a Millwall top face interview, but your question is favourite club in my life. This is a hard one its 70% Gers and 30% Wall. Glasgow Rangers I have to say as a Glaswegian. I was brought up with the Mighty Rangers FC and I have many childhood and teenage memories been taken to Rangers with my old man who actually was a Birmingham fan hence he was from Birmingham. I won't hold that against him (laughing). I also have a famous cousin that used to play for the Gers in the 1970s called Alex Miller. So, I am a true Blue nose I suppose, Rangers and Millwall. Both of these clubs are loyal and will stand by their club no matter what. Their fans are the best in the world. Seeing is believing. If you have never been there, get ready for a lively day out. We are the people! Why, because it is my religion.

- **What is your favourite football fashion wear?**

My favourite football fashion was... Now then that is a question from the 1980s it would be Fred Perry, Fila, Adidas, Burberry in the 1990s, to Stone Island, Ralph Lauren, mostly its polos, and Adidas and Fred Perry, but I'm glad you have asked this question. As a face in our world I have decided to launch my own brand of clothing, SD Clothing and my website this year 2017 www.footballfirmsclothing.com. This is really the new casual clobber gear which many football fans/Hooligans/ultras etc. are buying our gear and it isn't expensive. We must look after all of our own kind and not rip them off when it comes to football fashion.

- **What is your biggest dream related to the football team?**

That Millwall wins the Champion League and Rangers wins against Celtic at every Old Firm game, as well as reach their goals and have the last laugh. W.A.T.P. 'Don't be pushed by your problems. Be led by your dreams! Keep believing and it will happen and fuck off to all the haters. All those who never thought it would happen; we will have the last laugh.'

- **Which was the best team match?**

There are many, but recent times when Millwall beat Bradford at the FA CUP at Wembley stadium! Massive achievement for our hero Neil Harris watching his dream come through from being a player to a successful manger for the club. Steve

Morison's 85th minute goal handed Millwall a 1-0 win at the home of English football. The atmosphere was electric, the Lions' roar at Wembley that day was emotional, we did, it we came, we delivered, we achieved. "Winners turn setbacks into comebacks." and that is what Millwall did. Millwall were making their fifth appearance at Wembley in eight years. Bradford had the better of the chances in the first half but couldn't take them. Millwall played their way into the second half and controlled the game well. Steve Morison applied the killer blow for Millwall in the 86th minute. At the final whistle, Millwall fans invaded the pitch to celebrate promotion... Come on Mil....

- **Your favourite club player and your favourite other player?**

Neil Harris and Steve Morison have to be my best Millwall players by far! Say no more, look what they both have achieved while at Millwall.

- **Which is the worst & the best football ground you've been to and why?**

The second best compared to Glasgow Rangers at Ibrox has to be Millwall, the Den. Home to Championship club Millwall, has a reputation as one of the most intimidating, unfriendly grounds you could ever choose to visit. But we will welcome you all to show you that our club is a family club, and if you think it's going to be like the Football Factory movie, forget it. It is not the 80s or 90s anymore. As well as the less than warm welcome, away fans must also contend with being ferried directly from Bermondsey train station to the ground through a narrow alleyway. And, if that's not enough, there's also a waste recycling plant situated just around the corner. Lovely. But on a lighter note a day down the Den is mad loud if you aren't Wall and you are sitting at our end make sure you sing as you will lose your voice from singing "No one likes us, we don't care, we are Millwall super Millwall, we are Millwall from the Den!" The sound of the famous lion's roar gives a chill to your nervous system in a good way! MILL... Stick to that song, any other non Millwall song will stand out and be lucky to get out alive... just joking (laughing).

The worst ground I've been to is Gillingham's Priestfield Stadium. It was once voted the worst stadium in England with away fans criticising its poor facilities and terrible catering. Not to mention the wobbly scaffolding you had to sit on, fucking joke! The home of Gillingham has undergone a number of redevelopments in its 120 years history but there's still no roof on the away end, leaving us fans exposed to the elements. And as if that wasn't enough, opposition fans have to make do with portacabin toilets. This is what pissed me off with these football clubs charging a fortune for tickets. Every time Millwall travel we are made to feel like scum as they always think we are going to kick off, but not all of our fans are the same, if we are provoked we will. Let's just say some stewards cause a lot of the problems with us. Too controlled these days. I also have to say the old West Ham stadium in Upton Park the area is deprived and full of vermin. Say no more, could never live there.

- **How would you describe the situation with youths in the firm today?**

The problem we face in all English football with some of the youths today is that half of them think that they are living in that Football Factory film! Fuck all ever happens these days and everything is too controlled by the OB. We haven't got a war anymore against our own; it is against extremism. This is why it is important for all football fans to re-unite together as one nation all over Europe. We are all hooligan brothers that just want PEACE! That's it; no more. This is why I've set up the Facebook group Football Firms United for all of us to be part of as one nation, every country, every firm! It's time to stop this war we are all in with this sick evil that faces us! I'm sure you will all agree so join the group.

- **How would you describe the ultra-hoolie scene today?**

If it is European ultras you are talking about, they are mental and a bit behind... Not in a thick way, but as in they are living the way the UK firms where in the 80s and 90s era. This is the way it still should be in the UK, but it's to fucking controlled with the OB, they are the biggest firm now. All the top lads are on either life time bans or locked up inside. My dream if they were allowed to go to Russia and all future Euros then the European football firms will have a crash course on the way like it was back in the good old days of violence... Blood baths in the streets in the bars.... Was nothing. This is what hooligans are now enjoying. One thing I have noticed in some countries is they use knives, and this is shocking and just shows how much cowards so called hooligans can be. Nothing like good old bare-knuckle fight.

- **How old is your friendship with the Lokomotiv G.O - JRF (Jolly Roger Firm) fans, describe us how it all began and what do you think about BG supporters?**

I've known Tosh and Gilly for a few years now. They are part of my admin team on the 'Football Hooligans On Tour' FB page. We organise many events like 'Roll on Russia 2018' and we share the same old school ideas from the 80's-90's era... As for what I think of the Bulgarian Ultras: Greetings to all of them... They're my fellow brothers in arms... BIG RESPECT FROM MILLWALL AND RANGERS!

- **What do you think about English hooligans and their influence in hooliganism in general?**

Most of us are still on bans from years ago, and most of the old school lads that I know from all over England I have been meeting up with over the years have retired. Some of our bans are due to expire soon, so never say never, but as we get older things change and we play the game wiser. England fans get the blame for everything; we get the bad media... Let's look at the Euro 2016 the way we all got presented to the papers was a lot of bullshit... Most of us were having beers in Marseille and enjoying the French culture and then all of a sudden, an army of Russians came charging at us. Some English lads lost their lives many other English got badly injured; blame the Russian cunts, not us! 98% of the England away fans just go for the football, beer and culture and of course the women. Every club/firm in football will always have their small minority of hooligans and they are the ones that spoil it for the rest of the fans. Next year 2018 the World Cup, who knows what will happen, but I can say it will be good!

COME ON ENGLAND! RULE BRITANNIA, BRITANNIA RULES THE WAVES.

Remember to all join the biggest football hooligan group on Facebook. FFPU FOOTBALL FIRMS PISS UP AND ALSO CHECK OUT MY NEW FOOTBALL CASUAL CLOTHING AT

WWW.FOOTBALLFIRMSCLOTHING.COM.

We haven't got a War anymore against our own; it is against extremism and this is why it is important for all football fans to re-unite together as one nation! CHEERS FOR THE INTERVIEW.

RESPECT MILLWALL-RANGERS STEVE DOLIN

H. - Leeds United and Hertford Town (England)

Meet and greet

- **How old are you and when did you become a fan of the team?**

Raised in Islington North London, I started life as an Arsenal fan... Was taken to Highbury quite a lot when I was young but can't remember the first game I went... Wanted to support Leeds after 1972 cup final but was told by my old man you support Arsenal until you earn your own money then you can follow whoever you want ...

- **How did you get going with a football firm, did it have a name and how was the name established?**

Started getting involved in football violence around 82/83. I went to all Leeds games when they played in London and then when I got my first job, I started following Leeds all over the country. The 84/85 season was a very memorable season for me as I became very good friends with some top Cockney Whites (London Leeds fans). We could probably get around 30/40 good Lads on big match days, we then met up with other lads from Leeds, Wakefield, Doncaster, York and other places across England... Together we were known as the LEEDS SERVICE CREW and could easily get 500/600, sometimes more, on big match days.

- **How do you define yourself – hooligan or ultras?**

Defo a hooligan!

- **Who are your biggest rivals fan-wise and what do you think about them?**

Man. Utd. Quite simply SCUM BASTARDS!

- **Have you ever incurred any serious injuries or been badly beaten up at a match?**

Had a few injuries whilst travelling around the country, mainly cuts and bruises and a broken nose, but nothing too serious.

- **Where your favourite club stands in your life and how important is it for you?**

For me LEEDS was my life, but as I'm getting older, other things are more important (my wife and son), although LEEDS will always be in my heart and part of my life...

- **What is your favourite football fashion wear?**

Love the casual football scene from early 80's till now... Lacoste, MA. Strum, C.P. Company and many others all have a place in my wardrobe.

- **What is your biggest dream related to the football team?**

Don't really have one as LEEDS have shattered so many in the past.

- **Which was the best team match?**

Wasn't the best game, but watching LEEDS beat Man. Utd. scum in the F.A CUP at Old Trafford with Jermaine Beckford scoring the winner was one I remember well.

- **Your favourite club player and your favourite other player?**

The whole of the LEEDS team of the late 60's and 70's... LEGENDS!

- **Which is the worst & the best football ground you've been to and why?**

I hated Boro's old ground (I always seemed to come home from there with an injury... broken nose and black eyes).

- **How would you describe the situation with youths in the firm today?**

The youth firm at LEEDS is now one of the best in the country but the good old days of football related violence have long gone... Too many people with camera phones wanting to film everything nowadays.

- **How would you describe the ultra-hoolie scene today?**

Football will always be a big part of my life and the friends I've made through it will be friends for life, but with the unjust sentences that are handed out to anyone involved in football violence it's no longer worth the hassle.

- **How old is your friendship with the Lokomotiv G.O - JRF (Jolly Roger Firm) fans, describe us how it all began and what do you think about BG supporters?**

My friendship with the G.O lads is relatively new having met them at a Beyond the Hatred book launch in London, but I'm glad I did! ... PROPER OLD SCHOOL LADS and an absolute pleasure to know...

- **What do you think about English hooligans and their influence in hooliganism in general?**

The English were the original hooligans and I think many other country's lads now model them selves on us.

P. F. - Lazio and RC Strasbourg (France)

Meet and greet

- **How old are you and when did you become a fan of the team?**

I'm 53 and I became a football fan in 1974. I first watched my club RC Strasbourg playing. We went to the stadium with my father and my brother. I was 11 years old.

- **How did you get going with a football firm, did it have a name and how was the name established?**

We didn't have a football firm, but we tried to defend our club from other fans. At the beginning, it was only with chants for them. I didn't know what violence was, I only knew love and hate.

- **How do you define yourself – hooligan or ultras?**

In the beginning, I was an ultra because I had a fascination for the terraces and the tifos or banners. Growing up, I became a hooligan, ready to fight for my club, we were independent, no structure but only guys who wanted to fight and defend our territory. It was in the early 80s and I was working in Paris. Every weekend I went to Strasbourg to watch my club and at that time, I also followed the French national team. And there was an event I won't forget in my life: France played England at the Parc des Princes in 1984 before Euro 84. Extreme violence with English fans, I've lost some of my teeth this day and I understood what violence really was. English people were crazy, like animals and we, French, some skinheads with us, tried to defend our territory. I think it's the real beginning of hooliganism in France. For me, it was an experience, THE experience, which changed a part of my life!

- **Who are your biggest rivals fan-wise and what do you think about them?**

Our biggest rival is FC Metz because of the proximity of our towns and I think they have some good firms like our Meinau Boys. We both have good firms.

- **Have you ever incurred any serious injuries or been badly beaten up at a match?**

As I said, I used to follow the National team. And there was an event I won't forget in my life: France played England at the Parc des Princes in 1984 before Euro 84. Extreme violence with English fans, I've lost some of my teeth this day and I understood what violence really was. English people were crazy, like animals and we, French, some skinheads with us, tried to defend our territory.

But I remember when I was young, with my younger brother and my father, we were on holy days around Marseille, I was 12 or 13 years old and Strasbourg, our club had a game vs Marseille at the Velodrome Stadium. For my brother and me it was an unbelievable opportunity to see the Racing away. We had Strasbourg scarf and cap and in those times in France there were no away ends so we were with Marseille fans. In the first half, some people began to say to my father "Go home, fuck off, etc..." and at one point we had to leave the stadium because we were young and alone even if my father did what he could do for us. And it's THE moment I've have most hated in my football life. Even today I hate Marseille, I have always hated Marseille and everybody who is into football knows it!

- **Where does your favourite club stand in your life and how important is it for you?**

My favourite club is Racing Club de Strasbourg, the French team in my heart since 1974; it's the first love of my life. I used to fight for my Club when I was young, and I have followed the team in France and also in Europe.

- **What is your favourite football fashion wear?**

Stone Island of course, Lacoste and Lonsdale, Adidas.

- **What is your biggest dream related to the football team?**

Here, I must write that I've been also a Lazio fan since 1998 after a game at the Parc vs Inter in the UEFA cup final. Since 2003 I've watched a lot of matches of Lazio, in the Olympic Stadium or away in Italy.

I've discovered a real good family, and I was suddenly in the dream I'd had since I was young: to be someone in a good family, and Italian people are very kind with me, I go every year to watch the Rome derbies. The atmosphere was completely crazy in the past, we could drink inside the stadium, pay nothing to go to the Tevere Tribune and then fight with Roma fans. I've done it only once and it was very dangerous because Roma fans have weapons…

I realised another dream through football, i.e. to be in 2005 in Rome for the Racing vs AS Roma game with 12 or 15 goods friends of Lazio who were with us in the visitors end. A very good souvenir for me.

And it was in those years that I met a Levski and Lazio fan called Ivo, one of my best friends today. I got interested in the friendship and alliance between Lazio and Levski.

- **Which was the best team match?**

The best game I've seen is one of the "derby della capitale" with Di Canio playing.

- **Your favourite club player and your favourite other player?**

For me my favourite club player is Albert Gemrich, who played for RC Strasbourg when I was young, and he won the only title of France League 1, scoring and scoring for the Racing. My other favourite player is Johan Cruyff from Ajax and Holland, a really good player who had everything a modern player has.

- **Which is the worst & the best football ground you've been to and why?**

The grounds of my beloved clubs are the best, and the worst…, well, there are many poor grounds everywhere, I can't name them all.

Football has a large part in my life, friends, hope, the excitement before, during and after the game, a lot of beers of course and finally, when I take a look behind me, football is my life and a part of my family, not only football family, but like brothers.

- **How would you describe the situation with youths in the firm today?**

Well, I have watched a lot of football games in the last 5 years, Italy, England, Bulgaria, and France. And I was impressed with the young firms. They are more violent than us; they want to fight more than drink. I've seen some young lads, even in my first Club, Strasbourg, but also in England, Nottingham, Italy, Lazio or in Sofia, Levski. I like it and I think the movement is not dead, it will never die, but I'm now too old to participate (actually why not) and hope the young are our future, but more difficult for them because of new all those technologies, police...

- **How would you describe the ultra-hoolie scene today?**

In my view and opinion through all these years the ultras scene had a great evolution, in a good way I think... It's more innovative than before... Ultras in Europe are presenting beautiful spectacles nowadays with their choreographies. The last I've seen it was Lech Poznan. Ultras movement evolved with the technology and changed their state of mind. They're more infiltrated in the life of their beloved club and they can even discuss issues with the directors sometimes. It's a real progress for me to be recognised like a legitimate part of your own club! The evolution started in the late 1990s: more interaction with the club, club house, fanzines etc... I'm talking generally for the most passionate fans. Even if you aren't Ultras! I have some respect for those people and for what they're ready to do for their club in general. And finally, they're much more young people involved then in the 80s. It's a good thing that the mentality also changed and they're ready to defend their club with passion and by any means necessary.

When I was young (I'm talking about 70s and early 80s) it was different. I was fascinated by the small organised groups, then they became huge crowds and the hooligan years started. The Union Jack was a constant picture everywhere in Europe in and out the stadiums, because England was an "example" both on and off the pitch. I remember the famous game France vs England in 1984. There were English flags all around the stadium with the sentiment of glory of thousands of their fans. But, in general today England has no pyro, no ultras style at all. Only ordinary fans that can pay the expensive ticket prices. Police are always near and it's impossible to create a good atmosphere, because you can go straight in jail for a scratch.

Then most organised ultras are in Germany and Italy, but I was surprised by the Bulgarians and in particular Levski fans during my first visit for a derby in the capital of Sofia.

- **How old is your friendship with Levski Sofia fans, describe us how it all began and what do you think about BG supporters?**

I've been a Levski fan since their alliance with Lazio and have very good friends among Levski fans. I am fascinated by the Bulgarian terraces, especially Levski, pyro, etc... But I think the real fascination I have for Levski is because of their fans. Bulgarians supporters are proper fans of their club and do what they can for Levski. I like to see young people going to the stadium and also old school blokes. Levski Family is the best project I've done in my whole entire life, I'm really proud of it! I did it together with one of the authors of this book.

- **What do you think about English hooligans and their influence in hooliganism in general?**

I've told you a lot about English hooligans in this interview, I haven't got any animosity for them. I've a lot of very good friends, especially at Nottingham and West ham. I think today English influence is low because of the emergence of Eastern countries like Poland, Russia etc... But I also think that the English hools were at the top in Europe from the 1970s until the 1990s. I like to watch hooligan videos at work, if I can write it. And 1998 was their best in France at Marseille. And for me, it all started in Marseille if you remember, and the end of English hools was in Marseille also.

Epilogue
THE END OF AN ERA

THAT'S the way it is our game these days... We'd like to highlight our game because we believe that the greatest game ever belongs to us and was made for entertainment, to please ordinary football fans and not the modern arrogant businessmen! Clubs no longer seem to rely on their youth academies. What they mainly rely on is mercenaries, and with every season the number of players they hire gets bigger and bigger. Clubs crests and colours don't mean a thing for players now, they're nothing but a way for them to have yet another club in their portfolios. Our league has become a haven for anonymous foreigners and we simply can't see the point of them even being here. It's nothing personal, but when clubs keep on saying they have no money, it's ridiculous to pay those guys when their monthly income is much more when compared to our native players. Not to say that the quality of 90% of those foreign players does not contribute to raising the level of Bulgarian football. On top of it, our league has been so predictable in recent years that everyone seems to know the teams' results and final positions in the table. All of this football fans people lose their faith. It seems there are no more young players we can proudly call 'ours'. Boys that would do their best no matter they're not like Messi or Ronaldo. Anyone who's seen them play and gone mental after they score knows what we're talking about. Those were boys that we used to love watch because we knew they'd give not just a 100, but a 101% of their efforts for their club. These days... These days that's the way it is our game... These days fakeness on the pitch does not go unnoticed. More and more people stop going to football as they don't want to have anything to do with what our favourite game has become. Back in the days, there were all kinds of people standing side by side at stadia, i.e. professors, managers, workers, students, rascals and vagabonds. They all shared a single idea... an idea that made them feel like blood brothers. All one needed to hear was that the guy over there was 'one of us' and it would made them friends forever. These days... these days it's way too different! The cheap burlesque they've been playing on the pitch has had its disastrous influence on the crowds. Fans in their large numbers got repelled by what our football has become. All our stadia are in ruins! The thrill is gone! A shadow is also cast on derby games! People don't believe in them anymore. A handful of guys remained on the terraces to stand their ground as supporters. Bulgarian football is in need of a total change. It is in need of something that could bring back the thrill. We believe this won't last forever. The first step should be football grounds. They are the first sign that we are some 30-40 years behind the rest of Europe. The other things would be settled afterwards. We believe in that or at least we have hopes! Afterwards people would slowly come back to football and the magic would be back. What is important is that we believe, and we don't lose faith. And get rid of falseness and hypocrisy. We also need new people running our beloved game!

Only when the people who run the game settle this mess, they could turn their attention to problems we find insignificant, such as football hooliganism!

Hooliganism is still here and will probably stay here for good. For better or for worse it is closely related to football. However, it's time everyone looked beyond the very game before they fly their accusations and reproach. For our 'old school' generation, football was a kind of outlet, but that's not all there is to it. Violence and fights in the streets and terraces were something usual for Saturday afternoons and they simply reflected all the social chaos and disorder around us.

It's not a purely football disease, it's a way of expression. A way to boldly say you're sick and tired of all bullshit. A way to say you've had enough of it!

Nowadays attendance at Bulgarian stadia hardly gets higher than ten thousand and if it ever does it is considered as record breaking! But if you look at the papers or watch telly, you'll get the impression that it's much higher and the majority are hooligans and ultras, drug addicts, vandals, sociopaths and so on and so forth... You may wonder why!? Because viewers and readers are easy to manipulate, they read the articles and watch those heavily biased news reports and even documentaries that portray those people as dangerous criminals. They call them names and tarred with the same brush so at some point words like "supporter", "ultras" and "hooligan"are in a way devoid of their real meaning. Everyone gets stigmatised, even the rank-and-file scarfers. And that's the real reason for the absence of crowds. They were put off by the system, not by the hooligans. They were put off by the predictability of the Bulgarian version of the greatest of games!

It's high time those who on a daily basis use the phrase"They said it on TV..."opened up their eyes, read the appropriate books or watch the appropriate films on this topic because manipulating ordinary fellas and making them believe in such kind of bullshit turns out to be the easiest of jobs nowadays. We have no intention of proving that there are no thugs across Bulgaria stadia that could be described as "football hooligans". Surely there are, there's no point denying that and calling a spade a shovel. But the presence of such individuals is not necessarily a condition for the presence of the somehow abstract concept of "football hooliganism". Not to speak of its advanced form.

Can a country that has some 500 Buddhists, for instance, be classified as a Buddhist country?! Actually, it's a simple truth. In the 80s and 90s the situation with football hooligans was much more complicated, but not much talked about. Countries had much more important issues to solve. Bulgaria, in particular, has them now, but it seems much easier to turn the public attention to such topics so that people could have something to discuss and someone to put a finger at instead of blaming the ones who are really to blame for what is going on in the country. That's just a way of diverting people's attention from their real problems.

The football hooliganism topic is a favourite with our media, especially for those who have national air. When they have nothing to talk about, they start blaming football fans. For everything imaginable. With no exceptions. An easy way to attract attention. What matters for them is fans being given the worst possible publicity and portrayed as bigger criminals than those who are released by courts on a daily basis either because our prosecutors are assholes or take bribes (or both) or because our police is even more incompetent.

Surely there are incidents. Surely there are problems. Surely a visit to certain grounds could be dangerous... Sofia derbies, Minyor vs Levski, Plovdiv derbies and some others, but is it really more dangerous going to a football game than driving on Bulgarian roads where people get killed on a daily basis!? Who's responsible for that, where does responsibility stand, who pins it and who bears it?

We say all these words as we have been there; we've been at the very heart of it. These days if you don't come looking for trouble at Bulgaria stadia, the chance of getting into trouble accidentally is almost zero. Yes, there are occasional troubles, but the terraces are no longer a battlefield for the simple reason that they are … empty! The war described by Bulgarian hacks does not exist, but they see blaming football fans as their mission. Fans are supposed to be the bad guys, the criminals, who have to satisfy their need of ridiculous excuses. They are the country's greatest evil cause they are a pain in the ass of the system!

For some time now, the Bulgarian media have been holding a serious campaign against football supporters in general. In a few words, to sum up all that we've said, they make up and maintain a downright gangster image, which you'll easily recognise as a fake one if you are not one of those opinionated folks who like to generalise and call different people different names and if you have at least once set foot inside a Bulgarian football ground recently.

Nowadays football mobs do not consist only of skinheads, punks, metalheads and the like, blamed through all those years for being there just for the sake of looking for a fight. We won't use clichés like "intelligent boys and girls", though there are such individuals across Bulgarian stadia and anyone going to the football can see them. But it is those boys and girls on the terraces that, according to some, are the big threat for the all those coming to football grounds, which are generally as dangerous as any other places around us. Let's not forget the miserable, rundown conditions of our grounds, where one is more likely to get hurt by an iron bar sticking out of dilapidated structures than by a rival fan carrying a home-made bomb in his hand!

But actually, those boys and girls are really dangerous. And before you start thinking that we're out of our minds, we'll give you the ultimate answer. Dangerous they are, yes, but dangerous for the authorities since they have been the moving force in most large-scale protests the government in recent years. They are probably the last alert and public-spirited group of people remaining and without fear they keep on expressing their opinion on current problems the country is facing and respond to all injustice. They are dangerous cause they try to bring up issues in public while the rest of the society only comments on them sitting on their couch watching telly?

Surely there is aggro between mobs across stadia! Surely, they hurl abuse at and fight each other. Surely there are real thugs among them that do not belong there. Surely these are all facts, but there's also another fact. Whenever necessary, these people join forces and stand together behind ideas related mostly to that widespread injustice. They also build a common enemy's image for the state authorities, which, upon seeing that enemy getting stronger and united, tries to suppress, intimidate and disunite them. It is clear for all reasonable people that those phenomena and trends can be destroyed by creating a negative public image for them so that they do not get support. That's the major weapon authorities have always been using, i.e. the Divide and rule principle.

Another unwelcome by the authorities' effect can also be witnessed at stadia, where the fans' attention is more or less drawn by messages written down on banners, which express the attitudes of football crowds and they definitely disturb those in power. The media keep their mouths shut and cameras are turned aside in order not to show how the authorities' sharpest tool, i.e. the police, invades the stands. We have all witnessed numerous provocations by the full riot gear cyborgs beating women and children across stands in their efforts to capture the banners or writings in question! The media sometimes open their mouths just to distort or whitewash the truth about what happened, and they maintain the myth about football hooliganism or, if necessary, resort to complete media blackout. Grounds stay empty. Well, surely, they are, but the main reasons for that are not the very football supporters or their hardcore elements. They are just a part of a bigger and intentionally well disguised social problem.

So, the ordinary, manipulated fella is made to believe that words like "supporter", "fan", "ultras" and "hooligan" are near synonyms. And there's no more point in persuading this fella that some go to the stadium, watch the game and then peacefully go home, while others are part of organised groups that have dedicated their entire lives to football. They fly flags and create great atmosphere at football grounds, supporting their teams, and there are those blokes of a third 'disgusting' type, who incite violence and riots before and after the games. By the way, we've had the same 'distortion' regarding words like 'patriot', 'nationalist', 'chauvinist', 'Nazi', and 'racist', but that's a different story.

Nonetheless, we know damn well that in fact the entire operation against football mobs has been successful. We see it these days when we walk around wearing our beloved club's T-shirt and scarf going back to where we all started, i.e. to the rank-and-file supporter. It is sad. It is sickening. And some can't even realise how appalling it is. Because they are a part of all this destruction!

So that's why those fans who fight at stadia are supposedly mad: deserted terraces, strict police measures, court sentences and banning orders, suspension of passports, what not? If you get into a fight in a night club or bar downtown during the weekend, the biggest punishment you'll get will be a fine, but if you are a football fan, you'll get a year in prison for the same thing! It is this awkward link in our system of government and our manipulating politicians that nip in the bud fandom!

After all that's been said so far, here comes the eternal question that we, football fans, always ask ourselves, i.e. "Was it all worth it?" We doubt it, but after all, what is life? You spend one- third of it working just to get a meagre pension and survive. A second third you spend sleeping, so the rest of it is left to be enjoyed in some way and we chose to do it our way. Most people would find it ridiculous, but in addition to family (a major reason for living), these lads we've stood side by side through the years, gave life a new meaning. We don't regret it and what if we do, can we go back in time and do something different!? We doubt it. It's highly unlikely. It's impossible! The mobs made men out of us, they made us human and raised in us the sense of ethics, respect, love, hate, independence, and perseverance to fight for one's rights, beliefs and ideas. Football fans find it greatly significant, strong and righteous. It is the most genuine and natural thing, and nothing can beat it. Living on the razor's edge has always been an exciting and unique feeling, no matter who, what and where. Fighting for your club, town, country and mates is something supreme and for all interviewees in this book it was the meaning of everything!

Having introduced you to all those old-school lads, we keep wondering if this is really the end of proper fandom?! Most of them are almost 50 years old (some even 60). We also introduced you to some younger fans from the next generations to come and what we've got here is a mixture of several generations of supporters who have taken the special path of fandom in terms of style and even way of life. Looking at all of them and also turning our eyes to heavens where some of our best mates are now we keep on asking ourselves more questions like, "Is there any hope?", "Will there be succession and legacy?", "Aren't we a dying breed?", "Could this be the end of an era?!", etc. We leave those questions to the youngest generation of supporters as they will be the ones who'll answer them in the near future. Surely the men from the past will not be there forever, but they have given everything they've got for the cause. They used to follow their favourite teams everywhere, both in good and bad times, even when they were wandering between the different levels of Bulgarian football or had hit rock bottom. They used to fly their hand-made flags (often made in basements to the sounds of rock-and-roll and heavy music) as symbols of their love and devotion to their beloved clubs and embodiment of their own freedom and independence. They used to openly show their discontent with the past regime, and they paved the way for the freedom of speech, and rebelliousness, which was unfamiliar for the broad masses who seemed to be looking at the world through the prism of countless distorting mirrors.

After so many years spent at stadia all over the country it is clear that those people will always share a few feelings, and these are the feelings stirred up by that wicked adrenaline boiling inside them when they meet up with their like- minded fellas on Saturday afternoons. They still have this feeling due to their one and only love for football. Lots of the interviewees were literally gone from the Bulgarian stadia in the last several years, away from the public eyes, others were simply forgotten or disappointed with the football played in Bulgaria recently, still others were outcasts banished by their own lot and of course, there are those who were given long-term banning orders keeping them away from what they love and want to do...

Regardless of and to some extent in defiance of all tricks of fortune, a common idea and a common goal united us all here under those two awe-inspiring words OLD SCHOOL. This book tells slightly rusty, long kept secret memories of long gone football related adventures that some people still sigh for. All these supporters deserve our full respect not only for their influence on the native scene, but also for their loyalty to their beloved clubs, which the rank- and-file football fans seem to find incomprehensible. Most of them are now far away from the modern-day fashionable ultra scene, but you can still spot them at big games or fierce derbies, still flying their hand-made flags with the woven sacred club names and symbols, singing in line with the younger generation of fans without making any claims whatsoever. Children of the working class from the 70s, 80s and the early 1990s; they all have huge respect for each other though they support different clubs that are bitter enemies! They will always love and follow their teams, though that fondness of fighting they used to have is now a thing from the past. One way or the other, they are still up for it, but as time goes by, the harsh experience and their feeling of responsibility make them think twice whether getting into trouble is now worth it.

They are the real football fans, no matter how they are called in the press. Actually, who gives a shit about the media's fucking opinion? They used to live for the Saturday afternoons, for their mates and most of all, for their football clubs! Well, now their priorities may have changed, but they still really love the game though the game itself seems not to be real anymore.

In this book we let some proper, decent blokes do the talking. They've told their stories that you won't hear anywhere else. Some say we eulogise football related violence by writing such books without even making a single effort to read them. So, let them read first, enter into the issue, if possible, and then make their own conclusions and express their opinion!

In their prime those blokes were more popular than pop and film stars and everyone copycatted them because they were born to be leaders. Hopefully their stories and interviews set the beginning of a real national unification of Bulgarian football fans. We hope that finally everyone understands the nature of genuine football fans and stops believing the manipulative concepts of the so called 'mindless minority'. In our opinion, the only mindless minority through all those years has been the media, which have never been further from the truth during the last three decades. That's why our memories of the 1970s, 1980s and 1990s will always stay with us and we hope the stories in this book will revive, preserve and keep them alive.

Opinions

SOME THOUGHTS ABOUT THE AUTHORS
AND THEIR PREVIOUS BOOKS

'We were (in) Sector B ' & 'Beyond the Hatred '

FROM S.R.

We reach the point of frank confessions...

Lokomotiv Gorna Oryahovitsa

First, I'd like to make a few clarifications. Explicit ones!!!

To begin with, I know that whatever I write will be considered as a flattery, but in no way, it will be my personal flattery to anyone. Secondly, I'd like to point out that what I am about to write has been coordinated in advance with mates in Gabrovo, so it won't reflect my personal opinion only. Thirdly, I will be utterly honest, so, please don't be mad with me...

Now let me just outline the reason for me writing these lines. Here I am browsing through some FB pages and I get the shock of my life... Lokomotiv G.O. have written and published a book about their football related mischiefs! Furthermore, they have translated it and published it in English!!! Naturally, I immediately wrote some drunken comment, but I got quite a polite and reasonable response. And there we had a topic to discuss. However, it didn't come to my mind to look at the profile of the man who answered me. But when I actually did, the shock became even greater! I knew the man, but what I didn't know was that he came from Gorna Oryahovitsa. I added him as a friend and I also added him to our group and then I found out that he had been at parties with most of our lot! I leave the speculations to you (at least to those of you who come from the town of Gabrovo). I'll just say that he's no different from P. from the town of Lovech or J. from Tarnovo... So, my point was that the gauntlet has been thrown. And since it comes from G.O it feels like two gauntlets have been thrown (winking).

Yesterday I had a long and beneficial phone talk with The Joyce regarding the newly published Lokomotiv G.O. book. We made some things clear and he claims that 'We (Gabrovo) have never had a hooligan core. We used to drink a lot and go to home games mainly, occasionally on away games and whenever they'd have a go at us we'd fight, but it was never us who looked for trouble'. That partially stands behind my words above. What I and the Joyce mean by "we" is our generation and heavy metal gang only.

If I have to be honest, I'll start with this. Some 200 yards away from my current home in Manchester there is a bridge and under this bridge there is this huge writing on the wall that says "Death to Lokomotiv G.O.! ". I wrote it once when I was deadly drunk, but I didn't write it out of hatred for them (out of hatred I'd write something else), but simply because probably I didn't know them so well despite all our past encounters! But after 22 years of living abroad I recalled the name of Lokomotiv G.O. exactly and not Beroe FC, for example... Lokomotiv G.O. is different from all the rest of small town clubs. I'm not willing to tell any other club fans what I think of them, but I really feel the need to tell them Lokomotiv G.O. what I think of them.

It turns out that Gorna Oryahovitsais a town to which too much undeserved damage was done. In communist times it was privileged in terms of supplies with high quality goods due to a local communist party boss and that made people from the rest of the region jealous. On the other hand, the close vicinity of Tarnovo has taken its toll as Gorna Oryahovitsa was simply considered as a Tarnovo suburb. All those facts are insulting, to say the least, as we are talking of a thousand-year-old town that has had its decent contribution to our country's cultural and economic development! So surely this kind of attitude and the downright underestimation affected the small-town citizens' pride and they had to find a way to let off steam and so Lokomotiv G.O. football mob was their way of letting off steam. I can't find any other explanation for the rowdy behaviour of their mob when I take into account the fact that people who come from this area are traditionally known for being practical, hospitable and wise! I can surely say that G.O. football fans are among the top Bulgarian mobs! In addition to their fierce hatred for anything walking on two legs, to their vandalism and all their riots, they had bravery, honour and dignity. After the incident involving the stabbing of a Gabrovo bloke, they made their own internal investigation and their top boys came to our town to settle things. An unprecedented development for Bulgaria! Lads, you get all the RESPECT from Gabrovo and without a single trace of hypocrisy I'll tell you what. These lines are being written by a man who a few months ago said in public some pretty horrible things about your town, its club and fans. When I decided to check things, it turned out I was terribly wrong.

I'll tell you two stories, one of them a serious one and the other a funny story to apologise to Tosh and Gilly, i.e. two of the authors of this book.

I am absolutely sure it is the same brawl they described in their first book Beyond the Hatred. Lads, what you probably still don't know is that we always had someone at the train station in your town who informed us which train you had boarded and so the word would pretty fast spread all over Gabrovo. So that's why there was no "organised three-mob attack". It was just that the guys from the different quarters knew your estimated time of arrival and they had come to meet you in their own special way (winking). I was with the mob that arrived on the bus. We all had that adrenaline rush and so the entire bus-load just steamed out and into your ranks. It all went on for me for not more than 10 seconds. There was this long-haired bloke of yours, much bigger than me, wearing just a rocker jacket next to his skin. He punched me so hard that I just collapsed on the ground! When I recovered and looked around I saw the same guy fighting one of our top lads. So, then I did something that I'm still not proud of, though my young age can explain it to some extent. I came behind him in my meanest way, I grabbed his hair and pulled it back with all my might. As he was going down, I kicked him in the head. Next thing I saw were the cops arriving and I legged it as fast as I could, so I don't know what happened afterwards. If someone recognises himself or knows who this long-haired bloke was, I am sincerely asking for his forgiveness for the mean attack in the back made by a young coward.

The Prisoner

I'll finish with a funny story, in a typically Gabrovo style:

I go out to see some mates in the garden in front of my block of flats. Right beside them there is a metalhead sleeping on the ground in a terrible state of drunken stupor. So, I go asking my mates, 'Who the fuck is this?!' and my mate B. replies in a withering voice, 'Shhh! This bloke is our prisoner.'

- 'A prisoner?! What do you mean by that?!' I keep on asking. 'Oooh, you know nothing, mate! He spent the night at my place and now we're gonna have him on a national search warrant!'

-'Well, he's staying with you, isn't he? What search do you mean?'

– 'It's high time G.O. got what they deserve?'

The Background

As we all know, our town of Gabrovo has never seen a more drunken and disorderly mob than Lokomotiv G.O. I also believe in the opposite. Probably it's a matter of mutual respect (laughing). A few days earlier Yantra FC hosted Lokomotiv G.O. and after the compulsory attack at the train station that lad remained neither beaten up, nor nicked. He was left pissed as hell sleeping by the fountain. Then the right people came across him. (Later, he would come to the "Bird" pub many a time and he'd say, 'To hell with you, Gabrovo, why didn't you beat me up then!?') I can't remember his name or nickname; would anyone help me with it? So, he was just taken by our zombie mates and they made him get drunk for a few days in a row, in a way of sweet revenge against Lokomotiv G.O!

The Finale

I am convinced that everyone in Gabrovo has heard about the lad being seen off at the railway station, who, upon getting on his train started waving goodbye and shouting, 'I love you! I just didn't know! I love you all!'

So, the things I'll finish with are pretty important. And they are pretty important not for any other reason, but for the reason that we belong to one and the same generation. I'll put it this way: we are the generation that never got and will never get the right to speak out! So, let's be honest with ourselves. Gilly, Tosh, Milen... why are you writing these books!? Is it because it is so important how exactly we smashed the travelling support coach windows and we insist on people remembering that?! I highly doubt it. You're writing them because we all belong to one and the same generation that will remain unheard, misunderstood and unrecorded unless we not only speak out, but cry out. At the same time, though... Look at it from another angle, we belong to a generation that feels the need to write a book instead of just making a video with a smartphone. Write a fucking book!

So, PLEASE, let's tell the truth, let's openly admit it at least once, WE ARE SOME GODDAMN COOL MOTHERFUCKERS!!!

Tosh and Gilly... My last words will be in response to your dedication in your first book Beyond the Hatred. There has never been any hatred. There was something that gave birth to friendships and my participation in this one just comes to prove it. And it's only us who can identify this something and we cannot put it into words!

Bulgarian readers on `We were (in) Sector B`

Kristina Borisova

I read with great interest every word you wrote, and I am absolutely fascinated. You have described everything in an astonishing way, the games, the players, the supporters... I am writing this message to you with tears in my eyes. I've never thought I could love anything as madly as I love Levski... Thank you for describing the past life of Levski. I am so moved to have the great honour of becoming so closely familiar with the history of the club. Only when we know our past we will start loving our future!

Dyankov

Well-deserved congratulations for the authors of the book! I just can't stop reading it. Unputdownable, as the English say. Absolutely captivating, written in an incredibly interesting way. Every single Levski fan MUST read this unique book.

Petar Dinev

Please, start writing Volume II, please....

Ivaillo Zarkov

Well done for the terrific book!!! No doubt every Levski supporter MUST read it!!!

UL

Well, despite the limited amount of free time I get, I managed to devote 2 evenings to reading and I have almost finished it...I simply don't seem to find words, but what you did is unbelievable...This is a magnificent Levski read and every single soul who has ever been in Sector B must read it! At some point I caught myself thinking how it is really possible for a book, in our modern times, in our so materialistic and false reality, to be written as if you're having a chat with your mates and you're telling things straight and the way they really are. I have no words to express my gratitude to you for writing this book and I am really proud I know you in person! I won't go into details describing the pleasure I get and the big smile I put on my face when reading our purely Levski terms used for the communists, CSKA fans and all the rest of slang we all know so well, I find it so exciting that someone put them down on paper in an easily accessible and everyday speech. It is so hard for me to find the exact words, so ... JUST READ THE FUCKING BOOK!

Stefan Vandev

A unique book! I read it in less than two days. HUGE THANKS!

Diehard Levski fan

Mates, it's a fantastic book! I thank you on behalf of everybody! I read it with great interest. The book is so rich in content and so well describes the history of Levski mob up to now. Hopefully I have the opportunity to live through what you had the honour of experiencing. All the best, stay safe and sound and enjoy our beloved club for countless years!

Georgilsfc

Huge THANKS to the authors of this fantastic book! I'm speechless! I read it in three days while at work and my colleagues started looking me in a strange way, you know, but to hell with them! I think this book is an absolute must for all young generations of Levski fans. They must read it to understand what it was like in the past, what values people used to share, and they really should think twice about what they're doing now!

Kosjo

A fantastic book, I just finished it. I hope more people read it and begin to understand who they are and what they are fighting for while attending Levski games.

ITK

The book is scandalous, it really is! But it is exquisitely well written! Though clearly influenced by the so called 'vulgar literature', it has nothing to do with the twaddle of the modern cocaine gangster and mob authors... Highly recommendable! Even for those who think football is a total bullshit!

Stefan Sirmanov

I'll tell you fellas, I first read only 7-8 lines just to see what it's all about and I got goosebumps. The moment I opened the book I was in seventh heaven. Thank you, lads, for the idea to write this book. You don't become a Levski fan, you are born a Levski fan!!!

BlueLion

Your book deserves to be on our three-coloured national flag cause LEVSKI really is

BULGARIA. This is not just a propaganda slogan, it's a fact, WE are the people's club and WE ARE THE PEOPLE, the people of BULGARIA! I personally am not ashamed of my country, no matter how hard life here is! And your book fully deserves a place right besides the classic written by Rumen Paitashev describing Levski European games as those are the games that give rise to truly unique emotions for blue fans, be it good or bad, they are all authentic and real. And those emotions are the strongest exactly in Sector B! What is LEVSKI without its supporters? So that's why your book deserves to be put on a pedestal, because LEVSKI fans are the very heart of the club!

Georgi Ireland Georgiev

I just got obsessed with the book, I couldn't put it down for a second! It's a unique read!

TIhomir Hristov

AN ABSOLUTE MUST FOR EVERY LEVSKI SUPPORTER!

National Front

Hi there, first of all congratulations on the book. It's incredible, I read it in one breath. Thank you so much, for the book, for all the preserved traditions that we'll keep on defending. I thank God there are Levski fans like you. Levski till we die!

Lyubo Penov

Mates, it was only yesterday that I managed to get hold of this book and I really find it one of a kind. A legendary sector I am happy to have grown up in, a place that brought me up like no one and nothing else. Once again, accept my most sincere gratitude for reminding us who we are and what we have been involved in!

Blue Varna

The most engrossing book ever ... I read 144 pages in a single day!

Victor Iliev

I come from the town of Varna, I'm 30 years old and today, in my lunch break, I got your book and the moment I came home I started reading and I got soaked in, totally forgetting about everything else. I just wanted to say a big THANK YOU! I just hope we meet someday so that I could shake your hand, not only because I'm so grateful to you for writing something unprecedented a book about our Sector, a book written by someone who has had unbelievable experiences in this Sector. Huge respect and all the best from BLUE VARNA!

Iliana K.

The book is unique! I'm still at the beginning, but I have already been laughing out loud quite a few times. I don't know what lies ahead. Once again, congratulations and I really hope we do meet someday so that I could get your autograph. Be great! I got the book at 8 o'clock one morning, I was at a bus stop and I jumped out with joy right there and people gave me some really strange looks. I just wonder when someone last got so happy with any book...

AntiFootballFan

I've just finished reading the book... Whatever I say, it won't be enough. But I'd like to thank the authors for taking me into a romantic world far away from us, for reliving history through their own points of view and helping me understand how life and Levski mob have changed through the years and where the generation gap occurred.

Stefan Koncharski

The book is incredible! I read it in a flash of time! Once you start reading, you just can't put it down... Well done to the authors!

Martin Kotsev

A really fascinating book telling loads of truths about life in Bulgaria during the last three decades. Furthermore, after reading it, one gives new meaning of his philosophy regarding friendship, honour, loyalty to a cause and ideas. I wouldn't like it to sound like flattering, but you have really gone far beyond your original idea!

Zlatko1914

I've just finished reading the book and more or less I took part in the adventures in spite of the distance over time. I'd like to congratulate you on the great endeavour you've made and thank you for providing me with the opportunity to get a feeling of those difficult times, in which, however, the ideas you believed in were genuine and vital. Thank you for showing me that what really matters is standing behind those ideas instead of bowing your head or burying it in the sand. Thank you for what you really did not only in terms of Levski support, but what you dared to do in the fight against communism and its repressions. You have persuaded me once again that only actions matter because words are of some importance only when used to tell of some actions already performed and to learn and benefit from the mistakes we've made. Don't feel sorry about anything, feel proud!

Natural

I got so carried away by this book that I visualised, I imagined every single event described and I kept on telling myself "I wish I had been there"... We were really a great, a truly majestic society in the past! Nobody is larger than Levski! Nobody will ever be! Players, managers, presidents, they just come and go. Nobody is eternal! The only things eternal are Levski and our love for it! You could hardly imagine what unique experience you gave me with this book!

Viktor Todorov

I'd like to thank you for writing this unique book. I read it in 4 days, and it is really one of a kind. Thanks to people like you, old-school Levski fans, I feel proud that I support Levski, I feel proud that I am a part of Sector B and most of all that I am Bulgarian. It would be a great honour for me to meet you in Sector B. This book is the best Christmas present I've ever got and I read it in one sitting. Take my best regards for everything you've done and keep on doing in the name of freedom and in the name of Levski!

Helikon Bookstores readers on 'Beyond the Hatred' Bulgarian edition:

Stoyan /6th March 2018

Tosh and Phil, thank you for taking me back in time with this unbelievable book! I can't wait for your next projects and our future meets!

Radostin Mihnev /23rd February 2018

Whatever I say of Gilly and Tosh will not be enough. Respect, lads, for the wonderful book. For me you are the modern gladiators of Bulgarian stadia. Thanks for letting me get to know you.

The fan/10thFebruary 2018

A great book on football related hooliganism and casual culture in 1980s and 1990s in Bulgaria! Interesting events that do not only cover fights between rivalry fans, but also issues like honour, friendship and respect, so rare now among young football fans. I look forward to their next book. Full respect to you and the JRF.

Luchezar Pushkarov/24th November 2017

The only thing I can write is a big WELL DONE! The book is easy and pleasant to read and before you realise you will have finished it. It's a fascinating read and at times the vivid descriptions literally sent me back to where the events take place! No more praise to the lads because they have no time to waste as I can't wait to read their next books!

Victor Milanov /17th November 2017

Well done to my mates for this brilliant book. I was one of the first to buy it from Helikon Bookstores, though I had a signed copy reserved for me (a gift for participating in it). A wonderful, trustworthy and absorbing book that made me recall events from my youth. Great job, lads!

Todor Radnev/15th July 2017

I got the book by post last week and though I didn't have much free time, I read it in one sitting. It's nice and easy to read and it's a really classical piece of literature. In general, I've always been keen on football and whenever I find the time I go to watch games from all divisions, but it seems that I have not completely understood fan culture (the fighting and so on). I found answers in the book, the answers I've been looking for, for so long so thank you very much for introducing the full picture to me. I'd like to thank the authors Tosh and Gilly for taking me back to times long gone that I recall with a smile and a touch of nostalgia.

Gencho Danev /7th April 2017

A one-sitting read! A jewel for connoisseurs' collections! Great work by the authors!

Elena /25th March 2017

I find this a genuine book. A book about friendship, the crazy days of youth, honour and pride. Written in an exquisite style, it is full of events that take us back to the near past. It's so well written and presented that it makes me go back with nostalgia to times gone by that we all seem to miss now. I dipped into their small world and somehow, I experienced it all together with the main characters, i.e. boys crazy about football in every sense of the word. It's a story telling you how to live, pursue your dreams and make real memories.

I wish you good luck in all your endeavours, lads! Keep dreaming and make history...

Anatoly /21st March 2017

Good job, lads! A very well written book. I recommend it to all football fans!

Levski fan from Haskovo/20th March 2017

Though I support another club I liked the book a lot. I read it fast. Someone had to write such a book and I'm glad these are guys I know. I belong to their generation and while reading it so many memories came to my mind. I felt really good, especially about the train trips. We had no cars then, so we travelled mainly by rail or coaches. I'd like to see more books written by the authors and I wish them millions of keen readers.

Vladimir Iliev /5th March 2017

I recently met Tosh, or I'd rather say he met me on the occasion of our joint project for restoring the Rahovets fortress near the town of Gorna Oryahovitsa. I got the book and took great pleasure in reading it almost in one sitting! They've done a perfect job for amateur writers. Before getting acquainted to football hooliganism I strongly disapproved of such football related riots, which I used to think not only put off ordinary people from going to games, but also do harm to the very football clubs! However, the stories in the book made me realise that if one gets to know in detail the causes those guys fought for, one will no longer think the way I used to think! The book is a story of friendship, courage, and fair play, but most of all it says that you should do whatever your heart tells you to do regardless of the ways and means of doing it! Congratulations to Tosh and Gilly Black! Keep up the good work, lads! I look forward to their next book! I'd like to also thank Tosh for the fantastic fan items he's been supplying me with! Lokomotiv forever!

Stefan Stanchev/24th February 2017

At the beginning of September 2016 (before the official book launch in Bulgaria) I got a book, which is a brand-new genre for me as it provides a first-person description of football hooliganism. Its title was Beyond the Hatred. Never before had I seen a book like this on the Bulgarian market. As far as I know, such books are extremely popular in the UK, but surely not in our country yet. What I find even more remarkable about this book is that I've known its authors Gilly Black and Tosh McIntosh since we were all kids. They belong to Lokomotiv Jolly Roger Firm. What we all three shares is our love for Lokomotiv Gorna Oryahovitsa. These approximately 290 pages in Beyond the Hatred depict the authors' crazy football related adventures at and around Bulgarian stadia. All of this comes garnished with an interesting illustrated part. The book is highly readable and written in a simple and understandable language. It is divided into two parts separated by the photo pages. Some may find there is too much violence in JRF Beyond the Hatred, but that's the reality of fandom and its genuine brutal face. The read also depicts the casual fashion among football supporters, of which little is known in Bulgaria In addition, it also presents the opinions and views of several other supporters from Bulgaria and Britain. The authors also talk about their affiliation with British football fan culture. The real reason for writing this book can be traced back to English football hooligans. Probably everyone will find their favourite parts of this book and mine is the emotional introduction and the meetings I and Tosh had with an exceptional English character, i.e. Pat Dolan. Fan culture is actually a particular subculture that has its own strict rules (no matter how strange it may sound to some). And here we are not talking of some brainless MMA fighters, who fight to earn their living, but of people devoted to their ideas, people who follow their own code of conduct and their own principles. Probably Beyond the Hatred will appeal to all those who are into films like Green Street Hooligans, The Football Factory, The Firm, etc., people who are into fandom and would like to add to their knowledge of this subculture.

Mladen Spartak Varna/14th February 2017

I was pleasantly surprised by the book, which tells about the great years of Lokomotiv G.O. fans, when their active core featured the Jolly Roger Firm lads. Congratulations for the authors. My sincere wish is that the newly emerged JRF Youths can be their proud successors on the terraces, in the streets and of course during the derby games that everyone in Gorna is looking forward to, i.e. the games against Etar FC. Lokomotiv G.O. & Spartak Varna! Brothers till we die!

P.S. We're looking forward to your next book!

Marcho1914 /12th February 2017

It is a unique book and I can't wait to read the other projects that the authors have already started working on.

Yuri Lokomotiv Moskva /5th February 2017

Recently, in addition to the football fan books from countries from the ex-USSR and ex-Yugoslavia, I started collecting similar books written in Bulgaria. It turned out that reading Bulgarian is not much harder than reading Russian, Ukranian and Serbian languages. It would have been a pity if I had not taken advantage of that. BEYOND THE HATRED, which I bought immediately after its release, is dedicated to the hooligans supporting Lokomotiv FC from the town of Gorna Oryahovitsa. If you remember, in the early 1990s Rotor Volgograd played that team in one of the ECT. The book tells the story of a relatively small firm called JOLLY ROGER FIRM whose distinctive feature is the 'English disease'. Being sworn Anglomaniacs, the lads from that small Bulgarian town did their best to come into contact with the notorious then British hooligans and so they took advantage of each opportunity to do so like the games British teams played in ECT in Bulgaria and its neighbouring countries. You may remember how in December 1999 Spartak had to host Leeds in Sofia due to bad weather in Moscow. The hooligans from Gorna Oryahovitsa took their chance to meet like-minded lads from the UK. The first part of the book describes the relations between JOLLY ROGER FIRM, established in 1995, and British hooligan firms such as CHELSEA HEADHUNTERS, CARDIFF SOUL

CREW, FOREST EXECUTIVE CREW, BARNSLEY FIVE-O, etc. Copying, in their own words, the very best from their role models, they also went their own distinctive way in their native country. The details of all their experiences and adventures all around Bulgaria are extremely interesting. The second part tells of the relations of JOLLY ROGER FIRM with other similar Bulgarian firms. Among them they had their enemies such as Botev Plovdiv, Dobrudzha, Yantra Gabrovo, Spartak Pleven, Dunav, Beroe, Sliven, Shumen, Cherno More, Neftochimic and many others, and alliances such as Chernomorets, Spartak Varna and Levski. What was also interesting was that the copy I received was originally signed by the authors, which was a more than pleasant gesture.

Daniel Hristov /5th February 2017

I read the book in one sitting and I can assure you it is simply unique. The authors took me back years ago when there used to be real friendship, love and devotion to our favourite clubs. All the events and fights are just as real as our beloved LOKOMOTIV FC is. This book should be on the shelf in the home of every proper Lokomotiv fan and whenever he finds himself in trouble he should open it and feel the power it provides. This is a story of glorious times, First Division, momentous games, crowded grounds and off-the-pitch fights and riots. It is a book about strong people with strong characters. It is unworthy of some to backbite about the authors. Envy is a bad disease. We should respect their efforts. Thanks to them people all over the globe will know about Lokomotiv G.O. I fully respect the authors and I wish them the best of luck in their future projects.

Fuss /3rd February 2017

The book is unique, and I do recommend it to all football fans! Good luck!

Radoslava /2nd February 2017

A really interesting book for all those who, like me, have also been to our ground supporting our club from lower echelons to the top flight without being part of any mob. A number of interesting facts and events are presented and what really matters to me is that they provide a first-person explanation why and what made youngsters' act like that and whether nowadays such reasons and the society hypocrisy are gone or still exist.

M. from Youths /28th January 2017

An exceptional book that helps us young fans and hooligans understand what it was like back in the days. A book from which you learn all about hooliganism and with every page you read you become more and more addicted to it. An incredible one-sitting read. I highly recommend this book to every proper football fan!

Blue Terror Ruse /28th January 2017

This book is unique! It takes us back to years of complete freedom and depicts the nature of mobs in those days! It's a story how street fights and the unconditional love for a football club can result in friendships that last a lifetime. Highly recommendable!

I.D. /28thJanuary 2017

Beyond the Hatred is a great book! A perfect read written in a simple and easy to understand language recreating the events just the way they happened (I was present at some) tense, exciting, comic, sometimes repulsive, but genuine. As I was reading it I travelled back in time and I had tears in my eyes experiencing all of it again! Well done and thank you, Tosh and Gilly, you've done a really perfect job! I look forward to your next book!

LOKOMOTIV till we die!!!

Yordan Dulov /28th January 2017

Wonderful book for all football fans and everyone who remembers the dawn of organised hooliganism in Bulgaria! The times when loyalty and friendship were not just hollow words but were just as strong as one's hatred for one's opponents! Greetings from your Lokomotiv Plovdiv friends!

M.M. – G.O. /24th January 2017

Mates, I've just read your book. The whole of it! As you know, I'm not a big football fan and you haven't met me much at games, but I do know people from those circles and I've always had mates among them. Your book took me back to times and events that I only witnessed (without taking part in them), but it made me feel nostalgic for the long gone 1980s and 1990s, when I was young and full of energy, emotions and rebellious spirit. At the same time, being born in Gorna Oryahovitsa, the black and white ideas are not strange to me and they run in my blood and it's something that will never change. I hope everyone in Gorna Oryahovitsa feels the same. The book made me proud I was born in Gorna Oryahovitsa, a small town that has so many dedicated and loyal football supporters. And feeling proud that you come from Gorna Oryahovitsa, or from Bulgaria in general, is nowadays a rare feeling. Thanks for that, lads! You get my full respect for all your efforts you put into this book! I'm proud of you!

Simeon Rasheev/9th January 2017

It was high time! The first book of its kind! Great first impression with its intelligent ways of expression and presentation and the fantastic endeavour to get to the very roots of things. Cheers, Tosh and Gilly!

Marian / 26th December 2016

Beyond the Hatred is an interesting and exciting read! You simply dive into another world, another life that I didn't even know to exist, but I was greatly impressed. Wonderfully structured and well written! Great job by the authors!

Joyse (Gabrovo) / 17th December 2016

I just can't find the words to express my great admirations for this book! Beyond the Hatred is an incredible, a fantastic read for all football fans. I read it in a single night, I just couldn't put it down... I know both authors from the years when our two mobs fought each other, and I have always greatly respected the black-and-whites! This is the only set of supporters in Bulgaria that didn't betray their club even when they played in the amateur leagues! For me it's an honour to know them and I wish them good luck with their next book on football mobs in Bulgaria!

George the Cobble / 14th December 2016

My special greetings go to the authors. It's written for all those who have experienced the great feeling of belonging to a football mob, but also for those who fail to understand the special thrill of being at a football ground with the mob, with your mates who are more than a family to you, of supporting your club and generally being part of the world of football and living a life related to football.

P.L. /9th October 2016

Tosh McIntosh and Gilly Black are already working on the English version of a ground-breaking book (BEYOND THE HATRED) for Bulgarian fans and in particular for those belonging to the Jolly Roger Firm! I am honoured and I take real pride in being part of this firm. It was an unforgettable emotion for me that will stay forever in my mind. Once a JRF, always a JRF… JRF is a model for behaviour, friendship, virtues and ideas. Jolly Roger Firm will always remain a paragon, a predominant power and a great reminder of the golden urchin years! The lads who made this book also in a way made the firm and therefore their book is its most accurate and trustworthy history.

S.B. /4th October 2016

Beyond the Hatred is a one-sitting book. I didn't know much about football fans and so I was amazed by young people's love and admiration for the game and their beloved clubs. The book is fascinating and easy to read, and it provides a special insight into football hooliganism. I understood that football fans are a community devoted to that great sport. I wish the authors all the courage in the world!

G.B. /22nd September 2016

A fascinating book. Greetings to the authors! I'm looking forward to their next project! Good luck!

Friday / 14th September 2016

It's a terrific book! Written in the English style, the stories are well told and easy to read. Each mob in those times had its similar stories, great times they were. An absolute must-read for all young football fans. I hope it sells well and motivates other fellas to write books about their clubs. Gorna Oryahovitsa should be proud of this book and not let envy and jealousy prevail.

I.B./12th September 2016

A superb book! It's not only about off-the-pitch fights, it's about different club supporters' friendship and respect. Unfortunately, things are not the same any more. Go on lads, write some more. And for those who have not read it – buy this book, you won't regret it. Don't be the opinionated spiteful jerks. You should respect another people's work! And you should try and do even better. Good luck to the authors and remember: no one can take away from you what you have achieved! All the best, lads!

McStanchev /11th September 2016

Beyond the Hatred is written in a simple and fascinating way. As you're reading you keep on saying, 'C'mon, just one more page as this story is also pretty interesting.' Anyone into football and hooliganism will be swept off by this book. And I wish books like this give rise to some evolution among Bulgarian football fans who could gradually get rid of their boorish behaviour and start following some rules.

Uncle /9th September 2016

An extremely exciting book! It presents an original point of view to the phenomenon called football hooliganism and its effect on two men the way it shaped their personalities! It's a new genre for Bulgarian readers and I dare say I was immediately hooked on! Keep up the good job, lads, we can't wait for your next book! Huge respect to you!

Uncle Stan /9th September 2016

Great read. Written in a fascinating way, it's a one-sitting book. I thank the authors for taking me back in time with their adventures and for reliving memories of events gone by. Some of the stories are absolutely hilarious and described in a pretty funny way. I can't wait to read their next book. Good luck!

Come on LOKOMOTIV!

The Major /8th September 2016

Defo a one-sitting book. You simply dip into another world, another life that I was not well familiar with (though I knew about most of the events described), but I was greatly impressed. Also, the information is well presented to the readers and the book is very well structured. Each chapter has its meaning. Respect to the authors!

Milen Panayotov /6th September 2016

Without a single trace of doubt, I do define Beyond the Hatred as a must-have book for each and every football fan! Well, some may find it appalling and disgusting, while for others it will be intriguing and even exciting. On not less than 295 pages the authors provide a detailed first-person description of events they experienced while going to football games to unreservedly support their beloved Lokomotiv FC from the town of Gorna Oryahovitsa and ... the England national team. At the same time they do a great job trying to reveal the roots of hooliganism, explain that global phenomenon and most of all, shouting out loud, just the way they do on the terraces, they ask some awkward and hard to answer questions like "Who are you to judge or classify us in any way whatsoever?", "Who has the right to judge people for the free choices they make?", "Who has the right to label others?", "Do you understand what this is really about so that you can have any justified opinion on the matter?", "Who says what's normal and what is not?!" And Tosh and Gilly have the full right to state that no problem can be solved without being first understood, realised and considered. And that there are no big and small clubs, but there are big and small people with big and small hearts! And that it doesn't matter where you were born, but what matters is why you were born and how you're going to live that life of yours. It doesn't matter where you've come from; it matters where you're going to! And there's something else you learn from the two guys from Gorna Oryahovitsa, i.e. that concepts such as honour, dignity, courage, bravery, friendship, mutual aid, succession, etc. have not vanished from our contemporaries' vocabulary and value system. And that no matter how absurd it may sound to some, Beyond the Hatred there is friendship.

The book is completely easy and nice to read. Its style and language are reasonably simple and accessible for anyone since (thanks God!) there is no multi-word complexity and abstraction so typical of some elite and modern writers and aesthete. The scenes of violence are so well, so lively and vividly depicted that at times you find yourself unconsciously looking at your fingers you're about to turn the page with and checking whether they are not stained with the blood of someone from the rival mob or without even realising it, you touch your teeth to make sure they're still there and no one has knocked them out. And when we add up the wonderful colour pictures and newspaper cuttings, it seems you're not reading a book, but rather taking part in a film by Coppola or Tarantino, and a 3D film at that! So, by and large, it is the ultimate experience that is definitely not for the faint-hearted! But that's what life is, those are the times that destiny decided we are to live through. So, spare some money to buy this book. If you don't have it, save some! For Christ's sake, beg or even steal some if you have to! Because Beyond the Hatred is more than worth reading!

S.P. /4th September 2016

Beyond the Hatred is a fantastic book! Full respect to Tosh and Gilly! Everything they wrote is the truth and regards for writing about the good old times! Lokomotiv

G.O till we die!

Anonymous/13th August 2016

This is a really unique book for Bulgaria, where the topics of football hooliganism and casual culture are not so popular. And it's not only a matter of bloody fights all over stadia and streets as the authors consider philosophically and in great details issues like loving madly a football club, defending its ideas, paying respect to one's rivals and being bound by honour and friendship! The influence of casual culture and British traditions on the authors' lives is brilliantly described. In addition to the interesting stories about fights against the mobs of Etar, Spartak Pleven, Botev Plovdiv, Shumen and a number of other clubs and towns, there are also some humorous and sad stories. The authors complement each other in a rather unusual way and the blend is absolutely exceptional! And surely their firm is the typical one, in the good old English style, small and featuring proper die-hard fans closely related to one another! It's a fantastic book and you won't regret reading it! It's a must-have for any football fan and for your bookcase!

FanFace readers on the 'Beyond the Hatred' Bulgarian edition:

SofiaWest 2016-08-05 20:48

Beyond the Hatred is an amazing book. Respect to those boys, though a small firm! I do recommend this book to all football fans!

Amazon readers on the 'Beyond the Hatred' English edition:

Captain Flint:

Very interesting read, great insight into the reality of football hooliganism from Eastern Europe during the 80's and 90's. Really enjoyable read, it was very hard to put down. Brilliantly written and recommend to any football lad. Respect to you, Tosh and Gilly!!!

Francis Drake

Brilliant read. First impression makes of how well the book is structured and how stories run smoothly and with gradation. Unlike most of the books in the genre, the authors also show extraordinary statistical literacy such as names, events, dates, results off and on the pitch! While nowadays all can be found just Google it, they do skilfully tell in detail about the game itself as well. Yes, hooligans often say they are not interested in what's happening on the pitch... Gilly and Tosh also mentioned it a few times when the interesting events were probably outside the ground, but they definitely posses' high levels of erudition and knowledge in football in general, which makes them not just hooligans, but real football fans... If I have to summarise it: HooliFans

Annis Abraham

I have myself written 7 books. And for me 'Beyond the Hatred 'was a very honest written book by the Authors, with some excellent and interesting stories about their life's and how they got involved in the English hooligan culture. It's very rare you find so much truth nowadays in books and this one had it spot on. Plus, it was great to read a chapter on Fat Pat Chelsea RIP from so many names from the past. I strongly recommend this book, it's worth reading.

Todor Radnev:

Good book I find it very easy for reading. The story grabs you from the first moment and just follows the story. Also helping to the people like me who are football fans to understand "the hooligan culture". I believe if you read the book you will understand that the fans are sharing the same passion to the football wherever they are from.

Steve Hobley:

This is a fantastic read.... I've read a lot of books about this subject, but this has a slightly different perspective. Great accounts from all those involved, a fascinating insight of the Bulgarian hooligan scene ... congratulations Tosh & Gilly hopefully more books to come...

Blademan:

A great read and insight into the Bulgarian hooligan scene, written by two working class, knowledgeable lads, proud of their roots and their football team. It's not just a hooligan book, there's a bit of history in there, but what comes over most, is the camaraderie and love of the terrace culture.

Well done Gilly and Tosh

Matthew Rimmington:

This book and the photo materials in it, are yet more proof of the strong alliance between Lokomotiv G.O. and Notts County. Yesterday I had the privilege of being a part of a fantastic moment for Lokomotiv G.O and for Bulgarian football. After a lot of hard work by the authors Tosh McIntosh and Gilly Black I gratefully received my copy of their book "JRF - Beyond the Hatred" the first book written about Bulgarian football culture. It was also a proud moment for me personally as some pictures that I have taken are in the book, reflecting the friendship that has developed between Notts County and Loko G.O. Well done to Tosh and Gilly and all those that have helped to produce this excellent book.

Colin Blaney:

It's without a doubt the best overseas read from two proper good fellas in the know, starting with the clubs 'Steel workers' till present it paints a picture and I was hardly able to put this book down. I highly recommend lads in the know to read this book.

Authors

BIO

TODOR STOYCHIEV (TOSH MCINTOSH) was born on 15.02.1977 in the family of a steel worker and nurse, in the small town of Gorna Oryahovitsa, located in northern Bulgaria. He is married to Desislava and they have a daughter Nadya (aged 15). He is a graduated electrician and he practiced his profession in Bulgaria for 9 years. He has lived in London (England) with his family for 10 years now, where he works as a video surveillance operator in the control room of Arts Depot, Tally Ho, North Finchley. He has appeared many times in Bulgarian electronic media, radio and television broadcasts, such as Eurocom TV UltraSport, Tangra Mega Rock, etc., Interviews and articles in the Meridian Match 'newspaper and other editions. Author of two books (in Bulgarian and English) for football fandom in a relatively new, unknown and somewhat innovative for Bulgaria literary genre,Hoolie-Ultra-Lit '. Currently he and his creative partner, Gilly Black, are trying to re-write the story of their local football club 'Lokomotiv' G. Oryahovitsa, which is expected to be released in the autumn of 2019.

PHILIP BAKYOV (GILLY Black) was born on 18.03.1978 in the family of a construction technician and a piano teacher in the small town of Gorna Oryahovitsa, located in northern Bulgaria. He is married to Maria and they have two children: Daughter Elia (aged 2) and son Antoni (aged 11). He graduated with Master's degree in Shipbuilding, Marine Engineering and still practices his profession as a certified anticorrosive inspector of PG Protective & Marine Coatings with over 12 years' experience in shipbuilding and ship repair. He has had several publications in Bulgarian and foreign newspapers mainly in the field of his professional sphere. As well as his creative partner, Tosh McIntosh, he is an author of two books (in Bulgarian and English) for football fans, and in fact the two co-authors are bravely going together to publish two more books in the genre in their own words: "Seeing their dreams come true."

MILEN PANAYOTOV WAS BORN on July 9, 1971 in the family of an engineer and teacher in Shumen. Married, with one daughter, Milen has a Master's degree in English and Bulgarian philology. He worked as an English teacher and has been a freelance translator for more than 20 years. Publisher in recent years, he wrote two fiction books about Levski Sofia - We Were (in) Sector B and Blue Avalanche. Also he is the publisher of a collection of poems Levski-European. He has often appeared in television and radio programs such as: Become Rich (Who Wants to be a Millionaire) on NOVA TV, UltraSport on Eurocom TV, SKAT TV, as well as in broadcasts of Tangra Radio, Reaction Radio and some others. There are also several interviews in Meridian Match newspaper and other editions. He takes part in documentaries "We are Levski", "Love knows no bounds" and "50 years of Levski playing in the ECT". Co-founder of international charity association Levski Family. He was initially involved in these projects at the request of Todor and Philip mainly as a translator, as they were in need of a professional translator for their books double editions (in both languages), one of which is already on the English market and elsewhere in Europe and the rest of the world ... Later, however, his doyen's experience in this field was appreciated and he was invited to take part in this project as a co-author to help the two younger authors, who in return promised to help him publish his works in English, through their contacts abroad and here's another dream to come true!